W9-ADG-879

SPECIAL NEEDS IN ORDINARY SCHOOLS
General editor: Peter Mittler
Associate editors: Mel Ainscow, Brahm Norwich, Peter Pumfrey,
Rosemary Webb and Sheila Wolfendale

Educating the Able

Titles in the Special Needs in Ordinary Schools series

Educating the Able

Diane Montgomery

CASSELL

For A.M.L.
who was gifted and talented

Cassell
Wellington House
125 Strand
London WC2R 0BB

215 Park Avenue South
New York
NY 10003

First published 1996

British Library Cataloguing-in-Publication Data
A catalogue record for this book is available from the British Library.

ISBN 0-304-33598-3 (hb)
ISBN 0-304-32587-2 (pb)

Typeset by Action Typesetting
Printed and Bound in Great Britain by Biddles Limited,
Guildford and King's Lynn

Contents

Editorial foreword

A distinguished visitor to the UK, after studying plans and practice for the inclusion of children with special educational needs
into ordinary schools, concluded that this country would never
succeed in this aim because the education system as a whole was
too deeply divided by social and economic inequalities; that these
inequalities were increasingly reflected in children's achievements
from the age of five onwards and that the system as a whole was
best suited to meeting the needs of the one in six pupils who were
destined for higher education.

Why, then, a book on able and gifted children in a series on
special needs in ordinary schools?

If we are aiming for an inclusive education system which
includes all children, then the needs of able and gifted children
must be fully met within a comprehensive non-segregated system
of provision. In order to achieve this aim, able children will need
to derive benefit from 'a broad and balanced curriculum that
meets their individual needs', as outlined in the 1988 Education
Reform Act.

But not all able children are able to achieve this aim. Some are
not recognized as able and may only come to notice for other
reasons. Others are withdrawn from mainstream schools because
either they or their parents feel, rightly or wrongly, that schools are
not meeting their needs and may become disaffected or bored by
what schools have to offer.

Children who are able or gifted have little in common but some
of them do require 'provision beyond that which is generally available', as defined by the 1993 Education Act and can therefore be
regarded as having special educational needs. Some schools will
be able to meet these needs within their own resources; others may
find it difficult to do so.

Children do not have special educational needs because they are
able, but because there is a mismatch between what they bring to
the school and what the school and sometimes the family have to

offer. Such children deserve good teaching and support to meet their individual needs.

Diane Montgomery's book will prove an invaluable resource to all teachers, parents and governors who want to improve policy and practice for pupils who show evidence of high levels of ability but whose needs are not being adequately met at the present time. It summarizes a wealth of relevant information and provides examples of 'good practice' on ways in which able children can be helped to derive the fullest possible benefit from their experience of school and make a richer contribution to the development of inclusive education for all pupils, regardless of ability or achievement.

Professor Peter Mittler
University of Manchester
November 1995

Introduction

The following quotation is from a recent HMI Report. HMI surveyed a range of primary and secondary schools focusing upon the needs of able pupils in the maintained sector. Their survey confirmed evidence from earlier case work by a range of researchers and educators in this field, presented at the Chester Conference organized by HMI in 1990.

> When specific attention was given to the needs of very able children there was often a general increase in the level of expectation for all pupils and this was sometimes reflected in improved public examination results. The schools which were most successful at challenging their very able pupils consistently sought to encourage individual effort and develop independence. The judicious intervention of the teacher to urge pupils to a higher level of knowledge, skill, understanding and thinking was crucial.
>
> (HMI, 1992, p. viii)

There are a number of key words and phrases in this guarded conclusion which are crucial to investigating and understanding work with the able. These will be explained and developed and the underlying themes will be pursued in the rest of this book. Whilst purporting to draw conclusions the report really raises questions. For example, we must ask what kinds of *needs very able* children actually have and what is the nature of the *specific attention* they require. Is it useful or relevant to distinguish between *able* and *highly* or *very able* and make provision for different levels of ability in the upper ranges? Is there a distinction to be made between patterns of ability and talent or between creativity and giftedness – terms more easily understood by the general public?

It is to be noted that HMI state that the general increase in the level of expectation was *often* to be seen. We can of course conclude that it was often but not always to be seen. The general level of expectation was, we note, *sometimes reflected* in improved public examination results (but not always).

Schools which 'challenged' their able pupils *consistently* sought to encourage *individual effort* and *develop independence.* Clearly methods which offer such challenges and encouragement are to be applauded, but at no point is it made quite clear how the judgements were made and what the criteria were upon which they were based. In a recent publication by HMI, 'Primary Schools: source aspects of good practice' (1987), a careful analysis of their observational notes shows quite clearly that the teaching observed was quite ordinary: not intellectually challenging or a problem-solving approach, merely bearing the outward trappings of such. Approaches presented with enthusiasm and style can often be misconstrued.

'Good teaching', 'provision for different levels of ability' and 'challenging the able' are difficult concepts and constructs to unravel, and ones about which there has been considerable disagreement and debate even after a century of research and development. More specifics and detailed guidance are needed from a report if progress is to be made. All children need 'good' teaching to meet their individual needs and all children need 'challenge' in the curriculum. Teachers need to learn how to achieve it.

The final sentence of the report might easily be ignored, but implicit in it is something which will be seen to be fundamental to the whole debate. It tells us how to fail our able children, if this is all we have as a strategy – and this is often all there is. 'The *judicious intervention* of the teacher to urge pupils to a higher level of knowledge, skill, understanding and thinking was crucial.' This can be interpreted to mean that if the teacher is not able or not on hand to offer that judicious statement, comment, open question, to give that critical input, pupils will not be urged to higher levels. What if the teacher is not good with open questions despite training, is not in command of advanced knowledge or skill in some specific? What if there are thirty pupils all demanding such skill or levels of knowledge? Perhaps the small groups found in some fee-paying schools or in A-level classes and half-size practical classes may afford some opportunities for such close encounters. Where there are thirty-six children in a busy infant class the teacher will most likely be engaged in judicious intervention as s/he moves round the groups. However, the likely share of this high-grade input per child per day per need is observed to be very low. In reading research, for example, such qualitative input may amount only to 15 seconds per child per day at infant level and per two or three days in junior classrooms.

Overall, however, there is the sense of the Socratic ideal – the open ended questions appealing to 'cognitive stretch' grafted onto a content curriculum and a didactic method. Even if this were not there, these aspects of teaching and learning need to be examined.

Looked at from another perspective, perhaps we are asking too much of mass education. According to Resnick (1989) the development of higher-order thinking was never part of the brief for mass education. Its task was to provide an education in the basic skills of reading, spelling, writing and those core subjects defined by a particular society as useful for the conduct of its business. Even now there is a 'back to basics' drive by the legislature in the presence of a range of reports which indicate that a good education reaches far beyond basics.

When the English state education system was set up at the end of the nineteenth century, it was in the context of a well-established, gender-based 'caste' or class system. Family status and wealth determined who had access to higher levels of education beyond the age of 14. In recognition of the needs of a limited few highly able poor individuals, assisted places in the form of scholarships were offered by most colleges and grammar schools.

The 1944 Education Act was a major turning point, for it heralded attitude change and permitted partial restructuring of society on the basis of merit. Secondary education was provided for all children, with the opportunity for the top 20 per cent of the able to progress on the basis of an intelligence test and essay to an 'advanced' form of education in a grammar school. A public-school system still catering for its old élite was maintained. In the 1970s, comprehensive education was introduced in an effort to provide opportunities for educational advancement of a wider group of able pupils who had been screened out by 11-plus and 13-plus examinations. It was an attempt to remove both the feelings of failure of the 80 per cent not selected and also the socially divisive screening system. This still took place in the context of the maintenance of a public-school system, grammar schools, and selection processes in a number of areas. The grammar schools and selective streams in comprehensive schools offered a broad-based, accelerated content programme geared to the needs of a higher education university system. They were the primers of the structure.

The Plowden Report (1967) was one of the first major reviews of the operation of the 1944 Education Act and expressed a concern about the needs of the able thus: 'long term studies should be made on the needs and achievements of gifted children' (p. 308). Following this, Tempest in 1967 obtained a grant from the Leverhulme Trust for a five-year enquiry into the needs of the gifted child. It is significant that no major state funds were allocated to investigate these identified needs and problems. This pattern is typical of the rest of the century. Research grants can be calculated in thousands of pounds in Britain, whereas funding in North America for gifted education (and all other aspects of education) is allocated in millions.

Most of the research which has been undertaken either funded or on individual initiative in Britain differs from that in North America in a major way. It consists of descriptive surveys of what is available or commonly believed to be necessary, whereas in America the effectiveness of different methods and materials are tested in controlled designs to try to evolve the best practice.

Ogilvie (1973) did obtain funding for his survey of facilities for gifted children in Britain, and presented the difficulties inherently involved in first of all defining who is 'gifted':

> The term gifted is used to indicate any child who is outstanding in either a general or specific ability in a relatively broad or narrow field of endeavour ... where generally recognised tests exist as (say) in the case of 'intelligence' then giftedness would be defined by test scores. Where no recognised tests exist it can be assumed that the subjective opinions of originality and imagination displayed would be the criteria we have in mind.
>
> (p. 7)

He goes on to discuss the problems of cut-off points such as had been used in the 11-plus examinations, explaining that they could defeat their own purposes if set too high or too low. If they were set too high they could eliminate youngsters who for one reason or another did not test well; often these children were highly anxious. If cut-off points were set too low they might include such a wide range of abilities that 'highly advanced, challenging or different programmes become impossible' (p. 10) because they would result in frustration for some of the selected group. These two extracts incorporate problems which still exercise us today:

- What is the nature of high ability?
- How can we identify it?
- What type of programme is most suitable:
  - advanced,
  - challenging,
  - different?

The needs of gifted children, according to Ogilvie, were as follows:

- to have contact with average peers;
- to have contact with children of comparable levels of ability;
- to be stretched and challenged even to the point of experiencing failure and humbling experiences;

- to be guided rather than directed through a more academic approach to a greater depth of treatment;
- to avoid being set apart but have the chance to set self apart on occasions;
- to pass rapidly through elementary stages and use advanced resources;
- to pursue own lines of research;
- to be exposed to some forms of counselling – and for their parents to be so too;
- to be treated like other children;
- to have contact with teachers gifted in similar fields;
- to have abundant opportunity and encouragement to exercise specific talents.

Tempest (1974) made a significant contribution to the debate not only in describing the needs of the able child but in pointing out that teacher judgement was not always very accurate. He found that teachers made the wrong judgements for several reasons. They confused conformity with giftedness, and they still do. They tended to overestimate the intelligence of docile, diligent, conscientious or attractive children. They also failed to take into account sufficiently a child's background and therefore missed the underachievers. This also still happens today, and teacher judgement is only one of a range of strategies which have to be used if we wish to identify able individuals. It gives rise to further questions which need to be resolved:

- Should we identify even if inaccurately?
- Should we differentiate, and if so how?

The DES (1974) report pointed to another key problem which Ogilvie and Tempest had also identified. This was that if gifted children *were* treated as average children they would perform as such. If we need people of high ability then it would seem we do need to identify them. However, many teachers argued that if pupils were able they would identify themselves. Each of these positions will be examined, particularly in relation to underfunctioning and high ability. Despite the accumulated findings, a further DES (1977) survey stated: 'There is no overall policy for identification. Identification is a hit and miss affair, the initiative coming mainly from individual teachers', and: 'Giftedness ... is an ill-defined term. It is neither implicit nor explicit in the day to day dialogue of school life' (p. 13). Ogilvie (1980), in looking back at the position in schools during the 1970s with regard to the concept of giftedness, stated that it almost defied description. Some teachers felt very strongly (and still do) that the whole idea smacked of élitism, and hence were reluctant to discuss it or make special provision for it. Others were equally certain that the only difficulty lay in the problems of the reliability of intelligence tests.

All of these concerns, problems and interests resulted in the Schools Council (1980) establishing a set of programmes concerned to improve the education of particular groups of children. 'Programme 4: Individual Pupils' was directed by Helen Carter.

The Gifted Pupils project was one element of the Schools Council Programme 4. The programme was intended to help teachers identify and respond to the needs of certain groups of pupils, those with special educational needs identified by the Warnock Report (1978): disruptive pupils, pupils from ethnic minorities and gifted pupils.

The director of the gifted pupils project was Ralph Callow, and the period of funding ran for three years. The mismatch between the abilities of more able pupils and the level of work received from them in many of the country's schools was the focus of concern. The project's purpose was described as follows:

> The project is not solely concerned with the relatively small number of outstanding intellectually able children who are usually defined as 'gifted'. Our concern is also with a much larger group of pupils who are exceptionally able in a specific area of the curriculum, whose educational needs sometimes appear to be unsatisfied in the average school and who comprise approximately a *quarter* of the schools population.
>
> (Callow, 1983, p. 1)

The project began in September 1980 with the following objectives:

- to co-ordinate the work of existing local authority groups in the production and evaluation of materials;
- to initiate the production of a series of curriculum booklets for teachers of gifted pupils;
- to form a collection of materials suitable for classroom use;
- to encourage the formation of new working groups.

(Callow, 1983, p. 1)

The work was based upon the response of a group of local teachers to a perceived local educational need. LEA advisers and inspectors were encouraged through teachers' centres to provide support and encouragement and the initial impetus to get the work moving. Specialist lecturers from local colleges were to provide the background theoretical and research data and help in evaluation and course development. All would be involved in the development of methods and materials and would evaluate these with the pupils. It was a huge investment of time and effort by individuals in working parties formed to promote and develop work with able children. The target group was now considerably widened to include 25 per cent of children in schools.

It was as a result of this initiative that my work with teachers in a range of LEAs on making provision for able pupils began. Although funding ended in 1983, a set of books was published as results of the project by Longman. The titles covered identification, mathematics, geography and science. The networks, newsletters and regional resources centres still exist, and new projects and initiatives were developed as a result and in concert with it.

At the same time, the DES funded a two-year research project by the Oxford Educational Research Group, led by Denton and Postlethwaite (1985). It consisted of a study of teacher-based identification of more able pupils in physics, mathematics, English and French in eleven Oxfordshire comprehensive schools. The focus of attention was on the top 10 per cent of third-year pupils. This time it was discovered that the position regarding teacher assessment was not as problematic as previous research had indicated, and that subject-specific checklists could help in improving identification of a broad group of able individuals if used over a period of time.

A second project arose from the first – a three-year investigative experiment mainly concerned with *what to provide* as subject-specific enrichment and *what effect* this would have on the attainments and attitudes of the more able when classroom-based enrichment was introduced. It was acknowledged that at that stage the model accepted in a wide range of projects across the country was *enrichment*. The nature of acceleration, enrichment and differentiation will therefore need to be examined to determine their relative effectiveness. The results of the Oxford Research among others was reported at the DES Conference on Able Children at Oxford, 14–18 July 1986:

a) *Enrichment*
'There is some evidence that the kind of enrichment work that was done most frequently did have a positive effect: in Mathematics there were improvements in Strategies, Methods of Solutions and Making Generalisations: in English Attitude to Self-Motivated Writing showed a gain and some pupils increased the range of their reading and gave evidence of more enthusiasm for it: in Physics a general improvement in categories of Experimental Design can be related to a common theme of experimentation introduced into all the enrichment materials'.

b) *Attitudes of Pupils*
'Changes in attitudes towards the three subjects in terms of heightened interest, influence on hobbies or career aspiration were not detectable with the amount of enrichment given and the style of its introduction'.
c) *The Most Able (top 2%)*
'The success of the enrichment scheme with the most able was similar to that of the rest of the top 10% group'.

Project Report Phase II (p. 5).

'The project shows that much more preparation is necessary than was given before changes to established classroom procedures are made. Teachers need assistance with more detailed planning before introducing new materials or techniques for a special group. Further training in the management of human and material resources and the psychology of change may be pre-requisite to making effective alterations to teaching and learning styles'.

Project Report Phase II (p. 5).
(Denton and Postlethwaite, 1985)

Since that period there have been major changes in education with the introduction of the National Curriculum and changes in funding mechanisms, so that LEAs' ability to support initiatives has waned. Many teachers' centres have been closed and others have become cost centres, living off funds which they can attract directly from schools to pay for training. The needs of the able have not had a high profile in this period, but the work has progressed quietly, encouraged by the following networking organizations:

- LEA advisory teams;
- the National Association for Able Children in Education (NACE);
- the European Council for High Ability (ECHA);
- the National Association for Gifted Children (NAGC).

NACE and NAGC now have their headquarters at Nene College. Major contributions to funding research in the area have also been made by the Leverhulme Trust and in particular the Gulbenkian Foundation.

Recently (1993) the DFE have funded a three-year project by NACE, now directed by John Baker. The project is titled 'NACE/DFE Project: Supporting the Education of Able Pupils in Maintained Schools'. It is based at Park Campus, Boughton Green Road, Northampton. It has a remit and limited funding again (about £150,000) for the three-year period. Its aims are shown here:

A national project to support teachers with able pupils in their classes

Aims:

1. To mobilise the energy and expertise of those teachers who have developed successful strategies by:
   a. encouraging the formation and supporting the work of local networks
   b. recognising good practice and supporting its dissemination
   c. seeking opportunities for further personal professional development of the teachers by sharing their successes with others through school focused INSET
2. To assist teachers to:
   a. identify able pupils in their classes and have appropriate expectations of them in terms of levels of their performance
   b. recognise the need to offer differentiated work in terms of challenge and pace
   c. develop successful strategies to offer full access to the National Curriculum at appropriate levels
   d. recognise the importance of motivating able pupils by ensuring the work is stimulating and relevant
   e. provide opportunities for pupils to apply their knowledge and understanding in problem solving and investigative situations
3. To provide and promote INSET and support from NACE at:
   a. local level – for schools or clusters of schools
   b. regional level – for networks or LEAs
   c. national level – conferences and seminars
4. To co-operate with a variety of organisations in the provision of high quality INSET:
   a. to enable teachers to identify their able pupils and meet their needs
   b. to respond to Inspection Reports which call for the schools to meet the needs of more able pupils more fully
5. To publish through the NACE journal, or other appropriate means, the work of individual teachers or local support groups within the network for the greater benefit of all.

The Project Team and its appointed trainers will:
   a. actively encourage the formation of local networks amongst teachers and other interested parties to share successes and discuss anxieties
   b. stimulate interest and offer support amongst the networks by contributing high quality INSET and ideas
   c. encourage the members of the networks to identify the needs of local teachers and seek solutions through the expertise of the network and the wider expertise accessible through the Project data base
   d. identify and evaluate INSET offered by HE institutions, LEAs and consultants and bring successful practice to the notice of networks and the National and Regional Committees of NACE
   e. promote the aims and objectives of NACE.

(NACE/DFE, 1993–)

—1—

The nature of ability and talent

INTRODUCTION

The formal study of giftedness and talent has a history stretching back into the nineteenth century. Over this period the nature of the studies and the concepts have changed. In the nineteenth century, the researchers were preoccupied with genius and eminence and the conditions which created them. In the early part of the twentieth century, they focused upon intelligence, as measured by tests to identify giftedness in the school population, to examine the career paths of the gifted. In the last fifty years the notion of giftedness as a unidimensional concept has been redeveloped to include a wide range of personal, motivational, creative and intellectual factors, with creativity being a key construct in this multidimensional view of ability and talent.

Researchers now study patterns of ability rather than levels and include sporting achievements and gifts, leadership qualities and skills, and the problems of the realization of the abilities and talents of underfunctioning and disabled individuals. The development of the concepts are here traced to the present time to show that the way we perceive a quality can determine the way we assess it.

The way we view ability, of course, also frequently defines the kind of curriculum provision that we make. If, for example, we regarded it as a rare commodity, we might determine not to bother to make any special provision at all. This is in fact a common strategy in English schools. In higher education it is common to treat all students as though they brought the same knowledge and skills to a subject – which is patently absurd.

The first section of this chapter deals with the historical models, the second with the development of the multidimensional view, and the third and fourth with current perspectives in the education of the able.

GENIUS, EMINENCE AND HIGH ABILITY

The idea of the 'mad genius' is a popular one and perhaps enables people to cope with the challenges to the status quo which such people and their innovatory ideas so frequently bring. The concept of the insanity of genius has a long history and was enshrined in print by Nisbet (1891) and Lombroso (1899). Freud (1932) and Jung (1954) also suggested that there was indeed a narrow margin between insanity and genius, but there are no substantial reports or research studies which confirm this. There are of course examples of gifted individuals who have had a psychotic disorder, such as Van Gogh, and there are many stories built round the image of the mad scientist, but the extensive survey of giftedness undertaken by Terman over several decades revealed findings which were dramatically opposed to the view that to be gifted and talented you must necessarily be mad. He labelled the concept 'superstitious nonsense'. Suffice it to say that in any group of individuals there will always be a small proportion suffering from mental illness, and, in addition, when the majority fail to understand the ideas, explanations and actions of the 'genius', it draws the one possible conclusion – 'If I cannot understand it then s/he must be mad.'

One of the most famous and earliest studies was by Galton (1869) in his book on *Hereditary Genius*. It was a series of biographical sketches on the natural inheritance of ability. Galton himself was a perfect illustration of just this, being related to the Darwins, Huxleys and Wedgewoods and with the following biographical record, discovered by Terman (1917):

> Francis learned to read at the age of two and a half years. He wrote a letter before he was 4 which has been preserved. By 5 years he could read almost any English book and some French; could tell the time by the clock, knew the table of English money; he could cast up any sum in addition; had mastered all the multiplication tables except 9 and 11. He was devoted to the works of Sir Walter Scott and could repeat most of the epic poem *Marmion* by 5 years of age.

By the use of age norms, Terman later estimated that the lowest IQ which could account for all these facts was about 200.

In the early part of the twentieth century Cattell (1915) drew up a list of the most eminent individuals in history, and Cox (1926) used this list to provide further insight into the nature of eminence. She eliminated those born before 1450, because of the lack of written records, as well as those of noble or aristocratic birth and any others with no evidence of intellectual achievement (there were only a few in this category). The total of eminent persons left after this was 300, on whom she found 6000 pages of biography.

Cox used the biographical details to estimate the minimum IQ of each individual and also to provide a reliability rating of the estimate. The final IQs ranged from 100 to 200 with a mean of 155, *three standard deviations above* the mean of 100 which is typical for the rest of the normal population. Her low estimates only arose when there was little biographical data on early childhood. Her estimate for IQs of some of the particular categories of eminence were as follows: philosophers (170); poets, novelists, dramatists, revolutionary statesmen (160); soldiers (125); artists (140); musicians (145); scientists (155). From her studies it appeared that the genius who achieves highest eminence is one whom intelligence tests would have identified as gifted in childhood. However, *the converse of this is not also true* – very high IQ does not lead to eminence. Cox's data suggested that other factors were important in addition to high IQ if the person was to achieve eminence. The eminent also had personal attributes which contributed to their achievement: persistence of motive and effort, confidence in their abilities and great strength or force of character. Personality traits thus appear to influence the level and direction of achievement. She also found within these biographies that chance played a great part, and gave examples such as the following:

> Newton left school at 15 to look after his mother's farm. But for the visit of an uncle who had studied at Cambridge he would never have determined to obtain the education which made his later studies possible...
>
> Faraday left school at 13 and was apprenticed as a bookbinder. He chanced to read an article on electricity in one of the books he was binding and this started his interest in science. Humphrey Davy lived nearby and encouraged and stimulated his studies.
>
> (after Cox, 1926)

Cox's study indicated too that the direction of later achievement tended to be foreshadowed by the interests and occupations of early childhood: this was true of more than 50 per cent of the group. For example, Macauley began his career as an historian at 6, writing a compendium of universal history and filling a quire of paper before losing interest. Many musicians and artists gave indisputable evidence of their talents at very early ages, while few great poets did not show their unusual ability before the age of 15.

She found, however, a group of alleged dullards at school among the eminent. They were labelled 'slow' because they hated or would not bother with school subjects and school learning – in those days, mainly Latin and Greek. Examples were:

> Oliver Goldsmith was said by his childhood teacher to be 'a dull boy' but he was writing clever verse at 7 and reading Ovid and Horace at 8. [His IQ was estimated to be 140+ by Cox.] ... Walter Scott was said to be a dunce at his Musselburgh school. He never attended it if possible but at 7 was reading poetry and writing advanced prose... John Hunter, anatomist and surgeon, left Latin school at 13 and ran wild for four years.

Twenty per cent of Cox's study were forced by parents and guardians into other employment, and some almost starved before they escaped to their special field of interest. Other highly talented people must always have suffered the indignity of failure at school and in adult careers, where they suffered from specific learning difficulties in reading and spelling or poor handwriting – all problems frowned upon and barely understood even to the present day.

THE MULTI-DIMENSIONAL NATURE OF HIGH ABILITY

High intellectual ability by its very nature is general, and this versatility makes careers guidance of highly able pupils much more difficult. It is possible for these pupils to excel in many fields, not just one. People, however, like to believe that the highly able as a rule are not better than the rest of us except in one particular – in other words that ability is unidimensional – when in fact the opposite is true. Except perhaps in music and art, there appear to be few who have not displayed much more than average ability in more than one field. Biographers show mathematicians writing poetry in competition with poets of the day, and so on.

Cox's data has been used to look at this multidimensional nature of high ability, and it has been found that most highly able subjects showed more than average abilities in the following areas:

- science, mathematics, invention, handwork, art;
- poetry, novels, drama;
- philosophy, social theory, history and languages – a less compact group;
- religious leadership, politics, administration;
- music.

The supreme example of the art/science cluster was of course Leonardo da Vinci. While many highly able individuals may have multidimensional talent it is not the case that *all* do.

Intelligence and high ability: Terman's longitudinal studies

One of the most significant research studies of the twentieth century on high ability was conducted by Terman. He began his studies of gifted children by collecting data on 100 individuals between 1910 and 1920. He was attempting to find ways to identify giftedness early and to uncover its later relationship to eminence in adulthood.

His major study began in 1922, when 1050 subjects with an IQ of 140+ were identified in elementary school and a further 400 in high school. These were the children of mainly ordinary parents, rather than those from eminent families as in the earlier studies of Galton and Cattell.

The test consisted of:

- two IQ scores;
- twelve scores from four hours of tests of school achievement;
- three scores from tests of character, personality and interests;
- thirty-four anthropomorphic measures;
- a one-hour medical examination;
- ratings by parents and teachers on twenty-five personality traits;
- a case history of information on walking, talking, etc.

The results included the following findings:

- The medical and anthropological data revealed that typical gifted children were physically superior to average peers.
- On personality and character inventories, the gifted children's scores were far superior to their peers.
- On school achievement tests, their scores were almost as high as for the IQ scores and were on average from two to four grades ahead of peers.
- The mean IQ was around 150, and marked unevenness in achievement was found to be rare.

The mean achievement quotients for reading, spelling, literature information, historical information, scientific information, and aesthetic information were between 137 and 150. Terman maintained contact with 95 per cent of this group for a period of up to 25 years and undertook a series of follow-up studies.

Terman's 1937 findings

He found that the mortality of the gifted group was below average and so was the insanity rate, although suicide was approximately in the same proportions as for the rest of the population. Seventy-one per cent of the group were married, the same proportion of men as women, but the divorce rate was lower in the gifted group than in the general population. The group tended to marry spouses who were also very bright, but usually slightly less bright than they were themselves. By 1940, the subjects had produced 783 offspring, and tests on 384 of these children above the age of 2 years showed a mean IQ of 127. This regression to the mean was predictable on the continuum of genetic variation.

Retest IQ scores showed that the original subjects of 1922 had maintained their measured IQ to the extent of 99 per cent. In other words there was no evidence that any became progressively more stupid (burnt out) in late adolescence, as has often been suggested.

The devotion of many women in this group after marriage to domestic pursuits was observed, and robbed the arts and sciences of a large section of talent. Terman suggested from his results that the loss was due to motivational causes and loss of opportunity rather than lack of ability.

Terman's 1940 follow-up of the men

In 1940, when the men were 25 years old, they were rated on achievement in life; that is, the extent to which they had used their potential. One hundred and fifty subjects each were assigned to the A and C groups (those who had achieved most and least) with 300 in the middle, B, group.

An analysis was then undertaken on the differences between the A and C groups, with the results shown in the box.

The As were uniformly superior to the Cs in freedom from inferiority, emotional stability, self-confidence, integration towards goals, and persistence in accomplishment of ends. These findings confirmed those of both Galton and Cox that high, but not necessarily the highest, intelligence *plus* the greatest degree of persistence will achieve eminence. It also showed that the most able were more emotionally stable, not unstable as other research had suggested.

Terman's 1947 follow-up

In this study of the group, Terman found that they had retained their original superiority; none had developed 'burn-out' or post-adolescent stupidity as predicted by some. Of the men in the group, 800 had gone on to have distinguished careers, but only a minority of the women did.

Analysis of Terman's 1940 follow-up

A group	*C group*
Slightly higher IQ scores	–
97% went to college	68% went to college
90% graduated	37% (of the 68%) graduated
52% with honours	14% with honours
50% fathers were college graduates	15% fathers were college graduates
	At 16 twice as many of this group's parents had divorced.
Health same	
Higher in self-confidence	
Desire to excel	
Prudence	
Leadership	
Popular	
Sensitivity to approval and disapproval	

It was estimated that of the original 1450 subjects, 60 would attain a national reputation and perhaps a dozen would become eminent. Terman wrote that 'it would be surprising if in 100 years one of them should be among the eminent people of history. None of them showed the capacity of a Newton or a Shakespeare, many were the equal of a Washington [the 19th most eminent in Cattell's list]'.

Terman (1954) said that he took some pride in the fact that not one of the major conclusions they drew in the early 1920s about the traits of giftedness had been refuted. Getzels wrote in 1970 that even two decades later, the research continued to identify and confirm Terman's findings with a regularity bordering on redundancy.

The earliest studies of ability by Galton and others focused upon those whose performance was acclaimed as exceptional by peers and admired by the society of the day. Intelligence tests, although they became available at the turn of the century, played no part in these assessments. Retrospective estimates by Terman and Cox of the IQs of these eminent people were verbally biased because written work was most often the only data available. Terman's work, influenced by the development of psychometric testing, set a new approach by identifying able children and following them through their careers. It was notable that he was totally committed in the early stages to the view that intelligence as measured by the tests entirely accounted for high ability and achievement. As his subjects grew up and the pattern of results became clearer, he modified this view.

Regrettably, his major follow-up studies included only men. The collection of data on the women, even the small number of women who had gone on to have distinguished careers, would have been useful and revealing, as would an examination of the social pressures and attitudes of the day which excluded women from access to most careers of any kind. If the data had been collected, later researchers could have undertaken these analyses. Failure to collect it reveals the prevailing attitudes of the day and contributes to the conspiracy of silence on women of significance in history.

It was the work of De Haan and Havighurst (1957) which drew together a number of threads emerging in the studies of high ability, and broadened the concepts then in use. They identified six 'domains of excellence'. Hollingworth, as early as 1926 in her studies of high ability, identified 'special talents' or areas of outstanding potential or performance which appeared to be independent of general intelligence. Similar notions of *special abilities* began to appear in Terman's reports (Burke *et al.*, 1930). These were the precursors of De Haan and Havighurst's structured definition of multiple talents, which influenced thinking in the subsequent decades. They proposed that children could display unusual talent in one or a number of domains. Their work, together with that of Witty (1958) and Taylor (1968), was inspired by the work of Guilford (1950) and his model of the 'structure of intellect', with contents, products and processes as three dimensions in a 120-cell model (Figure 1.1).

Guilford proposed convergent and divergent thinking as two possible modes, each of which deserved consideration when assessing ability. (At some stage, of course, divergent productions do have to undergo some refocusing if something useful in human terms is to be produced.) 'Creativity' can refer to productivity in an artistic or scientific context where the product is innovative, inventive and original in terms not just of that individual but of society at large. In the 1950s and 1960s the term was used synonymously with *divergent thinking*. The earlier concerns with intelligence and intelligence testing had finally led many to criticize the convergent modes of thought required to get IQ test answers.

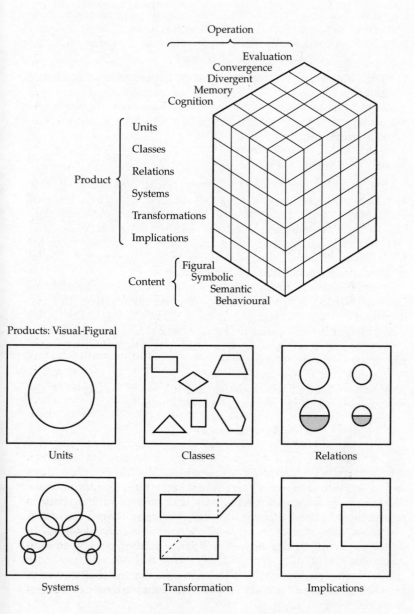

Figure 1.1 *Guilford's three-dimensional model of intellect* (1950)

De Haan and Havighurst's (1957) domains of excellence

De Haan and Havighurst stated that gifted children were those who, from kindergarten through to high school, showed unusual promise in some socially useful area, and whose talents might be stimulated. They distinguished between:

- intellectual ability – demonstrated in high-school or academic aptitude;
- creative thinking;
- scientific ability;
- social leadership;
- mechanical skill or ingenuity;
- talent in fine arts areas.

In the years which followed, many researchers adopted this approach and produced a range of *definitions of talent*. Each of them, however, now acknowledges the importance of the intellectual domain as a significant sub-category. A general threshold level of ability of about 120 IQ is thought to be necessary in order for talent to be made operational and enable the potential to be realized and directed in a productive way.

In 1953, Usborn emphasized the role of *deferred judgement* in creativity and developed the strategy of 'brainstorming' to facilitate and model the creative process. This process, also called 'synectics', is now popular in management training and collaborative problem-solving activities. Patterning and refocusing also play a part after the 'storm'.

Torrance (1963), in a series of studies of the relationship between creativity and intelligence, developed further the analysis of the processes. In his tests of creativity (1966) he defined:

- fluency
- flexibility
- originality
- elaboration.

as key activities in verbal and figural creative problem solving. The processes which seemed to correlate most with later creative productivity were originality and elaboration (Torrance, 1971). These two aspects are the most difficult to define and assess even when using the test guidelines; fluency and flexibility can be computed easily.

During this period, a number of researchers tried to distinguish between convergent and divergent thinkers on a range of dimensions. Significant figures in this field were Getzels and Jackson (1962), Wallach and Kogan (1965) and Hudson (1966).

The study of creativity expanded in the 1970s and 1980s to encompass packages and programmes to help develop creative thinking abilities, and other skills were added to Torrance's list, such as:

- curiosity
- openness to the ideas of others
- toleration and dealing with ambiguity and complexity
- risk taking
- imagination and use of fantasy
- humour
- finding essences and constructive resolutions.

During the 1970s, a series of programmes and initiatives were developed to guide students in creative and productive thinking. Some key examples were:

- the Creative Problem Solver (CPS) by Noller *et al.* (1976);
- the Productive Thinking Programme by Covington *et al.* (1972);
- the CoRT Thinking Programme by de Bono (1976), and his books and papers on lateral thinking (1971, 1975);
- the Purdue Creative Thinking Programme by Feldhusen *et al.* (1969);
- the Instrumental Enrichment Program by Feuerstein (1980).

Some of these will be discussed in Chapter 5.

MODERN CONCEPTS OF ABILITY AND TALENT

Giftedness, ability and talent

The most generally observed explanation of the term giftedness in current use is the following: 'the capacity for or the demonstration of high levels of performance in any potentially valuable area of human endeavour'. This definition is mainly based upon the conceptualization of Renzulli (1977). Over time it has remained consistent and useful as a working definition, but how we define 'high', 'levels' of performance and 'potential value' needs to be examined.

The model which Renzulli proposed, popularly referred to as the 'Renzulli Ring; (Figure 1.2), incorporates three essentials. The individual, in demonstrating high ability in some field of endeavour, needs to have task commitment or what Terman in his studies identified as persistence (Terman and Oden, 1947). The implication is also that only above-average ability is necessary in task

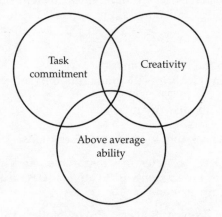

Figure 1.2 *The Renzulli Ring*

commitment and innovative creativity for a level of high ability to be demonstrated. Very high ability without task commitment and creativity is unlikely to lead to the achievement of a high level of performance in a potentially valuable area of human endeavour.

Mönks and Boxtel (1985) supplemented the Renzulli model with a dimension or frame of their own to illustrate the view that giftedness is not completely defined by what is within the individual in terms of creativity, ability and persistence (Figure 1.3). Rather, in realizing any part of that potential, the environment into which individuals are born and within which they are educated and interact facilitates or inhibits the demonstration of ability.

More recently, Tannenbaum (1993) has linked the concepts of *giftedness, talent, creativity* and *genius,* and provided a succinct set of definitions for each. If we substitute the term *'highly able'* where he uses 'gifted', his diadic model can be incorporated into our working definition, for although he leaves out persistence, he indicates a level of high ability and expands on the notion of creativity in a useful way:

> 'Giftedness' and 'talent' are used synonymously to encompass publicly valued abilities possessed by no more than one or two per cent of people at each developmental stage. 'Creativity' is regarded as representing one of two aspects of giftedness (or talent), namely innovation or invention that deserves critical acclaim in contrast to

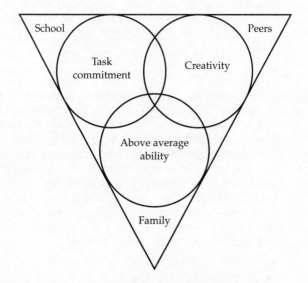

Figure 1.3 *A multifactorial model of giftedness*
Source: Mönks, 1992, p. 194

the other aspect of giftedness (or talent) which refers to highly developed proficiency in highly demanding tasks ...

Genius is the most advanced extension of giftedness (or talent) or creativity, denoting Olympian-level accomplishments by the rarest of adults.

(Tannenbaum, 1993, p. 3)

His view of giftedness thus has two aspects: innovation and high level of proficiency in demanding tasks. For a considerable period, as we have seen, the early literature adopted a *unidimensional* view of high ability, seeing it as wholly about high intelligence as measured by intelligence tests (Terman, 1945). Over time, other perspectives of high ability have emerged and other dimensions of ability and high ability have been recognized.

It is of significance that Tannenbaum's definition stands on the side of the innate capacities and leaves out the personality dimension introduced by Renzulli and the social perspective of Mönks and Boxtel, who were writing earlier. The notion of a gifted 1 or 2 per cent may also need to be challenged. Further definitions are examined below.

Highly able

This could be regarded as the more politically correct term for the gifted group, and is the one currently used in the field. It is the term which will be used in the rest of the text for the 'gifted' individual and group.

Able

This covers individuals on the continuum between average and highly able who also show some potential for or achievement in potentially valuable areas of human performance. This group can include large numbers of the population. It therefore may or may not prove valuable to make special provision for it in education; or it may be that including the widest numbers is the most efficient strategy. It is safe to say that there are a large number of able individuals in the school and college population whose needs are not being met, who remain unidentified and some of whom underfunction to a serious degree throughout their years of education because of lack of recognition and/or provision.

Talent

Talent tends to be defined as a domain-specific gift or ability such as musical, scientific, artistic, balletic or mathematical talent. The individual appears to have a high ability or a precocious talent in the presence of seemingly modest abilities in other areas. Peggy Somerville was a talented painter with a mature style at 3 years old. Mozart composed and played significantly well at 7.

However, many talented people do not show exceptional performance at an early age despite these well-known exceptions. Gaining success and being recognized for prodigious talent most often only comes after fifteen or more years of effort, according to Elshout (1990). Because of their personality characteristics, talented people stick at their tasks with intense motivation and persistence, and only then become outstanding. If this intense dedication finds direction at about 15 to 20, their peak performance is likely to be achieved in the 30–40 age span. Lehman's (1953) study of age and achievement bore this out. Although mathematicians peaked in their late 20s, scientists and others did so later, seemingly dependent upon the quantity of knowledge they had to master in the given field before they rose above it. Psychologists appeared to do their best work in their 40s and astronomers in their 50s.

Development of talent is not automatic. It involves a complex process of interacting internal and external factors such as the following:

- opportunity – contact with the particular field;
- diligence – long and concentrated practice and familiarization;
- fascination and interest – with that particular area;
- motivation – the urge to dedicate oneself to the study;
- belief in oneself – and the capacity to achieve something when all the odds and society might seem against it;
- models and mentors – not necessarily gifted themselves, but who facilitate the vision and crystallize the experience.

There are also many recorded instances where individuals are found to be multitalented. As mentioned above, mathematicians who were creative writers (Charles Dodson/Lewis Carroll), physicists who might have become poets, musicians who might have been writers, and some with four or five talents are to be found in studies of eminence and genius from previous eras (Cox, 1926).

Creativity

This describes an ingenious, innovative and productive response to ordinary problems and issues. The creative response is often typified by a flexible approach to thinking, a capacity for induction based upon a single or rare instance, and the ability to use analogies in novel and new areas in the development of new ideas, products and processes.

Necka (1986) proposed a triadic model of creativity. This goes beyond thinking to take in motives and skills:

- forming associations;
- recognizing similarities;
- constructing metaphors;
- carrying out transformations;
- selectively directing focus;
- seeing the abstract aspects of the concrete.

The creative person is very good at producing associations and recognizing the significance of a configuration which has occurred (Simonton, 1988).

Personality characteristics

Cox's early studies showed that Galileo, Copernicus, Newton, Keppler and Darwin, amongst others, in addition to having high intelligence, were characterized by tenacity of purpose and persistence. Terman's high achievers were likewise strongly motivated and persistent. More recent studies of creative mathematicians of the seventeenth to nineteenth centuries by Biermann (1985) showed that they had an early fascination with their subject matter and extreme motivation to study it. Hassenstein (1988) noted the obsessive nature of the work of gifted individuals and defined a set of personal characteristics in them as follows:

- flexibility
- sensitivity
- tolerance
- sense of responsibility
- empathy
- independence
- positive self-image.

However strong our abilities and capabilities, an education and a rearing context which damages the self-esteem could therefore damage the ability to achieve. Overnurturance and emotional abuse could also have harmful effects, although many famous authors were said to have been brought up in such environs.

Heinelt (1974) found that the highly creative were more frequently described as introverted, self-willed, intellectually mature, flexible, and possessing wit and a sense of humour. Schoolchildren identified as creative tended to remain aloof from classmates, preferred to work independently, were often socially isolated and unpopular, and were uninterested in conforming. These characteristics were frequently associated with a tendency to feel superior and appear arrogant.

If individuals are to be creative – and it is seldom groups who are – then they probably must risk censure and rejection in having to go against the accepted and traditional ways of thinking and doing. Creative productivity demands (Cropley, 1994):

- convergent and divergent thinking;
- drive to produce new and better solutions (motivation);
- openness to the new (personality);
- willingness to be non-conforming and not obey the social rules;
- communication skills.

In recent decades one can therefore see a radical change in the conception of high ability. It was Renzulli's strong defence of the 'ring', stating that giftedness embodies not only high intelligence but also creative ability and particular personality characteristics, that caused other researchers to reconsider their approaches. Mönks and Boxtel added the social and cultural dimension to this.

RECENT TRENDS

Now that we have come to use the term 'highly able' it may be that we shall lose this feeling for the multidimensional nature of what was formerly in our developing concept of giftedness. Cropley (1994) has reasserted this notion, stating that 'True giftedness' must include creativity. Creativity interacts with conventional intelligence to yield this 'true' giftedness. He also emphasizes the importance of the changes which have taken place to broaden the concept from 'schoolhouse' giftedness to non-school giftedness, so that it now includes not only cognitive aspects of gifts and talents but also personal, affective and motivational constructs. There is also an emphasis upon the need for able individuals to employ their talents in useful and productive fields, such as the social and political rather than just the academic.

Biographical studies have been on the increase again over the last ten years. Of particular note are the studies by Walberg (1995) and his postgraduate students on successful women. Each student combs the biographies of successful women in chosen fields to try to uncover what characteristics they have in common and what they have uniquely, and how these fit with models of giftedness. They trace life histories, mentors, influences, opportunities, motivation, personality, and signs and indicators of high ability and talent. A collection of these studies is due to be published shortly. Thus far the findings do not seem to differ radically from those on successful men in that the women were immersed in their subject from an early age, but they more than men needed to find a mentor or patron who encouraged them and facilitated some early recognition. Women have frequently found that this help has a greater effect if it comes from a man, indicating the strong structural biases still prevalent in our 'civilized' societies.

The contemporary perspective in special educational needs is that the origin of difficulties is ecological – an interaction between personal characteristics and those in the sociocultural environment. The same *ecological perspective* is now prominent in gifted education. Creativity research contributed significantly to expanding the concept of giftedness and challenged the traditional views of a giftedness associated only with intelligence. The ecological perspective emphasizes the view that intelligent behaviour and skilful thinking can be promoted, especially when it links people's natural abilities to real problem solving.

Creativity and creative problem solving are not reducible to a simple set of processes and stages. Creative thinking games and strategies can encourage productive, creative solutions in a wide range of business and educational settings, but as yet they do not produce a Rembrandt or an Anguisola:

> There are specific strategies and skills by which cognition or recon-ceptualization can be facilitated or enhanced ... Students who are above average intelligence, who exhibit signs of particular talents and who show signs of intrinsic motivation can develop the higher skills and strategies which facilitate creative cognition ... Students can acquire skill in recognising problems and using orienting or metacognitive skills while attempting to solve problems. They can be taught to monitor their own cognitive activity, purposely to seek alternatives, recognise new ideas to solutions when they come to mind and test the validity of potential solutions or new conceptions.
>
> (Feldhusen, 1990, p. 15)

There have been a number of shifts in the focus of attention and attitude to the concept of giftedness over time. As the focus has changed, so the concepts derived have been incorporated into the general definition.

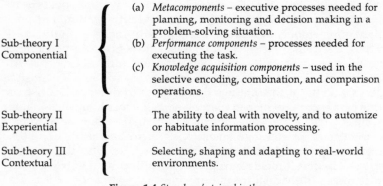

Figure 1.4 *Sternberg's triarchic theory*

Perhaps the most sophisticated conceptualization of ability thus far is Sternberg and Davidson's (1986) triarchic theory, which is constructed from three sub-theories (Figure 1.4). This theory draws very much on Gagné's (1973, 1977) earlier work and deals almost entirely with the control and executive mental processes which we could identify as *higher-order thinking* processes. As this century draws to an end, the identification of suitable learning and teaching environments to nurture higher-order thinking abilities in able pupils in schools and colleges has become a major preoccupation in the field of education. Conferences and research seminars on the subject have suddenly increased worldwide and particularly in higher education spheres in Britain. It could well prove that Sternberg's theory has found its time and could come into general use.

Gardner's theory of multiple intelligences

Just recently Gardner has revisited Britain and put forward once again his theory of multiple intelligences (1983, 1993, 1995c). This time it has gained wide coverage in the more popular education press. Whereas Sternberg's triarchic model represents a unified system with component systems interacting and operating in the world, Gardner views human intellectual activity as seven distinct intelligences using different parts of the brain:

- linguistic
- musical
- spatial
- logico-mathematical
- bodily kinaesthetic
- personal intellectual about self
- personal intellectual about others.

Each intelligence, he believes, is a system in itself, and he emphasizes the separateness of the skills, which he regards as independent of each other. A person's abilities can be high in one and low in others, high in all or many, and so on. These intelligences do interact, otherwise there might be problems for the individual and the theory in cases where, during surgery for epilepsy, the corpus callosum is severed and the two hemispheres of the brain have to function independently without sharing information at a conscious level (Gazzaniga, 1967).

For Gardner, intelligence is an ability or set of abilities that permits an individual to solve problems or fashion products that are a consequence of a particular cultural setting. This position is not new, although it sounds so. For over a hundred years the debate has gone on as to whether intelligence is a unitary or a multiple construct, ability or trait. Thorndike (1913), variously considered to be the father of psychology and/or the father of behaviourism, regarded intelligence as the ability to make good and accurate responses from the point of view of fact or truth. He postulated three types of intelligence: mechanical, abstract and social. An individual could be high on all three or at various different positions on them. He developed the idea that intelligence is only given meaning by its observable products, and constructed a four-factor test consisting of comprehension, arithmetic, vocabulary and directions items.

Spearman, a British psychologist (1927), proposed the existence of an overall general mental factor (*g*) which interacted with several more specific factors (*s*) or abilities in areas such as art, music, mathematics and so on. Using factor analysis, the Thurstones (1938) identified several primary mental abilities but not one general one. Thurstone's Test of Primary Mental Abilities had six separate sections:

- verbal
- numerical
- spatial
- word fluency
- memory
- reasoning.

Whether these can truly be regarded as independent is questionable, for memory is required in all the tasks, as is a certain amount of reasoning. Guilford's (1950) three dimensional model of intellect hypothesizing 120 separate abilities, discussed above, was a further step along this path. It is possible, indeed, to argue for a fourth dimension, the underlying driving force, which was not susceptible to detection because the model determined the items and statistical techniques used.

Gardner is in the forefront of the authentic testing movement, which seeks to evaluate children's gifts in terms of what they produce. They have to demonstrate their ability not just by the potential to produce; they must actually produce. In these methods children must write the poem or story, design and make the object, draw, paint, compose and play, solve real-world problems and so on. In this there is little to disagree with, except to regret that our current systems of assessment do not go far enough in this respect, especially if we are seeking to provide a differentiated curriculum which is going to motivate the able. It also calls in question the use of IQ tests to identify the able.

Gardner has proposed eight criteria by which independent intelligences may be distinguished. These are as follows:

- the potential for isolation by brain damage;
- the existence of idiots savants, prodigies and other exceptional individuals;

- an identifiable core operation or set of operations;
- a distinct developmental history;
- a definable set of expert end-state performances;
- an evolutionary history and evolutionary plausibility;
- support from experimental psychology investigations;
- susceptibility to encoding in a symbol system.

It is, however, equally possible to apply these criteria and confirm another theory such as Sternberg's. According to Mönks and Mason (1993), Gardner's theory is a trait-orientated definition and is 'primarily based on anecdotal findings rather than empirical tests' (p. 92).

The differences between multiple intelligences and the multiple abilities of the earlier theorists are subtle, and possibly those theorists might have used the newer terms today to communicate to a wider audience. Gardner's own background has no doubt contributed to the way he has perceived and interpreted his anecdotal evidence and the manner of their expression. He was formerly a historian, and moved into developmental psychology inspired by the work of Piaget and Bruner. He became interested in children's artistic development and spent half his time working with aphasic adults in hospital, where he could see examples of isolated abilities preserved in different parts of the brain after stroke and injury. The brain would then seem to act as a collection of machines. The results of brain injury, however, do no allow us to make direct inferences about the functioning of intact brains. Controversy is nevertheless good, for it can lead to more focused research and theory which can clarify the issues.

A similar debate took place in the nineteenth century between physiologists about brain function. Gall and Spurzheim favoured localization of functions and held that there were multiple abilities, leading to certain areas of the brain becoming very well developed where there were high abilities. (By overextension it was argued that this led to swelling, producing bumps on the skull which might then be 'read' – phrenology.) Hughlings-Jackson favoured the notion of the 'mass action' of the brain.

Gardner has been so persuasive in his argument that a number of schools in the USA have been reborn as 'MI [multiple intelligences] schools' – schools which believe that children have multiple intelligences and are strong in some but not in others. Gardner himself points out the dangers inherent in typecasting a child as a linguist or a scientist. The approach overall assumes that the majority of children have some talent area or intelligence which is developed through 'focused curriculum attention'. It favours the use of diagnostic information to develop appropriate curricula rather than identifying children as able by IQ tests. (Examples of such approaches are discussed in Chapter 2.) According to Bolanos (1991), it has been successfully implemented in several schools. It can only be helpful if teachers are encouraged to value a wider range of pupil's abilities than traditional academic subjects, even if it is because these have for the first time been dignified with the term 'intelligence'. Gardner is himself critical of schools and suggests that by the age of 5 children have developed very powerful theories about mind, matter and life. These are often charming but wrong. Schools, he says, are supposed to help children think in a more sophisticated way, but when people move from them into adult life most revert back to the theories they held at 5: 'School learning does not become part of the mind. Schools everywhere fail to develop understanding' (Gardner, 1995a, p. 15).

In a recent paper, Gardner has turned his attention to creativity and distinguishes between two different ways the word is used. In the first and true meaning, there are feats at the height of a profession – composing, dancing, scientific investigation and so on. There is also the everyday meaning of the term, when we refer to a child's drawing or story and call that 'creative', meaning it is an original production for that individual. Each form of intelligence harbours within it its own form of creativity (Gardner, 1995c, p. 35). He suggests that creativity is an interaction or dynamic between three distinct constituents:

- the individual's distinctive abilities, styles, needs, etc.;
- the particular domain or discipline within which the training has occurred;
- the field: the context of other individuals and institutions which offer training, positions and awards, and which eventually make decisions about merit or lack of it – the vested interests.

Creative individuals change the nature of the domain, and the next generation study this. To illustrate his theory, Gardner investigated the biographies of seven recognized creatives in his different fields. He selected T.S. Eliot (linguistic), Einstein (logico-mathematical), Picasso (spatial), Stravinsky (musical), Martha Graham (bodily kinaesthetic) Mahatma Gandhi (interpersonal) and Freud (personal). He found a number of common characteristics of the group. They were born removed from the centre of their society in a reasonably supportive home which required disciplined work. By the end of adolescence, before a career had been chosen, they moved to a metropolitan area where they sought the community of other talented and energetic people. They were relatively gregarious during early adulthood. They discovered or returned to a domain and mastered it, which took them about ten years. Their personality was the type that pulls towards novelty and often isolated them. They all needed someone who understood the nature of the domain and the breakthrough. They also needed affective support from someone who loved them unconditionally and assured them they were not mad. Typically, there was resistance to their breakthroughs and these individuals were excellent in more than one area. The breakthrough often depended on an unusual combination of high intelligences and nearly all were weak in one area. Most were not infant prodigies and when they were 20 no one could have predicted their eventual achievements (Picasso was an exception). They later became workaholics.

This is an interesting analysis, and appealing for one can think of others who fit into these categories. Equally, however, it is possible to think of many more who do not, and of course we need more cases and more data from biographical studies to clarify these proposals. There are in fact a number of such studies in progress, again in the USA, where funding is available for such projects.

SUMMARY AND CONCLUSIONS

Research over the last hundred years has shown an increasing emphasis on the application of ability and talent towards useful ends. At the same time, there has been an extension of the conceptual framework to cover wider aspects of ability than just high measured intelligence. Studies of genius and talent have in the main been replaced by studies of ability and talent in the wider community, and the influence of social and cultural factors is gaining in importance as a field of study.

The theoretical models have also undergone significant changes over this period. They have moved from narrow, unidemensional models to the multidimensional frameworks which include personality and creativity as well as cognitive, metacognitive, motivational, social and environmental perspectives.

For teachers concerned with the pragmatics of everyday classroom life, these newest models can provide a much more useful basis for curriculum development and teaching methodology. The notion that we can perhaps teach for promoting high ability, talent and creativity is empowering teachers to try to make a difference in these areas. These changes also enable clearer training goals to be set for the teachers themselves.

Current trends in gifted education show that identification and curriculum provision based upon these new patterns of ability rather than level in the cognitive, metacognitive and creative areas will repay our attention. We need to offer opportunities for the development of the higher-order thinking skills in the context of real and simulated problems within the school curriculum.

2

Identifying the able

INTRODUCTION

Just as models and concepts of ability and talent have changed over time, so the methods of identification have changed, but not necessarily in keeping with theory. There has been a tendency to stay with testing for ability using intelligence tests, despite their well-known limitations. This has meant that other methods have not always gained the acceptance which they should have. There are of course many reasons why educational administration falls back on tests. Perhaps it is not felt that teacher judgement is reliable; tests results can give a false sense of scientific security and accuracy when subject to challenge by parents and teachers; the administration process and costs can be kept to a minimum if a short, paper-and-pencil test can be used; and of course a 'magic' score can be inserted on a form to overawe a lay person.

The earliest method of identifying the able was to look at publicly acknowledged achievement and then undertake biographical meta-analyses. In the last ten years, there has been a reawakening of interest in this method. Following its early popularity, there was a long period of intelligence test development and testing which included the analysis of mental abilities. From these studies the first models of intelligence and ability were developed.

The first results seemed to show that they were highly successful in distinguishing an able population, and thus after the 1944 Education Act (England and Wales) they were used to screen the children so that an able 20 per cent could be creamed off to be given a grammar-school education. This was to be a more academic and fast-tracking route than the rest would enjoy in their secondary technical and secondary modern schools. Within these schools, pupils were also streamed by ability, and thus there is extensive reporting of this form of acceleration and testing and of its effects in the literature of the period. Although it opened up education to a large group at 11 who before would not have been able to afford it or go on to higher education, it had serious emotional and social consequences for those who had failed to obtain the required baseline score. It also missed large numbers of able and talented children and consigned them to a less favourable and less well-resourced education. The system was changed in the 1970s to one of comprehensive education, and selection points were deferred to allow children more time to reveal their ability through the challenge of the curriculum. There was, however, little retraining offered to the teachers for the new mixed ability groups; over the years 'setting' by ability in English and mathematics was instituted, and streaming within many secondary schools never really went away. In the 1990s we have witnessed a return to the old system as schools opt out from LEA control and gain grant-maintained (GM) status. These new GM schools are beginning to use tests, interviews and baseline scores to keep out the less able and the awkward. In a few LEAs the grammar-school system was allowed to continue.

The education of the able in the comprehensive schools when the intake factors were held constantly showed that they did as well as peers in grammar schools, and often enjoyed far better facilities and opportunities for choice. However, it is not always the evidence which sways political opinion.

In the research field, dissatisfaction with the test instruments began to grow. The IQ test was criticized for the convergent nature of items where only one possible answer was recognized as correct. It was at this stage that interest in creativity began to come to the fore, and tests for creativity and divergent thinking began to be developed. Links between creativity and intelligence began to be investigated. Nevertheless, satisfactory screening instruments to determine who was likely to become able and probably gifted could not be satisfactorily produced, and all the while the concept of ability and giftedness kept on expanding whilst better methods of identification were sought. During this period, there was a return to methods of trait identification of common characteristics, and checklists based upon them were developed. Trait rating and checklists became popular on inservice training courses in the 1980s, and they are again being developed with teachers in the latest NACE/DFE inservice project.

Researchers began to use multiple methods to assist in identification, and many more techniques were devised. Current practice has evolved the methods of process analyses, self- and peer selection, performance-based identification, and identification through provision. Each of these would seem to have more to offer to teachers who are engaged with the pupil on the curriculum activity than a formal test, for they give many opportunities to observe pupils at work.

What we can now see instead of a quantitative approach is an emphasis upon qualitative methods. Researchers now ask what kinds of ability constitute giftedness, how these abilities are organized and how they interact. Traditional tests of cognitive abilities are being used to define patterns rather than levels, and there is an increasing interest in and emphasis upon cognitive structures and processes. The analysis and development of metacognitive abilities, problem solving, and non-cognitive aspects, such as motivation, values and attitudes, self-image, confidence and dedication, social abilities and values, are some of the more recent and most important areas of investigation and development in identification of the able. All of these newer developments put identification more in the hands of teachers than before.

Sternberg's theory emphasized the triarchic nature of ability and showed that subject knowledge and skills, although an essential part of human mental functioning, were only a part. Of equal importance were the other components: the metacognitive and the performance. How these newer conceptions of ability can be built into identification procedures will be discussed in subsequent sections. However, before this it is necessary to consider some of the barriers to identification, which are social and personal. These barriers are our own views and stereotypes about what constitutes an able or gifted person. If identification were easy and straightforward, checklists and tests would not have been necessary. Freeman's (1985, 1988, 1991) extensive research into giftedness provides plenty of examples of such problems. Her case studies of 150 gifted children, following them through into adulthood, make her work some of the most extensive carried out by an individual researcher, and certainly the most important longitudinal study in Britain in this century. She describes the stereotypes of giftedness or high ability still operating. According to Freeman (1991), to be brilliant is in a sense an affront to good manners. It is contrary to the natural order of things. Being termed 'gifted' creates expectations that the child will have stereotypic characteristics and problems. If the stereotype is not confirmed, then teachers and parents alike can overlook giftedness. Stereotypes, however, appear to be culturally defined, and Freeman defines the differences found between those of the United States and Britain: 'The American stereotype is of a superchild: he (for it is always he) is a brilliant sportsman, a natural leader, and a straight A-scholar. He is expected to be physically well-formed and good to look at' (Freeman, 1991, pp. 21–22). By contrast:

The British stereotype is a weedy lad (for he is still male): is bespec-
tacled, lonely, and much given to solitary reading. This stereotype
is in fact of a juvenile intellectual, at times referred to by his school-
mates and maybe his teachers as 'the little professor'. He will look
old-fashioned, move awkwardly, be difficult to bring up, and will
find it hard if not impossible to make friends. He is certainly not a
leader for in Britain talent in leadership and sport are assumed to be
the province of non-intellectuals.

(Freeman, 1991, p. 22)

These pen portraits would be amusing if they were not true. If you
drop a grade below 'A' you can thereby become a failure! Women in
both countries, by definition, are not gifted whether or not they
wear spectacles. Being small, weedy and bookish can attract the
label of 'the professor' or 'boffin' and give a stereotype to live up to
that may prove impossible, as well as resulting in victimization.
Similarly, blonde, good-looking adolescent girls by stereotypic definition cannot possibly even be able: they must be 'dumb blondes'.
The grades of these 'dumb blondes' were found to have been
systematically lowered by teachers when a group of pupils forged
essays so that all had written the same one (Montgomery, 1957).

In order to bring some equality to the treatment of boys and
girls, and of disadvantaged young people of all kinds, it is thought
to be necessary for educators to use tests, inventories or checklists
and curriculum identification strategies to find out who are the
able and highly able and what are their needs. In this chapter, a
range of identification strategies will be examined for their relative
merits, and the question will be posed as to whether it really is
important to single out the able for educational purposes. Consideration will also be given to levels of ability, talent and creativity,
and to whether or not it is helpful or useful to distinguish between
able and highly able or between one level of IQ and the next.
Differences in patterns of ability will be examined for relevance in
relation to curriculum provision and pedagogy.

IDENTIFYING THE ABLE USING PSYCHOMETRICS

During this century, intelligence tests have been developed from
the early work of Binet (1905), Terman (1925), Cattell (1915) and
Wechsler (1945, 1974) into a wide range of sophisticated modern
tests. It is the revised version of the Wechsler test which has been
used in recent years worldwide in the identification of the able for
special programmes and research, and there are modified versions
in various languages, including a British version. Each country has

also developed its own intelligence tests. In Britain, the British Ability Scales (BAS: Elliott, 1983) are well established, and are often used by educational psychologists to assess levels and patterns of ability. The Wechsler Intelligence Scale for Children – Revised (WISC-R) is an individual test and takes about 50 minutes to administer. Thus it is usual only for individuals about whom there is some concern to be assessed with it, or for it to be used in research and special programmes. WISC-R and WAIS (Wechsler Adult Intelligence Scale) consist of two major subsections, verbal and performance scales, each of which is made up of five sub-tests tapping both right- and left-hemisphere types of intellectual processing. The sub-tests are made up of items which it is thought contribute to our mental abilities, such as information, similarities, arithmetic, coding and block assembly.

Individual administration enables the tester to read the question to the pupil and receive an oral answer, which cuts out errors especially associated with reading problems. The tests also usually require that a trained expert both administers and interprets the results. Group tests are more economical of tester and administration time, but can require reading by the pupil and a written response. Responses also have to be codable in written terms within a short space, which can limit the types of item used. There are some group tests, such as Young's and Raven's Progressive Matrices, which are non-verbal. The Alice Heim (AH) tests are paper-and-pencil tests often used to identify levels within the high-ability range. Schools and LEAs interested in identifying or screening out able pupils are obliged to use group tests because of the time and cost factors.

When administering a test to a group, there are more opportunities for response errors to occur. The tests themselves are more narrowly focused on items which can be responded to by marks on paper. It has been shown that group tests are useful *only as rough screening devices*. They can identify able groups from less able groups, but are less reliable when predicting an *individual's* level of ability. Group tests on the whole have a lower ceiling (top score) – usually about 134 IQ – than individual tests. Thus in one LEA school visited, twenty out of the thirty-six pupils in the first-year 'top' class had IQs of 134, when quite clearly, from their responses to the mathematics and problem-solving work given them, some of them were less than that and a number of them were most certainly 150 and above.

In a comparative study in Terman's research (Terman and Oden, 1947), 332 pupils scored 130 or above on the Stanford-Binet test (Form L-M), but when tested on a group test only 48.5 of the pupils scored over 130 IQ. When the researchers looked at the percentage of pupils on the group test scoring over 125, they would still have excluded 82, or 25 per cent, of their able subjects. If we apply these findings to LEAs still selecting pupils on the basis of group IQ-type tests, we can infer they are leaving out 25 per cent of the able population and presumably including 25 per cent who are not able. Within the middle and lower ranges, the IQ individual and group tests gave similar results and so proved more reliable. LEA tests also tend to be more biased towards verbal reasoning, and so this can exclude able performers. However, since these schools tend to have a curriculum which is verbally biased, this may result in less heartache for the able but learning disabled.

All tests, even 'good' ones, have an inbuilt test error (standard error) of plus or minus 3–5 IQ points. Poorer tests have a larger standard error. Standard error is significant in that it contributes to creating identification errors when strict levels and cut-off points are used. The test items indicate the general theory of intelligence held by the test constructor, and the most widely held view currently is that intelligence is *'a general problem-solving ability'*. This underlies performance in many areas of human activity, and the test items usually centre on:

- verbal reasoning questions;
- numerical reasoning questions;
- spatial reasoning questions.

When devising a measuring instrument such as a test, the test writers and publishers have many other assumptions under which they operate. The following assumptions are made:

- At least to some extent each item on a test and all the words in that item hold the same or similar meanings for different people.
- Test behaviour and actual behaviour are consistent over time.
- The test measures what it is supposed to measure.
- An individual's observed score is equal to his or her true score and thus measures 'true' ability.

> Paper and pencil tests do not measure what has been learned in school in any way that is useful in the social arena. Thus to make functional use in the societal arena of what has been learned in school is difficult to ascertain. Should schools not emphasize what is relevant and useful to society?
>
> (Ediger, 1994, p. 172)

Relying upon psychometric measures alone to identify an able group for whatever purpose would seem to be an unwise practice, given what we now know about the broader nature of ability and talent and the limitations of even the best test instruments. Passow (1990) summed up the problems of test identification thus:

> Despite the acknowledged critical significance of identification and selection processes in the school's efforts to nurture potential to performance, there is little research to ascertain the effectiveness of our procedures or, more important, whether we are diagnosing the right characteristics and behaviour.

(p. 16)

Levels of intelligence and ability

When large groups of subjects have their intelligence 'measured', the majority, or about 68 per cent, fall in the middle or average range. Fewer have low IQ (14 per cent) and fewer have high IQ (14 per cent), and their scores spread more or less evenly on each side of the average group, with an approximate 2 per cent each side falling at the extremes of what is considered to be the normal range at plus 130 IQ or plus 2 standard deviation.

As can be seen from the 'normal distribution curve' in Figure 2.1, only 2 per cent of the population can be expected to have an IQ above 130 points. The DES figures in 1980 predicted about 3 per 100 in actual terms. Some local authorities identify the small proportion of children with IQs of 145 (plus 3 standard deviations

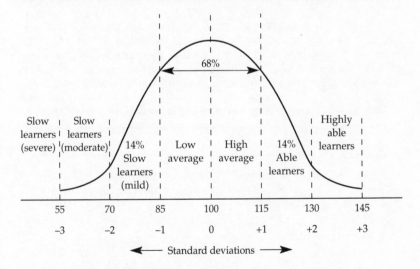

Figure 2.1 *Distribution of intelligence in normal individuals*

above the norm of 100 or mean IQ score) as 'gifted' and perhaps in need of special consideration, in the form of special projects, clubs or the use of enrichment materials, even special schooling. The higher the threshold is set the fewer pupils are identified and the less costly special provision becomes. Table 2.1 shows a range of thresholds.

Table 2.1 *Examples of the thresholds used to determine giftedness and ability*

Threshold	Source	Pupils identified
100	Montgomery (1990) UK. Any above average ability, talent or interest in any definable area	50%
115	Callow (1983); Montgomery (1985)	25%
120+	Havighurst (1961) US; Wallach and Kogan (1965) (creativity threshold) US	8%
125+	Parkyn (1948), New Zealand	
130+	Ogilvie (1973) DES project; Painter (1982)	Top 2% UK
132+	Getzels and Jackson (1962) US; Lovell and Shields (1967) UK	
140+	Terman (1926–47)	Top 1% US
145+	Some LEAs	

Researchers in a number of countries have noted that there is a bulge at the upper end of the IQ range, with the actual numbers with very high IQs exceeding the table of expected frequencies. (There is also a 'bulge' at the lower end of the range, probably associated with pre-, peri- and post-natal injury.) See Table 2.2

Table 2.2 *Expected numbers of pupils in the general population at various IQ levels*

No. of pupils		IQ level
3 per	100	130
1 per	100	137
1 per	1,000	150
1 per	10,000	160
1 per	100,000	168
1 per	1,100,000	180

Source: DES, 1980

Bearing in mind what has already been said about cut-off points, standard error and levels, it can be seen that any attempt to select with a high degree of precision is bound to fail.

In an analysis of wide-ranging data, Flynn (1987) has shown that IQ numbers of highly able appearing in the IQ range are consistently much higher than the earlier statistics predicted. He has found that individuals grow more intelligent by six points on average every decade in his studies in The Netherlands. If this is borne out by classroom performance, in fifty years' time there will be a most interesting problem for education to resolve.

Flynn (1987) found that IQ gains of present 20-year-olds in Holland were twenty points higher than those of their counterparts thirty years ago. This means that in his samples the numbers with IQs over 150 must have increased by a factor of nearly sixty, yet the number of patents had fallen to 60 per cent of the rate of the 1960s. The question this raises is whether IQ is as relevant to inventive achievement as it once was, or whether we have to have even higher IQs to achieve in this area these days. Alternatively, is the Dutch education system changing and working heavily against invention?

The heritability of intelligence and high ability

In *Hot House People*, Walmsley and Margolis (1987) repeatedly claimed that the majority of young children were capable of gaining abilities that most people would regard as exceptional. The book and TV series created a great deal of excitement and debate. The evidence that average infants can be converted into child prodigies by sufficient of the 'right sorts of enriching education' was confirmed by Howe (1988) in his analysis of the evidence, and Radford claimed as recently as 1993, at the British Association for the Advancement of Science meeting, that he could create child prodigies.

Howe argued that no genuine masterpiece had ever been produced without a huge amount of conscious effort, there were apparently no short cuts to greatness (even for Mozart), and each prodigy's early background provided an environment that gave rich opportunities for learning, when there was sufficient evidence available for analyses in the biographies. Unhappiness, poverty and disruption were not uncommon, but virtually all prodigies had adult encouragement to accelerate the development of their talents. A contemporary example of such acceleration was the success of the Suzuki-trained child violinists.

Whilst for most of the century parents and educators have been led to believe that intelligence and ability are heritable, contrary evidence exists that they are *highly malleable commodities* which early enriching education could facilitate, particularly if it continues and is not cut short at the end of a special programme. The malleability of intelligence is such that over a generation or two it has been found to increase by one standard deviation (15 IQ points). Intellectual acceleration cannot, however, guarantee that the individual will gain the non-intellectual qualities upon which success depends. These qualities Howe (1988) defined as self-direction, self-confidence, a sense of commitment and sheer persistence. He says that in the absence of these the cleverest individual is likely to achieve nothing, and quotes *The Prodigy*, Wallace's (1986) biography of William James Sidis, 'the world's greatest child prodigy'. Freeman (1991) in her longitudinal study found that it was the most able and the least able who suffered the greatest disadvantage from a poor-quality cultural and educational environment.

On the other side, the most longstanding intervention programme, Head Start (Head Start Bureau, 1985), published an extensive meta-analysis. Overall, the results indicated that only a transitory positive effect was gained: an immediate post-training gain for pre-school children of nine or ten points, which disappeared within the first year of formal schooling. The effect seemed stable despite subtle differences among programmes: how many hours per day they ran, the number of children in the class, the minority composition of the group, the socioeconomic status of the families, etc. In a review of eleven other more extensive pre-school programmes, Lazar and Darlington (1982) found that in adolescence the children from their pre-school project averaged 5 points below their pre-test IQs (average 83 points) and controls 1 point below (average 82 points). Both were disadvantaged, low-average groups to start. The Milwaukee pre-school project was different. It started at age 3 months and continued seven hours per day, five hours per week, to school age with children of black mothers whose IQ scores were below 75. At 3 years, the children as a group scored a mean of 122 IQ, 30 points above the control group. At 14 years, the IQ was 10 points above the controls. Later analyses by Flynn (1987) reduced these gains to 10 points. The study could not be repeated by others, however, and questions were raised not infrequently about the quality of the data and its interpretation. The nature–nurture issue has been in continuous debate since the early years of psychometrics, and clearly must remain under review with regard to methods of 'enrichment' and those by which gains might properly be assessed.

Case studies and levels of high ability

In 1942, Hollingworth reported a small subsection study of seven-teen children, twelve with IQs of 180+, in the Terman project. Ten were first-born and five were only children. All showed normal physical development, but the rest of the developmental mile-stones were passed astonishingly early. They were talking by 14 months and reading by 36 months. Their response to school ranged from truancy to enthusiasm. Hollingworth found that the earlier the giftedness was identified the more favourable the development. She suggested that the optimum IQ for integration with peers was between 125 and 155, but that those with levels of 170–180+ suffered problems of severe isolation, for they were too intelligent to be understood by their peers.

She concluded that the highly able or gifted person is generally superior in all aspects of development and attainment to average peers. Being intellectually gifted, however, does not necessarily mean that these people will become successful or eminent in later careers. Such success depends greatly upon personality factors like independence and persistence, together with some occasional favourable chance effects.

Pickard (1976) followed up fifty-five very able pupils identified by the Stanford-Binet intelligence test. She too found that not all the children were happy in their school experience and this followed a particular pattern as follows:

IQs 131–40	There were eleven children in this group and all were *reasonably happy* in their ordinary school.
IQs 141–50	There were nineteen children in this group. They were not doing as well unless a particular teacher took an active interest – the *significant adult*.
IQs 151–60	Fourteen children ⎫ Almost no child in this
IQs 161–9	Eight children ⎬ group was happy. A few had
IQs 170+	Three children ⎭ found places in progressive public schools which were *flexible enough to help to some degree*.

Pickard maintained that most of the children had lost any chance of realizing their real potential because they had not learned *how to study* in their junior school. The work of Bridges in the Brentwood Experiment (1969) underlined this view. Very able pupils needed to learn *how to think about* what they studied or read, so that they did not have such a limited view of learning that it directed them to memorize all the rivers and seas of the world or simply accumulate information about topics in which they were interested. Their capacity for appraising evidence and thinking creatively and exploratively about data needed to be inspired and encouraged to action, so that they became active learners rather than passive recipients. They needed to know that it is both important and 'good' to question what others may wish to consider accepted fact, or an authoritative source.

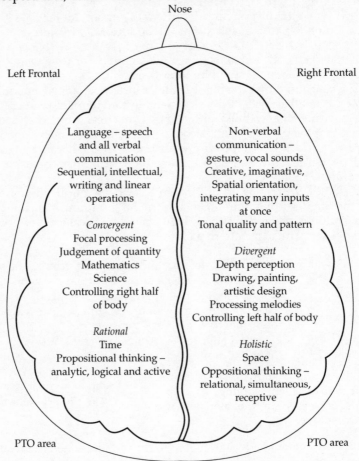

Frontal areas: voluntary movement and plans and programmes

PTO areas: pattern analysing in vision, hearing and other sensations

Figure 2.2 *Differing functions of the two sides of the brain*

In the last twenty-five years, brain research has revealed two main types of processing, each associated mainly with a particular hemisphere. The Wechsler test had already heralded this in giving separate verbal and performance quotients for its two separate clusters of sub-scales. These are summed to give a full score. These two main forms of intelligence must be assessed if an effective identification procedure is to be established. These are variously called right- and left-hemisphere thinking, simultaneous-spatial and sequential logical thinking (Gazzaniga, 1967; Bogen and Bogen, 1969). Useful summaries of right- and left-hemisphere functioning can be found in Calder (1970), Blakemore (1977), Springer and Deutsch (1985) and Ornstein (1982).

Figure 2.2 illustrates some of the most frequent findings. There are approximately 10 per cent of the population who are left-handers; 50 per cent of this group also appear to have language functions located in the left hemisphere. In the rest of this group of left-handers, the roles of the two hemispheres are reversed. Handedness is controlled by the presence of a gene for the 'right-shift' factor, making the majority of the population right-handed and left-brained for language (Annett, 1983). Research has begun to indicate that being left-handed can carry with it extra facility for creativity and originality, particularly in the arts.

The cerebral hemispheres in humans are two huge lobes of the brain that flop over the rest of the lower brain structures, which carry out the vital functions of running the body on autopilot. The cerebral hemispheres are the seat of the intellect and thinking processes, which the 'split brain' studies of Gazzaniga (1967) first began to unravel. Previously, little had been known about the 'silent' right hemisphere, but now it is realized it has important functions and works in harmony and harness with the left. Individuals with well-developed creative abilities appear to have a greater facility in the right hemisphere and are more flexible in their thinking. Creativity has been linked with right-hemisphere activity and a more relaxed, wakeful state (Ornstein, 1982) in creative problem solving, as opposed to alpha-wave blocking, which is seen in the alert, problem-solving states of the left hemisphere.

SAVANTS

The term 'idiot savant' was originally used by Down (1887) in describing a mentally handicapped person who had an isolated area of high ability, most often in art or music. Such individuals are now more frequently called 'savant', as the term 'idiot' has been long ago replaced as a scientific/medical label. A person with severe learning difficulties might have an isolated area of high functioning such as calendar counting ('On what day of the year 2310 will 29 November fall?'); music, particularly piano playing; rapid calculating; memorizing facts; painting, drawing or sculpturing; and mechanical abilities. The phenomenon is rare in cases of severe learning difficulties, according to O'Connor (1989), and has an incidence of about 0.6 per cent in that group.

Savants are more frequently found in autistic populations and form about 10 per cent of that group. However, autism is itself quite rare, occurring in only four births in 1000. Out of 100 known prodigious savants worldwide, from twelve to fifteen are still alive. One of the most recent was the gifted artist Nadia, born in Nottingham in 1967, who was studied by Selfe (1977, 1983). Nadia's talent manifested itself at about 3½ years despite her severe linguistic difficulties.

An interesting explanation of the prodigious savant has been put forward by Treffert (1989). He suggests that pre- or post-natal damage to the left (language and analytic thought) hemisphere stimulates compensatory growth of the right. The right hemisphere, responsible in the main for musical and spatial abilities and analogous activities, gains an increased capacity, which in certain individuals coincidentally results in high ability. This high ability or prodigious performance is in the presence of severe learning difficulties in other areas. From comparative studies, Treffert argued that the prodigy also has heightened right-brain functioning differing from the savant in possessing intact left-hemisphere functions. No doubt new techniques in brain research will be able to shed further light on this relationship.

CHILD PRODIGIES

A child prodigy shows an astonishisng and adult-like mastery of some demanding aspect of human endeavour, such as musical or artistic ability. The definition of a prodigy given by Feldman (1986), following detailed analysis of cases and the rather sparse literature on the subject, was that a prodigy was a child who, before the age of 10, performs at the level of an adult professional in some cognitively demanding field. Such abilities were in former times considered freakish and unnatural. Later, precocious abilities were linked with high IQ, as IQ testing gained widespread acceptance. Then any 6-year-old who could compose a sonata or play a grandmaster at chess was assumed to be also of high ability.

There are, according to Morelock and Feldman (1993), only three scientific studies of prodigies in world literature to date, and these show similar patterns. Baumgarten's study in 1930 characteristically shows, like that of Revesz (1925) and Feldman (1980, 1986), that the prodigies had a mixture of adult-like and child-like qualities. They had an extraordinary ability which showed itself at an early age, often at 2 or 3 years. The talent was in an area which did not demand a vast degree of prior subject knowledge before it could be exercised. Typically it occurred in music, fine art, performance arts such as dance and drama, poetry, mathematics and chess. Baumgarten's subjects' IQ scores ranged from 120 to 160 and beyond, but she concluded that the intellectual abilities reflected in the IQ tests failed to explain the prodigies' high-level performance in their particular field. Their other characteristics were ambition, pragmatism, passionate devotion to their careers, and a total lack of fear of public performance. In other respects, they were like any other children.

From his studies, Feldman also concluded that prodigious achievement could only occur in domains accessible to children where little prerequisite knowledge was needed. The area had also to be attractive to children and adaptable, so that child-sized versions of instruments could be produced. Thus far, the most frequently reported instances of child prodigies have been in chess and musical performance. Feldman proposed that coincidentally the meeting of many sets of forces interacted in the development or expression of human potential. He used this principle and the forces of coincidence to explain how natural ability, an appropriate nurturing environment, and the encouragement and services of key individuals such as tutors, mentors and so on would from time to time cause child prodigies to occur in these particular domains. Radford (1993) lays claims to being able to create a child prodigy given the full direction of 'his' education and nurture from a very young age. Once again, nurture and its potential role in the development of ability have emerged as an issue for consideration.

CREATIVITY AND INTELLIGENCE

During the 1960s, a number of concerns were raised about the use of the IQ alone to identify and define high ability. Torrance was one of the key researchers raising questions during this period:

'If measures of intelligence alone are used in identifying children for special classes, 70 per cent of the most superior on measures of creative thinking will be missed'. This is one of the early warnings which suggests that high intelligence was not the only form of gift- edness which might be observed.

(Torrance, 1965, p. 39)

Teacher judgement ... Not only were more than half of the gifted missed but ... almost a third (31.4 per cent) chosen were not in the gifted or superior range but in the average range on Stanford-Binet.

(French, 1964, p. 78)

The later work of Painter (1982) confirmed this: she found that secondary-school teachers could only identify one-third of the very able pupils, but nominated one-third *who were not very able.*

The dispute concerning the relative independence of intelli- gence and creativity still exists, but, as mentioned above, the consensus position is that there is probably a threshold point on the IQ scale, perhaps about 120 points, below which an intelligence score is the best predictor of academic achievement, and above which measures of creativity become more significant for the prediction of the achievement of some children. Identifying creativity itself by tests or practical demonstration of ability is still a matter of personal and more subjective judgement, which ex- perience can hone.

Woodland animals

Woodland animals often live in woodland, the fox, the squirrel the woodmouse and the shrew. The largest of these animals is the fox. The fox carniverous which means he eats meat. The shrew is the smallest of the animals mentioned, and he is about two inches long at most. The pigmy shrew is about one and a half centi- metres. The squirel is often a pest because he will dig up roots of various plants. Squirrels eat nuts and sometimes pine cones. Ocasionaly rabbits are seen in the wood, they are greay brown and have very large ears The rabbits sense and hearing is very good too. A warning call is a thump made by a rabbit sensing danger. The rabbits home is called a warren. Many rabbits will live in one warren. Rabbits eat berries and other fruit. Adders live in woods too It is the only british poisness snake. An adder is brown and has crosses down its back.
I once found a dead adder.

Figure 2.3 (p. 42)shows a drawing by a boy aged 5.3, with a mental age 11, in the Goodenough–Harris 'draw a person' test. Mark's WISC-R rating was off the top of the scale. He was referred for behavioural problems in class. He was unable to read and thought to be a slow learner.

The box shows an able pupil's free writing. The writer was a girl aged 5 years 11 months with a memory span of eleven digits. Compare this piece of writing with that of a pupil of your own or whom you know of similar age but average ability or of older average ability, on factual report.

IDENTIFYING CREATIVITY AND TALENT

Although the terms 'high ability', 'giftedness' and 'talent' are used interchangeably by some researchers, the relationship between 'giftedness' and 'talent' has always been problematic. After an extensive review of the literature, Gagné (1985) defined giftedness/high ability as above-average competence in one or more domains of human *ability*. Talent he defined as above-average performance in one or more fields of human *performance*.

The most recent definition by Feldhusen (1992) proposed that talent refers to superior aptitude or ability in any worthwhile line of human endeavour. Talent, he suggested, was a developmental phenomenon emerging out of general aptitude into specific, career-orientated abilities. Creativity can be regarded as a form of talent as well as a set of fundamental attributes underlying a number of performance areas. The identification of both creativity and talent at an early age has been found to be problematic.

One of the most famous definitions of the creative process is that of Wallas (1926). He proposed four stages, which have been verified many times by those who have experienced creative insight.

Model of the creative process by Wallas

Wallas proposed that the creative process consisted of the following four stages:

(a) *Preparation* ➜ (b) *incubation* ➜ (c) *illumination*➜] (d) *verification*. Kekule's description of his discovery of the benzene ring (in Koestler, 1966) is an example of this process in operation. He spent years trying to unravel the molecular structure of benzene, but none of his models worked. He gave up trying to work it out, but he was so immersed in the problem that he began dreaming about it. In one

Clown

Figure 2.3 *A drawing by a boy of high mental age*

of his dreams, the molecules all got up and began to dance around in a circle. When he woke up he had forgotten the dream, but then suddenly during the work on the molecule the dream image of the molecules dancing in a ring came into his consciousness, and he had that sudden illumination or insight, that 'aha!' realization, proposed by the *Gestalt* school of psychology as early as 1913. The verification stage followed as the idea was tested for its validity. This model has popularly been reinterpreted as 'Creativity is 1 per cent inspiration and 99 per cent perspiration'. (A *Gestalt* is a configuration or organized whole, a set of structured configurations or patterns which have to be organized and understood as a totality rather than a collection of parts. Thinking develops through insight and a sense or feeling for patterns and new resolutions of different configurations. Westheimer was regarded as the initiator and leader of this approach to perception and thinking.)

Guilford's model of intellect (1959, 1967), in which he proposed the notions of divergent and convergent thinking, was highly influential in both the research and educational fields. Creativity became synonymous with divergent thinking for many people. For the first time, the focus of attention in identifying the able shifted from highly able as defined by high scores on intelligence tests to looking for other characteristics, such as fluency, flexibility, originality, and elaboration (Torrance, 1963, 1966); 'brainstorming' (Usborn, 1953); and personality attributes (Mackinnon, 1965).

The relationship between creativity and intelligence was investigated by a number of researchers. Some of the key findings were as follows.

Torrance (1965) devised a range of tests for creativity to study verbal and figural fluency. One sub-test, 'circles', can be used to illustrate his main ideas. Subjects were given a sheet of forty or so circles of about 3 cm diameter and invited to draw as many interesting and unusual things involving the circle as possible in ten minutes, giving each a caption. Torrance suggested the following four ways of marking this subtest:

- *Fluency:* the number of circles used or incorporated into other pictures. Count the total number of different things drawn.
- *Flexibility:* the number of different category changes. For example, face, clown, ball, sphere, would count as a score of one, as the categories changed from face types to spheres.
- *Originality:* The scores range from 2 to 0. Everybody draws faces, so this scores 0. Only a few draw screws, so this scores 1. Objects which only one person in the group draws score 2 (such as the underside of a Tilley lamp).

- *Elaboration:* the amount of detail given in the picture. It is extremely difficult to mark objectively.

Torrance found that high scores on originality and elaboration gave the *highest correlation* with creative ability. He also found some very individual and creative responses which did not score highly at all on any of the measures, such as those of the pupil who made all the circles into hexagonal cells in a honeycomb and drew a bee in the bottom corner. One individual simply wrote a different caption under each without drawing any distinguishing detail.

A large number of circles completed suggests a fluency of ideas and an ability to think in spatial terms, especially with scores above 20–30 in five minutes. More characteristic is the completion of 12–14 circles with careful thought, the products of our literal education system. Art students in general proliferate more designs and symbols rather than produce recognizable objects. Any individual who performs very well by comparison with peers can be considered to be unusual, with a talent worth exploring.

Case data at the beginning and end of our courses was regularly reviewed and teachers' feelings of competency were assessed in interviews and questionnaires. The problems of identification of creativity were always more complex and more dependent upon personal views. Development of evaluation schedules made the judgements more reliable and consistent, but *validity* remained an overarching problem.

Wallach and Kogan (1965) compared samples of children having high or low measured intelligence and high or low creativity on a number of educational, psychological and social dimensions. They summarized their findings as follows:

- *High creativity – high intelligence:* These children can exercise within themselves both control and freedom, both adult-like and child-like kinds of behaviour.
- *High creativity – low intelligence:* These children are in angry conflict with themselves and with their school environment, and are beset with feelings of unworthiness and inadequacy. In a stress-free context, however, they can blossom forth cognitively.
- *Low creativity – high intelligence:* These children can be described as 'addicted' to school achievement. Academic failure would be conceived by them as catastrophic, so that they must continually strive for academic excellence to avoid the possibility of pain.
- *Low creativity – low intelligence:* Basically bewildered, these children engaged in various defensive social activities and regressions, such as passivity and psychosomatic symptoms.

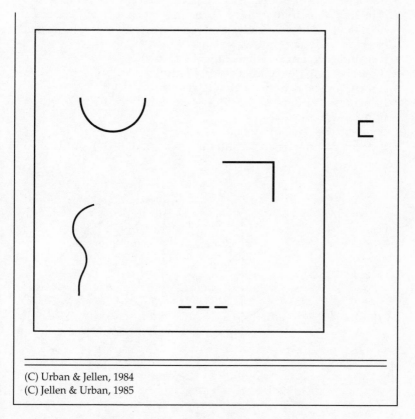

Figure 2.4 *TCT-DP/TSD-Z test sheet* (reduced)

The Torrance tests of creative thinking are still used worldwide in creativity studies, according to Urban (1990), who reviewed 200 research studies. Most European studies used the Torrance test, the Wallach–Kogan tests, the Mednick Remote Associations test or items from the Guildford battery of tests, which was the predecessor. Urban concluded that recent trends show a more holistic view of creativity. It is not now regarded as just a form of divergent thinking in which quantity of response is the crucial factor. Earlier, Urban and Jellen (1986) had developed their own test instrument, the Test for Creative Thinking–Drawing Production (TCT-DP: see Figure 2.4). They based their identification on defining creativity as follows:

- It is the integration of divergent and convergent thinking.
- It is a balance of opposites or dialectics in creative processes.
- It includes creativity in science, technology and mathematics.
- It involves process analysis of creative problem solving and invention adaptor–innovator approaches.
- It includes creativity in management and business.
- It involves creativity in everyday settings.
- It includes social and collective creativity.
- It includes content- and activity-orientated creativity in education and training
- It covers the developmental life span.
- It needs diagnostic and evaluative instruments to identify it.

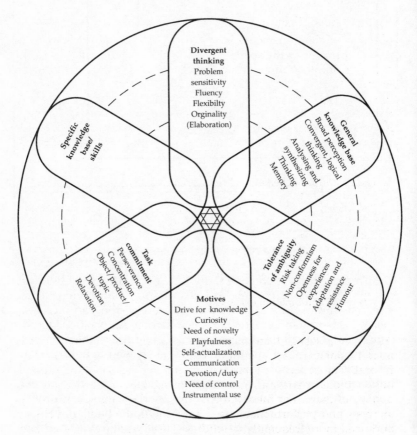

Figure 2.5 *Urban's component model of creativity*

From various authors such as Necka and Cropley, Urban developed a components model of creativity to assist in the development of the assessment procedures (Figure 2.5).

Part of the mystique attached to creativity stems from the difficulty in defining it. Since the early attempts, there have been definitions such as the following:

• expert problem solving (Weisberg, 1988);
• ability to apply heuristics across domains (de Bono, 1976);
• synergistic application of creative resources (Sternberg and Lubart, 1991);
• ability to form new declarative (knowing that) and procedural (knowing how) knowledge by using the total cognitive system (Glaser, 1985).

Glaser's (1985) view was that good problem solvers and experts possess efficient metacognitive skills, so that they are able to reflect critically on the appropriateness of the strategies they select and can employ different ones where necessary. They can also monitor their progress while engaged on the task. An extension of the metacognitive process for creativity is that of 'metacreativity'. It includes emotional and physiological processes as well as cognitive ones. Most recently, Yashin-Shaw (1994) has suggested that there are three orders of schemata or cognitive process underlying creativity:

> The first order schemata represent familiar knowledge, skills and procedures that have been mastered and checked and assimilated. The second order are the knowledge, skills and procedures used for relatively unfamiliar schematas and need conscious control. Operations in this order possess a high cognitive load. The third order represents metacognition which is the cognitive control mechanism enabling the operation to switch between knowledge as it is needed. Creativity is not located in any one order but results in a combination of all three being used in various degrees. Synergy is created where the combination exceeds the sum of its constituent parts.'
> (Yashin-Shaw, 1994, p. 35)

As can be envisaged, an instrument for identification on this scale is not contained in a simple paper-and-pencil test, verbal or figural. The processes which are being used have to be tapped, observations made and questions raised about the nature and quality of them. For these sorts of reason, the methods of process analysis and performance-based assessment are being developed and used more frequently in studies. These will be discussed later in this chapter.

Identification of talent

Talent can be regarded as a general ability which is non-specific until it finds a particular focus, when the investment of time and, if necessary, a great deal of practice enables the learner to become expert. Some talent, however, seems to be domain-specific, at least in some individuals, and the performance in that field is recognized by a body of experts to be 'talented'. Even to the inexpert observer, the ability of a 7-year-old to play a musical instrument like an expert is a demonstration of a high degree of talent, and this is most often how we identify it – as an unusual ability, particularly in music, art and design, dance and drama, or sport. Experts often vary in their assessments of the degree and nature of the talent, but there is a general recognition of some special ability based upon current performance.

More difficulties arise when identification has to precede any opportunity to learn to perform, as is often the case in selection for ballet schools. The experienced selectors, however, seem to have no difficulty in looking at some skills performance and assessing who should be offered places. Their choices often appear to be surprising – they do not always choose the trim little precise performers but often a plumpish, dumpy one. Their criteria seem to centre on flexibility in the skeletal structure, freedom of movement, and whether or not the bones have more growth potential. (Specialist sources will need to be consulted on the subject of the early identification of special talent.)

Tannenbaum (1993) identified a prestige hierarchy in giftedness and *talent* in Western society based upon admiration value at particular periods in history and rarity:

- *scarcity talents:* talents in short supply which makes life easier and safer or different, such as Salk's polio vaccine, Luther King's leadership, Freud's work on psychoanalysis;
- *surplus talents:* people whose talent is considered great by many but whose work only a small proportion may study or enjoy, such as Van Gogh, Dickens, Scott, Platt, Woolf, Bach, Britten, Mozart;
- *quota talents:* specialized, high-level skills required in response to market needs, such as those of teachers, doctors, lawyers, politicians and currently managers and accountants;
- *anomalous talents:* talents which may be appreciated or ignored, such as Mastermind abilities, creative cookery, craft, speed reading, sexual prowess, tightrope walking.

IDENTIFYING ABILITY USING TRAIT DEFINITIONS OR CHECKLISTS

When able individuals are said to have unusual persistence or task commitment, be highly curious, and have a wide variety of interests, these psychological or personality traits are thought to characterize these individuals and form the substance of trait definitions. The checklist or trait inventory is a good example of this approach. The inventory may be devised and scientifically constructed from looking at able individuals' clustering of scores on personality tests, but in these cases the able are first selected on the basis of an IQ test. Inventories may also be informally devised traits and scales put together from the clinical and practical expertise of those who have worked with the able. Experience is formalized into a checklist.

The checklist then needs to be validated. This can be done in a variety of ways, but it is particularly important to use it to identify an able group and then to investigate this group further with tests, examining the results of school, work on special projects and classroom observation. From all this a profile can be built up of the pupils, and judgements made against the criteria to assess whether or not the pupils are able.

In using a checklist the *more items included* as characteristic of a particular able person, the more likely it is that there is ability. The *more strongly* the characteristic is shown, the more highly able the individual. Single traits are unlikely to be strong enough indicators by themselves of high ability. Several – even five or more – traits, should be taken together to indicate ability.

An example inventory or checklist for identifying able individuals

The Learning Difficulties Research Project (Montgomery, 1985) put together the following checklist of characteristics:

- a wide range of interests and hobbies;
- curiosity and investigativeness in approach;
- an interest in and knowledge of questions about the origin of the universe, God, planets and the solar and stellar systems at an early age;
- keen powers of observation, noting mismatches and analogies;
- a facility in hypothesizing and dealing with abstract ideas;
- originality and initiative in intellectual and practical work;
- unusual imaginations and plenty of ideas;

- pursuing subjects or a subject in great depth;
- a very powerful attention and attention span, concentrating and persevering for extraordinarily long periods;
- frequently having learned to read or being 'self-taught' before going to school;
- superior reasoning powers and also powers of induction;
- superior development of verbal skills and vocabulary, using complex and advanced sentences at a very early age;*
- working effectively independently, using the library with ease and frequency;*
- following complex directions easily;
- maybe a very good memory span for age;
- maybe high superiority in a particular area, such as mathematics;
- a good sense of humour – unusually so for age;
- maybe very rapid speed of thinking and working.

Asterisks indicate areas of learning disability which may mask high ability, i.e. a gifted child may not learn to read at all, may not have advanced verbal skills, avoid library work and any writing and spelling tasks (see also the section on dyslexia on pp. 200–207).

This particular checklist was validated by teachers and educational psychologists working with them and the pupils. The final list was compared with items on other checklists produced by similar groups active in the field at the time (Ogilvie, 1973; Kerry, 1983; Denton and Postlethwaite, 1985).

A range of children begin to read and write before attending school. It is generally regarded as a sign of high ability when the child's reading and writing is at least *five years* above chronological age. Literacy skills two and three years above chronological age may be an indicator of ability, but not necessarily of high ability. The same can be said of verbal ability.

Early reading ability and high scores may fall away. It is, however, very common for children who read well soon after entering reception class to be promoted to the able learners' table, and maybe to carry the label of 'highly able' throughout infant and junior school. This 'early promise' may fade and fail to be fulfilled when the child is found not to be advancing as rapidly in a range of areas, such as mathematics, science and humanities, as these become more demanding. The phenomenon of slower learners who have a facility for reading is not unknown, but tends to be overlooked in the period of schooling when being able to read counts for more than being able to think.

Being put at the 'red table' because you are able to read well in reception class may be little to do with later promise or high ability. But it has its advantages, for children who are expected to achieve and do well will have more chances to do so than others of the same or higher ability at any of the other colour tables.

Highly able children often develop vocabulary at 6 months and speak soon after in coherent and even complex sentences. They may also reach the other developmental milestone, walking, much earlier than other children. When they arrive at school, their complex sentences make them sound a little old for their age, even quaint, and they can be labelled as 'the professor' or 'boffin'. Children from families with elderly parents may also sound and look quaint and be similarly labelled.

Children with *learning disabilities* in language and literacy areas may have very high intellectual ability but fail to show this. Their problems in language, reading and spelling may hamper their entire careers in school. Only in later life may they achieve in some area not demanding literacy skills. If they have an understanding tutor and are given an effective remedial training, they can over-come their difficulties.

Children with high intellectual ability but poor language and/or literacy skills still have a very difficult time in schools, and it is important to bear their special problems in mind and have a second checklist to help identify them. Two general patterns of high ability and learning disability may be most commonly identified, and there are doubtless others. Pattern one applies to children who are good verbally, but have poor literacy skills. They:

- are highly able orally, and seem very intelligent;
- are able to engage in a mature way in adult conversation;
- are very good at oral problem solving;
- answer all oral questions well and ask difficult and often impossible questions;
- have very poor handwriting;
- read at a level that is possibly average for their age but well below their mental ability;
- spell very poorly;
- refuse to write anything down;
- as soon as they are asked to write, clown about, do very little, make excuses, and avoid writing when possible;
- as more stress is placed on written work, become difficult and a 'behaviour problem', maybe becoming emotionally disturbed and candidates for a special unit by secondary age;
- may prove highly able in mastering and using the computer, especially to support the poor written work.

Pattern two applies to children who are poor in verbal and written work. They:

- are very good at design problem solving;
- have very advanced drawing and painting abilities;
- spend a lot of time on constructional activities, maybe later building motor bikes from old parts, or clocks and computers;
- have surprising insights and gifts in certain kinds of creative problem solving;
- do not contribute much in oral work;
- were late talking, maybe having mild difficulties in expressing ideas and in forming words;
- are poor at reading and spelling;
- may be good at handwriting and copying neatly, which conceals spelling difficulties for a time;
- have behavioural and emotional difficulties which emerge as the curriculum becomes more didactic and emphasizes written work;
- may develop special interests or gifts in sports, musical and artistic activities, often outside school;
- may become exceptionally able in computer programming.

These two checklists were validated after referring pupils exhibiting these problems to the educational psychologists for assessment for potential statementing. In each case the administration of WISC-R or BAS showed that the pupils identified by a cluster of positives were able disabled learners.

Checklists by themselves will not enable us to identify all the able individuals. They are useful, however, in identifying areas and behaviours on which to focus. They indicate that characteristics which identify the able or highly able have to be seen in the context of the other individuals of the same age in that group. What tends to happen is that a teacher fails to identify an able child because s/he is comparing the child's knowledge or expression of ideas with the adult's. Children do not have to know more or solve cleverer problems than adults. Adults have a far wider experience and knowledge store, so that even very able children may seem not too bright by comparison.

Often it is found that some teachers fear able children and will try to compete with them; of course they win and 'put the child down' by superior wit, knowledge or status. None of this should be necessary. There is nothing to fear from having able pupils in groups and everything to be enjoyed and gained by all the group.

Checklists may be 'homegrown', as are these examples, when

interested groups get together and share knowledge and expertise in drawing up a list of agreed attributes from case experience. There may also be a list of attributes drawn up from quantitative research studies based upon test items and questions given to highly able individuals. In these instances, the definitions can prove circular, for most often the individuals are first identified by being screened in an IQ test. The resulting checklists are thus ones of those attributes of highly able individuals defined first by the IQ test. Denton and Postlethwaite (1985) found that the discussion and use of checklists enhanced teachers' identification, especially when used over a period of time.

The characteristics of highly able learners

Shore *et al.* (1991) identified seven ways in which highly able children differed from others. They acted as *experts* do in a field of knowledge in the following ways:

- *Memory and knowledge:* they knew more, they knew what they knew better, and they could use it better.
- *Self-regulation:* they expertly guided and monitored their own thinking on task.
- *Speed of thought processes:* they spent longer on planning but arrived at answers more quickly. Their solutions times were shorter, like those of experts.
- *Problem presentation and categorization:* they extended representations beyond the information given, identified missing data, excluded irrelevances and grasped the essentials of the task more quickly.
- *Procedural knowledge:* they used organized rather than chaotic and unsystematic approaches to problem solving, and engaged in flexible switching.
- *Flexibility:* they had an ability to see alternative configurations and adopt alternative strategies.
- *Preference for complexity:* they increased the complexity of games and tasks in play situations to increase interest.

These characteristics enable us to identify able learners whilst they are engaged in curriculum activities. This of course can only be done if appropriate cognitive process pedagogies are being used within the curriculum.

According to Nickerson *et al.* (1985), 'Experts not only know more, they know they know more, they know better how to use what they know. What they know is better organised and more readily accessible and they know better how to know more still'

(p. 101). Shavinina (1994) concluded from a critical review of research and biographical material on scientific geniuses that their thinking processes were determined by a specific feeling of direction. The data showed that the mind-work of highly able creative people was determined by subjective, internal, developed standards and orientations, which were intellectual intentions. Their negative reaction to any attempts to impose external standards on their intellectually creative behaviour was not surprising. Shavinina identified three sorts of intellectual intention:

• They had a specific feeling of direction in their creativity and in life as a whole.
• They had specific beliefs which were diverse and included feelings of truth and faith in the power of ideas. These determined their self-confidence and the extraordinary stability of their intellectually creative work.
• These individuals were characterized by specific preferences, including the aspiration to harmony and beauty, the understanding of mind-work as very valuable, and the consideration of thought as an important aspect of human life. The feeling of the 'eternal', the aspiration to 'endlessness', and clarity in everything were among these preferences.

PROCESS ANALYSES IN IDENTIFYING THE ABLE

IQ tests measure the products of prior learning, and individuals are compared with respect to these products. A process of maturation of innate abilities interacting with learned functions gives us this product quotient. The assumptions are that:

• each has had an equal opportunity to learn;
• long-term memory is an essential component;
• all people are more or less equal in relative ability.

However, Haywood *et al.* (1968) found that when the strength of learned associations was controlled, people with severe learning difficulties retained the learned associations with no less efficiency than normals. In 1934, Rey had pointed out that the *way* in which one person achieves a score of, say, 110 may be quite different from another's. Not only may the pattern and structure by which the score is achieved be different, but so may the *process* by which the pattern was learned. We therefore need to look at *patterns and profiles* of an individual's abilities when planning educational activities. Vygotsky (1962) emphasized that, since the development of intellectual function was closely related to the social interaction between child and adult, we needed assessments which told us the degree to which individuals can *benefit from the help* of an adult, and a comparison between this and their independent performance. He emphasized the need for both quantitative and qualitative measures.

In pursuing process assessment further, Frank (1970) tested a group of subjects on their ability to assemble Koh's blocks (as in the WISC-R test) to a set of basic patterns. The portion of the group who failed to do this successfully he gave coaching to, and another set from this portion then passed, but some still failed. To the failed group he gave special tuition as follows:

• Rules for making the designs with the blocks:
  – all blocks must touch;
  – all designs must be square.
• Make as many such designs with the blocks as you can.
• Now child or tester draws child's own designs.
• Later child constructs own designs from the plans.

After this form of *teaching* the children, the double failures could solve 9- and 16-block problems whereas before they were unable to solve simple 4-block designs.

Teachers are on the whole interested not in children's position on some latent IQ variable but in what they need in the form of education. They are much more concerned with *learning efficiency* and ways in which to make the *process* of learning more efficient, or how to facilitate the *learning to learn* process.

One of the most important ways to identify the able in this respect is to set them something new to learn – a problem to solve, a design to evolve – and record the efficiency of the learning by direct observation of their behaviours and outcomes. From all of this derived the interest in the process approach generally and in learning to learn and learning sets in particular. Curriculum identification and assessment (CIA) arose specifically from studies in this area of process analysis. Interestingly enough, Feuerstein, whose work is discussed later in Chapter 5, was an associate of the Budoff (1967) and Frank (1970) group and developed the Learning Potential Assessment Device (LPAD; Feuerstein, 1970), which he uses as part of his work on instrumental enrichment with disadvantaged groups. He listed twenty-eight different skills which might be lacking or deficient in a culturally disadvantaged child, and his methods for improving their performance will be discussed in Chapter 5.

Performance-based assessment

Performance-based assessment (PBA) was described by Shore and Tsiamis (1986). Any children who display high achievement are deemed gifted and are then given special provison. This appears to be an open system, but there are problems with it. Children from disadvantaging environments and low socioeconomic groups will most often be missed out; they may have far more to learn to catch up in school, and so their performance remains unexceptional. The school tasks themselves might be of a mundane variety that do not motivate able children, and so they underperform. School tasks also tend to provide a limited range of performances to judge from and they are definitely of the 'school-house' variety. Where an extended definition of giftedness is in use and notions of performance extend outside school activities, more successful PBA can be undertaken, especially where, according to Shore and Tsiamis, it can cover endeavour and uncompleted tasks.

Curriculum-based assessment

This is a variation upon performance-based assessment, which we used to begin to develop alternatives to testing and checklisting for identification. Here the curriculum consisted of all those normal school-based activities, and additionally performance on the enriched curriculum tasks defined as suitable for the able, and the extra-curricular activities and the hidden curriculum of attitudes and values. These curriculum activities were specifically designed to elicit higher-order thinking skills. Higher mental processes are more concerned with qualitative activities than with quantitative ones. These processes include reasoning abilities, planning and predicting outcomes, and making judgements based upon relevant criteria. These are often called mental executive and control processes. They manipulate the data or the contents of thought, which in schools are the curriculum subjects. Emphasis upon the passive acquisition of content material and simple applications can exclude the development and use of these higher mental processes, and this can disable even the ablest of learners.

Designing curriculum materials and teaching strategies which enable learners to develop and use executive processes on the content is an important goal for teachers, but it has not yet been made part of mainstream teacher education. Nevertheless, significant developments have taken place in the area of problem-based learning and 'real' problem solving to enable general principles and practices to be evolved. The key aspect of this type of provision is that it is enriched by having multiple sources, not just the teacher providing input, and it enables differentiation of learning inputs and outputs to meet different learners' needs. How this can be achieved will be discussed more fully in the next two chapters on curriculum and pedagogy. There are some examples in the chapters, with teachers' and pupils' comments. What was elicited were different patterns of ability and different nominees in the able group when they were set to work on the new-style materials which were not always apparent using traditional methods.

The children's processing of information and the ways in which they worked on the data were the key focus. CIA is perhaps too restrictive a title to use now, although teachers need something which will empower them again.

The assessment of learning potential and ZPD

Vygotsky introduced the Zone of Proximal Development (ZPD) as a new concept in 1978. It takes account of the capacity of individuals to learn from another, more capable or expert person. Some children appear to be able to learn more easily and to high levels of performance when their problem solving is facilitated or supported by the teacher. Vygotsky explained ZPD as follows:

> this new concept ... is the Zone of Proximal Development. It is the distance between actual developmental level as determined by independent problem solving and the level of potential as determined through problem solving under adult guidance or in collaboration with more capable peers.
>
> (Vygotsky, 1978, p. 86)

He illustrated this with the case of two children who were both 10 years old chronologically and 8 years old in terms of mental development. This meant that they could deal with items up to the degree of difficulty that has been standardized at the 8-year-old level. Their subsequent development might be assumed to be the same except that one child might have been ill and absent from school for six months, whereas the other might never have been absent. Vygotsky stated that if he had begun his study at this point (the testing of the IQ) instead of ending it he might have found some further important differences:

> Suppose I show them the various ways of dealing with the problem. Different experimenters might employ different modes of demonstration in different cases; some might run through an entire demonstration and ask the child to repeat it; others might initiate

the solution and ask the child to finish it; or offer leading questions ... In these circumstances it turns out that the first child can
deal with problems up to a twelve year old level, the second up to
a nine year old level. Now are these children mentally the same?

(Vygotsky, 1978, p. 86)

He argued that what is in the ZPD today will be the actual developmental level (ADL) tomorrow. He quoted the work of McCarthy
(1930), in which she found that what her subjects could only do
under guidance, in collaboration, and in groups at the age of 3–5
they could do independently when they reached the age of 5–7
years.

As can be imagined, the ZPD is an important concept, but one
which has only just found its time. It causes us to question again
the bases upon which all intelligence tests are founded, for they
only take into account ADL. ADL can be curtailed for many
reasons – sociocultural, educational and economic. If we can incorporate some notion of ZPD into our assessments of ability in
future, this could lead to the identification of perhaps a new and
different group of able individuals. This group might not prove so
disappointing in their achievements as others identified only by
IQ tests. How this can be done by the busy class teacher needs
some thought. Exponents of Vygotsky's methods from the Eureka
University in Russia use individualized assessment procedures
and graded tasks in their demonstration classes, and offer worldwide seminars on the subject.

Adaptive assessment

Strong emphasis is now being placed upon integrating assessment
and instruction, according to Birenbaum (1994). These changes are
part of school restructing processes, in which the learner is an
active participant and the methods are geared to developing self-
regulation, thus making the learning more meaningful. Birenbaum
does admit that these new methods are in their infancy and are
used alongside traditional methods. It is perhaps possible to view
adaptive assessment as another version of process analysis.

In England and Wales there has been a return to formal and
closed assessment procedures under the National Curriculum.

IDENTIFICATION BY PROVISION

Recently, a number of methods have been developed under this
heading to try to get the provision to those who need it. Originally

it was teachers who were responsible for nominating children whom they thought were suitable for gifted education, and then these children were tested to see if they had high enough IQs to receive it. The problems associated with such methods have been discussed. The new strategies are as follows:

- *Self-nomination:* children who wish to take part in special provision for gifted and talented nominate themselves. If they do not do well they drop out.
- *Parent and teacher nomination:* again, the children drop out if they wish to or do not do well.
- *Peer nomination:* This is being researched by Gagné (1994) using a questionnaire covering all facets of giftedness and making the instrument pupil-friendly. He has found that peers also know who the able children are.

The portfolio approach

This is seen as a compromise solution to the complex problems of evaluating learning and pupil achievement. In Vermont, the portfolio method has been adopted and is now part of the law.

Records of achievement

These are well-developed evaluation methods in a few schools (Pole, 1993), but the national initiative for England and Wales has been dropped. The format and design will vary but the DES (now DFE) statement on ROAs in 1984 suggested that account should be taken of a pupil's progress across the whole educational programme of the school, both in the classroom and outside. This meant that the reports could contain statements about progress in subject areas, cross-curricular studies, personal and social skills, practical skills, membership of clubs and other organizations, leisure interests, work experience and so on. Each section should contain statements of what had been achieved with evidence recorded where practicable. Pupils and teachers might contribute to the record and should meet to discuss and verify the contents.

The purpose of the ROAs was that they should make a positive contribution to schooling and would recognize achievement in school and in the wider social and skills context. They should also make a contribution to the pupils' motivation and personal development increasing their awareness of strengths, weaknesses and opportunities.

The Profile is not a new method of assessment but a method of reporting assessments giving a record of information about pupils. The early work on profiling began in Scotland in the 1970s because there was an absence of examinations to record the achievements in school of many lower attaining students whereas in England and Wales the Certificate of Secondary Education (CSE) could do this. Nevertheless even CSE grades were not attainable by some pupils who had made modest progress in their studies in a number of areas. Profiles were developed to record this progress and also included the wider area of personal and social skills so that pupils would have a Record of Personal Achievement (RPA) on leaving school. The Schools Council, the Further Education Unit and the DES all became interested in researching and promoting their use (Broadfoot 1986; Pole 1993). ROAs can be equally beneficial to all children including the able if the process is well conducted.

OBJECTIVE ASSESSMENT AND TESTING: STANDARD ATTAINMENT TASKS

Feller (1994), writing in support of open methods of assessment, reported on a three-year, million-dollar study which investigated objective tests. The one overall conclusion was that they hurt the educational process. The results showed that many standardized tests and textbooks heavily emphasized lower-level skills and rote memorization instead of measuring high-level skills such as conceptualizing and reasoning. They found that this influenced instructional practices and curriculum content to emphasize the same low-level goals. It was concluded that such practices rob time from curriculum activities which could be used to develop higher-order thinking. Although it is not likely that in England we shall see half a million pounds put into evaluating the efficacy or otherwise of the National Curriculum and its Standard Attainment Tests, there is considerable concern that it is not meeting the needs of able children and that it has far too much content still which can only be rote learned.

SUMMARY AND CONCLUSIONS

The main approaches to the identification of the able have been described, and some of their shortcomings pointed out, as follows:

• biographical studies

- psychometrics
- creativity tests
- trait definitions and checklists
- process analyses
- performance-based assessment
- provision-based identification.

What is quite clear is that unidimensional methods and tests are not successful in identifying the able. Teachers' identification on its own has also been shown to be error prone, but if teachers are given clear definitions and some training (Denton 1986) then they can learn to do a reliable job. Hany (1993) also reported that teachers' skills in identification were more judicious and insightful than previously supposed. They appeared to be objective, searching, reasoning and evaluating, yet they still relied on some gross stereotypes and models.

Overall, it would seem that if we can offer an appropriate curriculum, which is challenging and attempts to develop cognitive and metacognitive processes in the learners, then process analysis or adaptive assessment techniques used by the teacher will be successful. These can be reinforced by reference to checklists, test data if available and discussion with colleagues:

> Selection for giftedness which is developed indistinguishably from segregation of pupils in grammar schools or special express streams is not an exercise in identifying genius or releasing gifts in all types of pupils. Indeed it stunts our chances of helping the gifted. We give up the commitment to looking for gifts in the vast majority, once we have accepted the argument that giftedness is limited to the hunt for the few. We also fail the few, particularly true genius. For true genius cannot be limited to the world of IQ testing and formal education.
>
> (Benn, 1982, p. 84)

3

Curriculum provision for the able: acceleration, enrichment and differentiation

INTRODUCTION

The curriculum is generally regarded to be all the planned experiences provided by a school or college to enable students to attain designated learning outcomes to the best of their abilities (Neagley and Evans, 1967). For the philosopher Hirst (1966), the curriculum consisted of programmes of activities to enable pupils to attain, as far as possible, educational ends and objectives. Over time, the curriculum concept has been extended to include extra-curricular activities provided by institutions in the form of clubs and societies, and the *hidden curriculum* (Broadfoot, 1986).

Whilst the main curriculum is concerned with subject knowledge and skills thought by a particular culture to be essential for its members to learn, the hidden curriculum consists of all the attitudes and values embodied in the presentation of the rest of the curriculum to learners by teachers and tutors. This hidden curriculum can prove to be very strong and purvey images and models of success and failure. Its stereotypes can also be disabling to the able and talented wherever they are not regarded as 'mainstream' or 'regular guys'.

The curriculum itself is a *selection* from the society's culture which is regarded as important or worthwhile to transmit to its young. The selection of curriculum subjects and curriculum contents had, until recently, been left to professional educators, trainers and administrators, although the general framework and direction had been set by legislators. The British system was not then formalized as a national curriculum and written down, although there was a consistent and coherent view of what the primary- and secondary-school curriculum should consist.

At a national conference on exceptionally able children, organized by the Department for Education, Pyke (1993) reported that teachers of very able children had told Sir Ron Dearing, who had been charged with modifying the National Curriculum, that their pupils were being disadvantaged by it. Dearing was told that the overload of material prevented able children from developing quality and depth in their thinking. Teachers felt that it should not be a race to get through the curriculum content, but that there should also be time for pupils to investigate and build their capacity for creative thinking. The emphasis on speed of progress was at the expense of investigative approaches. The teachers also believed that the programmes of study for·the higher levels were not suitable for the younger children who were nevertheless intellectually very able.

Since that period, the National Curriculum content has been cut by 20 per cent, but as it was already overfull it is still unlikely that there will be sufficient time for able pupils to work at an appropriate level. It also holds out little hope for any of the less able children that they will ever have a chance to learn anything properly.

PRODUCT-BASED CURRICULA: THE CONTENT MODEL

Already the National Curriculum has had to be pruned radically (Dearing, 1994), for the programmes of study contained so much content there was insufficient time to teach it. This had been foreseen by teachers and teacher educators, but had to be proved in practice before changes were permitted. Similar problems arose in relation to the multiple assessments required and the huge amount of recording involved, which interfered with teachers' ability to give time to teaching. This problem is typical of any curriculum which is product-based and in which there is an overriding concern for the teaching of subject content. Subject content naturally expands as new studies and concerns arise within its area. Each subject competes for time in an already crowded curriculum, and debates in schools ensue endlessly on how much curriculum time can be expended on each area beyond the minimum guidelines laid down by the legislation. The pressure of the assessments once again, as in past eras, comes to define what is taught, and eventually can become all that is taught.

Content models emphasize the importance of learning skills and concepts within a predetermined domain. When making provision in this system for the highly able, the basic levels of the content area are covered very quickly and the students are *accelerated* through towards higher levels. In these systems, a large amount of rote learning (learning content material by heart) is seen.

According to Gibbs (1990), a considerable amount of such learning is of a superficial kind even in higher education. These types of curriculum and didactic teaching methods promote what he calls *surface learning*. The characteristics of surface learning are said to arise from:

- a heavy workload
- relatively high class contact hours
- an excessive amount of course content material
- a lack of opportunity to pursue subjects in depth
- a lack of choice over subjects
- a lack of choice over methods of study
- a threatening and anxiety provoking assessment system.

(after Gibbs, 1990)

Although many of the most able can cope with the lecture style of learning, it leaves little room for reflection upon what has been learnt.

The content mastery model, according to Van Tassel-Baska (1993), can enable the basic reading and mathematics skills programmes to be condensed and covered in one-third of the time, leaving time for more challenging learning experiences. Even so, the approach has to be modified by the intervention of the 'effective teacher' to recognize and unify the content area for the individual. This principle of *acceleration* is a key construct in content curricula for the able.

PROCESS-BASED CURRICULA

Process models cannot operate without a content base upon which to perform their processes. These approaches emphasize the explicit teaching of social and/or investigatory and problem-solving skills. The students are required to work collaboratively and to a large extent independently, whereas in the product model the activities are teacher-dominated. In the process approaches, they are learner-orientated. Learners' interests and needs determine the direction of study in key content areas, and learners construct knowledge for themselves. These programmes have mainly taken place in the USA in special scientific programmes for the highly able. In Britain, the process approach is best illustrated by the Nuffield Science Curriculum and Nuffield Mathematics approaches, where the notion of the student as a scientific investigator adopting the scientific approach to research and problem solving was the dominant theme. It was, however, coupled with a closely specified and also overfull curriculum content upon which the investigative and collaborative skills would be practised.

CURRICULUM STRATEGIES: ACCELERATION, ENRICHMENT, DIFFERENTIATION

McClelland (1958), whose work was widely influential in education in the 1960s and 1970s, argued that intelligence was a much more widespread characteristic than was then believed. It was, he said, transformed into talented performance by various of the *right sorts of education*. He said we should concentrate upon learning environments which link learning opportunities with identification rather than rely upon intelligence tests and school attainments to predict who would benefit most from advanced education. A wide range of researchers had at that stage come to the conclusion that a large number of able and gifted individuals were never identified and encouraged to enter higher education. Lowering the threshold for entry into higher education may have assisted somewhat in giving these individuals opportunities, but once in it the progress hoped for was not achieved.

Having reviewed 176 research studies on gifted education, Goldberg (1965) came to the conclusion that there were two great research needs, namely to find:

- what would stimulate a love of learning among able students;
- what kinds of assignment would most effectively develop independence of thinking and independence of effort.

Twenty-five years later, Passow (1990) in his review of research of gifted education was still able to conclude that the two major areas for research and development were:

- what kinds of educational and social opportunity are needed to promote high ability;
- how we can identify and nurture high ability in disadvantaged populations.

These problems are currently preoccupying us in higher education as we broaden and deepen access.

Goldberg was also unclear about whether able children needed acceleration through some early phases of programmes or depth in others. It was concluded that differentiation of some kind was a priority for all able learners. Nearly thirty years later, these issues have not been resolved, and they have become a high priority for consideration in the recent HMI Report (1992) on the teaching of able children in maintained schools. These three issues will be considered under separate headings.

ACCELERATION

Acceleration means that the student moves through lower levels or sections of the standard curriculum at a much faster rate than age-matched peers. It is probably the cheapest and simplest form of curriculum provision for able learners. Some typical examples of accelerated provision are as follows:

- *Early entry* into a new phase of education: nursery, infant, junior, secondary, college.
- *'Grade skipping':* promotion by usually one or sometimes two years over age-matched peers.
- *Subject acceleration:* joining students in older age groups for particular subject areas, such as mathematics or music, matching knowledge and skills competencies.
- *Vertical grouping:* entry into classes which have students of, for example, 5–7 years of age, enabling the able 5-year-old to work at the level of the 6- or even 7-year-olds in the same classroom for all or part of the curriculum, usually language or mathematics.
- *Extra-curricular studies and clubs:* able students join special groups such as NAGC (National Association for Gifted Children), explorers groups and summer schools. Able students are often identified by the large range of extra-mural studies in which they are involved.
- *Concurrent studies:* at the same time as the normal primary curriculum is being studied, the student may be pursuing a study of secondary-school curricula in algebra, geometry and trigonometry or even A-level studies in pure or applied maths, physics or music. Modular school and college systems can permit multiple modules to be studied, so that a university course might be completed in nine months by a highly able individual.
- *Telescoping studies:* students follow the normal programme but the studies are compacted into a much smaller time span, perhaps one-third of the usual length.
- *Self-paced and/or self-organized instruction:* students design their own programmes of studies and follow them, often whilst waiting for the rest of the class to catch up.
- *Mentoring:* students, however young, are introduced to and work with an 'expert' in the field of interest on a regular basis.

Class teachers may be mentors or parents may come in to mentor, and schools can be linked to local universities to provide a range of mentors.
• *Correspondence courses:* these can be followed by a student whilst pursuing ordinary school studies during normal school hours.

It is questionable whether acceleration is capable of providing the 'right sorts of education' which McClelland felt the able needed.

In the post-war period, acceleration, particularly 'grade skipping', was the major form of differentiation offered to meet the needs of able students. Selective education and acceleration were strongly opposed by those who regarded the concept of giftedness as both élitist and a myth established to maintain the class system and a 'two-nations' philosophy (Benn, 1982). Acceleration was criticized on the grounds that it would damage academic progress and create socioemotional problems in those who were accelerated. These concerns were mainly raised by educators, teachers and administrators, but their criticisms were based upon extrapolations from theories about holistic learning and deeply held attitudes to selective education rather than research evidence. When the subject of accelerated provision is discussed even now, teachers' first responses are to express concerns about the child's socioemotional well-being.

Research originally lacked adequate definition and controls for any generalization to be made from it. However, Kulik and Kulik (1984) found that students did not suffer harm from acceleration, but maintained academic progress in the new and more demanding settings. Southern and Jones (1991) found that few parents, teachers, students, psychologists and co-ordinators of gifted education programmes in the USA gave any instances of academic harm. The evidence about socioemotional damage according to Cornell *et al.* (1991) was more equivocal. In Britain, hard evidence from long-term follow-up studies did not exist. Why problems said to result from acceleration should be greater than the problems which could ensue if the able student were to remain with the age cohort is difficult to imagine. Failure to accelerate could increase problems arising from boredom, monotony and lack of curriculum challenge, and lead to a range of behaviour problems arising from frustration.

Acceleration options are rarely used without consultation with all concerned for the child's well-being, and it is generally used in a conservative fashion because something clearly needs to be done. 'Radical' acceleration, as when 10-year-olds take A-levels and enter university at 12, is rare. These cases are frequently given wide press coverage, and seem mainly to occur in cases of outstanding advancement in areas such as mathematics and music. The case of Ruth Lawrence was one recent example, when once again the issues surrounding acceleration were raised in a highly emotionally charged context but in the absence of much evidence.

The case of Ruth Lawrence

Ruth Lawrence obtained a 'commended first' (1985) in mathematics at St Hugh's College, Oxford University. Ruth never went to school and had little contact with children of her own age. Her father gave up work to accompany her to Oxford and went with her everywhere, lectures, coffee parties, tutorials, badminton and dining out. His theory was that intelligent adult company provided the best learning environment for a bright child, and he tutored her for her A-levels. Since infancy, she had been treated by her parents as an adult. They believed in concentrating children's mental energy and Ruth only took exams in maths and physics. She was deliberately denied any formal literary education: Mr Lawrence said, 'Not only does literature not help you to live your life, it positively impedes you. I feel there's a kind of obscenity in the way most literature attempts to live people's lives vicariously and purports to show their innermost feelings. We should live our emotions ourselves.' Ruth's tutor at Oxford said that she had the quickest mind at comprehending mathematical ideas of any student she had taught. As well as gaining her brilliant first, in two rather than three years, she had covered a wider range of subjects – fifteen lecture courses instead of the usual eight in part II of the course and seventeen special subjects instead of the usual four in part III.

Ruth likes Kipling, Walter de la Mare and science fiction. In her case there seems to be a high correlation between intelligence and emotional maturity. Her sister Rebecca passed O-level maths at 11 and is training to be a musician. Ruth's case is an example of high ability, acceleration and mentoring.

Freeman (1979), writing on the education of the gifted in Britain, was able to conclude that most able children could be well educated in mixed-ability settings and that too much emphasis on the academic side of education could harm socioemotional development. This reflected the move away from acceleration towards enrichment and improved teaching strategies for including and challenging all students.

Personal experience of acceleration resulted in no academic disadvantages, no gaps in knowledge or lack of experience, and no diminishment of extra-curricular experiences. The socioemotional problems appeared to belong to others: temporarily being the smallest child in the secondary school drew the unwelcome attention of bullying peers and the oversolicitous maternal responses of senior girls.

Perhaps of greater significance and concern is that acceleration strategies assumed that the normal curriculum was valuable and worthwhile and provided what the able student needed. Accelerated students could also soon become bored and frustrated in their new environment, once the novelty had worn off, if the system was traditional and didactic, as was so often the case in the thirty years after the Second World War. During the 1970s and 1980s, much greater emphasis was placed upon mixed-ability teaching and changing the curriculum to meet the needs of all learners through integration, topic work and interdisciplinary methods. Where separate provision for the able was regarded as important, the emphasis was placed upon *enrichment*.

Acceleration of itself does little more than shorten the length of time the child spends in education. Several hundred studies have been undertaken on the subject, and the results show considerable consensus. The clearest results and recommendations show that:

- mathematical talent and foreign-language ability can be most effectively and economically developed through acceleration (Clarke, 1988; Feldhusen, 1985; Van Tassel-Baska, 1985);
- acceleration is not appropriate for every able child but should always be an available option (Southern and Jones, 1991).

Gagné (1986), in a thorough review, concluded that it works and does no general harm, academic or social. The benefits which arose were mainly from curricular density, and in Kulik and Kulik's (1984) meta-analysis of twenty-six controlled studies of elementary- and secondary-school subjects it was shown that those accelerated moved nearly a full grade ahead of controls.

Rogers and Span (1993), in a meta-analysis of thirteen research syntheses including that of the Kuliks, summarized their main conclusions and then listed five guidelines for educating the able.

This is probably the most up-to-date position based on research currently available. The guidelines were as follows:

- *Ability grouping:* students who are academically or intellectually gifted and talented should spend the majority of their school days with others of similar abilities and interests.
- *Cluster groups:* if schools cannot support a full-time gifted programme, cluster grouping of approximately one-third of a class load of similarly gifted will suffice. The class cluster teacher needs to be well trained and to be given preparation time, and should be willing to devote a proportionate amount of time to the cluster group.
- *Acceleration or setting:* In the absence of a full-time gifted education programme, pupils should be offered specific group teaching across grade levels according to knowledge levels, either in cluster groups or instead of them.
- *Options:* pupils should be given experiences involving a variety of appropriate acceleration-based options, which may be offered to groups or individuals.
- *Enrichment:* pupils should be given experiences which involve various forms of enrichment that extend the regular school curriculum, leading to more complete development of concepts, principles and generalizations. This could be provided within the classroom through numerous curriculum delivery models, or in the form of pull-out programmes.

They concluded that mixed-ability co-operative learning should be used sparingly, perhaps only for social skills development programmes.

Ability grouping and segregation

Ability grouping in Britain is called 'streaming'. Able pupils are often put into 'A' streams or classes and are taught as a group for the whole of their school career. In other countries, this method is sometimes called 'tracking'. Where able pupils are put into fast tracking groups for specific subjects such as English and maths, this is called 'setting'. Both methods are really only a variant of acceleration and have been widely used as the only method of differentiation, with all the attendant problems.

The wide range of studies from which the meta-analysis of Rogers and Span was drawn were equally broad based in terms of their conceptions of what were enriching and suitable materials for gifted education programmes. Some of them would offer no more than what in England and Wales would be called good standard curriculum experiences. For example, in one German pull-out programme the novel experience for the group was to write poetry, and in another to engage in multimedia creative artwork. Until the present developments become the mainstay of gifted education programmes, it is unlikely that the last word has been said on the subject of curriculum organization. This is probably a good thing, for the really useful and relevant work has only just begun.

ENRICHMENT

In a general sense, all forms of adjustment for the able are forms of *enrichment*. The term came into fashion in the 1930s, when Hollingworth and others decided that it was better to keep the able with their social age group rather than accelerate or segregate them (Gowan and Demos, 1964, p. 14). A number of early studies reported improved achievements of the able with enrichment (Dransfield, 1933; Ziehl, 1962; Arends and Ford, 1964).

Enrichment has become the most widely developed strategy in Britain for making provision for the able in the last twenty-five years. It is a process which was designed to extend beyond the confines of the normal curriculum. It was targeted at developing initiative and originality in early American studies and at leadership education programmes in more recent times (Sisk and Shallcross, 1986).

Passow (1992a) recommended four guidelines for the development of enrichment programmes:

- modification of the curriculum to provide additional breadth or depth of coverage;
- modification in the pace of presentation – speeding up the rate of progress through the curriculum to suit the individual's need;
- modification of the nature of the material which was presented, to take account of needs and interests;
- development of process skills such as those of creative and critical thinking, heuristics and problem solving, and affective and interpersonal communication and social skills.

As can be seen, at least two of these guidelines would be in accord with the views of progressive educators and would draw criticisms from traditionalists. Progressive educators would, however, regard enrichment as a necessary part of *all* children's education, not just that of a talented élite.

Whilst in the USA enrichment programmes received substantial funding, in the UK it was left to individuals and concerned groups to develop provision for the able.

Passow's definition of enrichment shows that acceleration can be regarded as a form of enrichment and differentiation. However, in my view it would represent a weak version of the concept. Clarke (1988) noted that: 'Enrichment in many classrooms often means just more work, sometimes more of the same work' (p. 202). This is not always the intention of the enrichers, but it has been widely observed. The Brentwood Experiment by Bridges (1969) provided a weekly afternoon club for highly able junior school pupils in Essex, linked with the college of teacher education course. The teacher education students were matched with able pupils and developed methods and materials for them for the club sessions. The results showed the students' responses were to present the pupils with content of an older age group, typical of O-level examination programmes. Similar approaches can be observed in many of the hundreds of enrichment packs available in Britain. Topics for infant classes draw on secondary-school curricula, and secondary-school 'extension projects' draw upon degree-level material.

This approach is *content acceleration*. Other enrichment packs and materials present subjects which are outside the main curriculum areas, and are truly *extension* projects. They broaden and deepen pupils' knowledge of an area. The intention of most of those who prepare the packs is that teachers who have individual or small groups of able pupils may give the package as it is to the learners and more or less leave them to organize themselves and work on it. Some of the packs provide 'answer books' so that they can be self-checking and save teachers' time.

Good literacy skills are demanded by these types of material, and there is a wide range available. Listings of the materials may be obtained from the National Association for Able Children in Education (NACE), established with the headquarters of NAGC at Nene College. Essex County Council, Manchester and Croydon LEAs also market hundreds of extension packs designed by local teachers.

Able pupils in our case studies have nearly always found both these types of study package interesting and useful. The materials are used when the able individuals have completed all the assignments set by their class teacher and are running far ahead of the rest. Giving them their own project, which is structured and has all the supplementary materials included, enables the pupils to opt to work on the 'project' rather than waste time waiting for others to catch up, doing extra examples, reading around interest topics, annoying and distracting others and daydreaming.

Over a period of years, students on initial and inservice education courses at the college evaluated enrichment materials as part of their training programmes. The instrument of evaluation used was Bloom's (1956) taxonomy of educational objectives, as laid out below. It was found that the vast majority of the enrichment packs achieved only level 3 status – 'application'. There were of course notable exceptions, and these had quite a different quality and intention from content acceleration. The principle embodied in these superior work packs was that they were to promote the use of advanced intellectual skills and abilities of the pupils. They were *process* enrichment materials.

Description of the major categories in the cognitive domain (Bloom, 1956)

1 *Knowledge.* Knowledge is defined as the remembering of previously learned material. This may involve the recall of a wide range of material, from specific facts to complete theories, but all that is required is the bringing to mind of the appropriate information. Knowledge presents the lowest level of learning outcomes in the cognitive domain.

2 *Comprehension.* Comprehension is defined as the ability to grasp the meaning of material. This may be shown by translating material from one form to another (words or numbers), by interpreting material (explaining or summarizing) and by estimating future trends (predicting consequences or effects). These learning outcomes go one step beyond the simple remembering of material and represent the lowest level of understanding.

3 *Application.* Application refers to the ability to use learned material in new and concrete situations. This may include the application of such things as rules, methods, concepts, principles, laws and theories. Learning outcomes in this area require a higher level of understanding than those under comprehension.

4 *Analysis.* Analysis refers to the ability to break down material into its component parts so that its organizational structure may be understood. This may include the identification of the parts, analysis of the relations between parts, and recognition of the organizational principles involved. Learning outcomes here represent a higher intellectual level than comprehension and application, because they require an understanding of both the content and the structural form of the material.

5 *Synthesis.* Synthesis refers to the ability to put parts together to form a new whole. This may involve the production of a unique communication (theme or speech), a plan of operations (research

proposal) or a set of abstract relations (scheme for classifying information). Learning outcomes in this area stress creative behaviours, with the major emphasis on the formulation of new patterns or structures.

6   *Evaluation.* Evaluation is concerned with the ability to judge the value of material (statement, novel, poem, research report) for a given purpose. The judgements are to be based on definite criteria. These may be internal (organization) or external (relevance to purpose), and the student may determine the criteria or be given them. Learning outcomes in this area are highest in the cognitive hierarchy because they contain elements of all of the other categories, plus conscious value judgements based on clearly defined criteria.

These set a standard for others. Notable amongst them were these pioneering packs:

- 'The Motorway Project' and 'Townscapes', published by Learning Development Aids and written by the Maidenhead Group of Teachers led by Johanna Raffan, a local headteacher. The packs were designed for 8–11-year-olds.
- 'The Battle of Islandhlwana', a secondary-school package written by Julian Whybra, formerly a county adviser on gifted education, published by Essex County Council Education Department.

Evaluations of both are given below.

An evaluation of 'The Battle of Islandhlwana'
We consider this to be an excellent example of the process approach to teaching and learning applied to project work. It provides information to be studied but demands the use of cognitive skills at the highest level in Bloom's hierarchy in that study. It also allows pupils to work co-operatively if they wish so that communication and negotiation skills can be practised. We should like to see it extended further to offer the opportunity for a keen group to present it as a 'courtroom drama' and to research the nature and format of courts martial and military tribunals. This allows others to shine whose best work is not always in the form of the written word.

(Concluding summary from a group evaluation by teachers, 1991)

An evaluation of part of 'The Motorway Project' in use with a group of able 8-year-olds

Activity 3: 'Ashwell Manor and Home Farm'

This was attempted by all the eight children. (The group was 8.6 years old and with mental ages of 11.5 years.) The criteria for the evaluation of the subjects' work is as follows:

* Evidence of ability to discuss, criticize, evaluate and judge the situation.
* Evidence of extrapolation of main points including mention of consequences and reasons for decision making.
* Composition of logical and persuasive speech.
* Ability to role play.
* Evidence of understanding the life situation.
* Understanding of alternative points of view.
* Ability to present argument and communicate point of view orally.
* Evidence of decision making and productive thinking.
* Presentation and general standard of work.
* Evidence of investigation of the information and going beyond given data.

This was the first time the group had been given any form of enrichment work. They began with Activity 1 from the pack and worked through. The children all completed the work and seemed to enjoy the role play, arguing their points of view and evaluating others. At first they seemed daunted about the length of the information sheet.

Ruth and Michael both re-read the information sheets without having to be reminded, and Michael tried hard to select relevant facts and apply them to his argument.

Peter worked on his own without asking any questions while the rest of the group chatted about the pros and cons of the proposed motorway before putting their ideas down on paper.

Most of the children put forward a good valid argument to support their points.

Michael was the only subject who mentioned conserving the historical ground around Ashwell Manor, which he obviously extracted from the information sheet.

None of the children showed any understanding of alternative points of view and no child mentioned any positive points about the opposing motorway route nor negative points about their own choice, nor of human behaviour, and appeared self-centred in their approach, and apart from Michael they thought not so much about the land but their own future. For example, some suggested Mr Williams may be deaf and Mr Broadhurst may not live much longer as he was old, so the motorway could go through the opponent's land.

The work of Michael, Susan and Ruth emphasized their ability to play a role imaginatively and to select relevant information from the two sheets. Michael again showed his sense of humour and Susan showed the greatest understanding of real-life situations.

(extract from report by Sarah Pollard, 1989)

An evaluation of 'The Motorway Project' pack produced for able children in middle schools in relation to the model 'Teaching thinking skills in the school curriculum'

This project pack consists of six separate worksheets, a game and a set of teacher's notes based on the theme 'Motorway'. It has been designed for bright, middle-school children to use either individually or in a group. The pack is intended to be self-sufficient and each worksheet is complete in itself and could be used in isolation. There is a list of useful, additional reference books included at the end of the teacher's notes but most of the essential reference material is provided. The aim of the designers of the pack was 'to provide challenging and interesting material on as broad a based curriculum as possible' in order to 'help the children develop an enquiring mind'. The teacher's handbook contains a short resumé describing the materials, their intended use and the title and objectives of each worksheet. There are also suggestions for the teacher's possible role in the clarification, discussion and explanation of certain ideas and a list of the equipment required. Each worksheet has a name and is printed on a different colour paper together with the extra reference sheet relevant to it. All the necessary equipment is easily accessible in school, e.g. calculators, tracing paper, graph paper, plasticine, straws, etc. There is also a set of answers to the computational work involved in one worksheet. Two of the question sheets use information appertaining to the M4, one mentions the building of the M1, and the others are concerned with imaginary places and situations.

The worksheets do not have to be worked in any particular order.

In the fourth sheet, Activity 3: 'Ashwell Manor and Home Farm', the pupil is told that there is a need for a motorway in the area where these estates are. There are two suggested lines along which the motorway might pass and the pupils must consider the proposals and their effects on the two estates. Working with a partner, the pupils take an estate each and prepare a report explaining their preferred line. Then they present their case to the class who act as decision makers at the court of enquiry. The sheet includes details of the two plans and a description of the estates and their owners. The object is to present an argument representing a given viewpoint with the intention of persuading an audience as to the validity of one's case. Teachers may want to discuss bias and information manipulation with their pupils.

This sheet requires the pupil to become intellectually involved in solving a problem by reading and assimilating facts, selecting alternatives, thinking reflectively and arriving at a decision. Considerable skills of persuasion are required to explain and justify one's point of view to others. The list of study skills involved in this task is endless but includes reading for the main point, appraisal, comparison, investigation and discrimination. The pupil has to consider alternatives, imagine self in the role of landowner and identify and comprehend the main issues at stake. S/he must inhibit the first response and write a succinct report.

My observation of the group of 10-year-olds at work proved the value of the problem-solving exercise. They were instantly keen and much valuable and pertinent discussion ensued. Group leaders evolved naturally but they found it difficult to come to mutual decisions. Listening but not interfering in the conversation, I was struck by their immaturity. There was no mention of conservation of areas of beauty or agricultural land. It might have been better to let them work at a sheet alone first and then discuss. The written work was fair considering their inexperience with open-ended topic work.

Expressing arguments to others gave them confidence and stimulated discussion, ideas and debate amongst the whole class. They will all be called upon to *evaluate* when they appraise and judge the reports. The 'landowners' must also synthesize, analyse and apply their knowledge. The group worked well at this task, quickly made a decision and justified well. They enjoyed presenting their case to the class and the subsequent discussion was enthusiastic. Two of the girls really 'became' the landowner and became rather irate when others disagreed with them. Much '*real*' thinking occurred.

The six worksheets of the 'Motorway' pack are all good examples of the process approach to teaching, because they use the strategy of starting from what the child knows and has experienced and present the subject content as a problem for the child to solve. They require the child to study the conditions of the problem and form hypotheses which must be tested in order to make a decision. Real thinking rather than fact memorizing or rote learning will occur at all levels of Bloom's Taxonomy and, since the tasks are intrinsically interesting, underachievement should be avoided and even the most able child should be motivated. A gifted child or group of children could work through the pack at their own pace thus avoiding dead time and could produce work at their individual intellectual level. Little teacher assistance is required since the pack is virtually self-sufficient.

The variety of problem-solving tasks is wide and illustrates the flexible way of acquiring information which the *process approach* advocates. Since the topics covered in the pack are openended, novel and inventive, the pupils cannot rely on old solutions or copying from books; they must devise new answers. To be successful they must do what the process approach suggests in order to think effectively – inhibit the first response, select an appropriate scheme and strategy, use tactics to obtain the solution followed by verification. Having reached conclusions about the task, the pupil must then communicate answers verbally and on paper. The worksheets require different types of written work – memo, brief, factual account, imaginative conversation, persuasive or informative reports. If one refers back to the model of the central objectives in practical teaching in the paper (Montgomery, 1982), it is obvious how the questions in this pack meet those criteria. The children must think and communicate within the social and developmental context and need to acquire knowledge and skills which they can use to do that. By working through the pack they will gain knowledge of motorways, statistics, social considerations, etc. and will learn, use and develop study skills, including higher-order reading skills, i.e. research and cognitive skills, social and intellectual skills. They will take on the role of people they have come across on the television and in newspapers, e.g. ministers, civil engineers. In only one case are there correct or incorrect answers, otherwise the answer depends on personal viewpoint or values, which, when they become accustomed to it, gives children confidence.

The pack needs more coherence of elements rather than a series of separate tasks. It would be better if the whole pack was concerned with one actual stretch of motorway. The pack being self-sufficient is certainly easier for the teacher but bright pupils might be stretched more if some individual research was required. A child unaccustomed to problem-solving activities might benefit from an initial introduction to the techniques involved. Some adult/pupil interaction must occur in order to share ideas and to show children that their opinions are valued. Perhaps there could have been more illustrative and craftwork required, although of course this could be part of a wider project evolving from the pack. A motorway building site could be visited and more map work, modelling, art and craft could be included. The layout of the sheets is clear and thorough and the game at the end of building a motorway without going bankrupt (Monopoly type) proved fun and rounded off the project well.

In my opinion the 'Motorway' pack would serve as a vehicle for developing and encouraging thinking skills in able pupils of middle-school age because it meets many of the criteria expressed in 'Teaching thinking skills in the school curriculum' paper.

(evaluation by Christine Hale, Junior Schoolteacher)

The children's evaluations of the experience were as follows:

- 'It was good fun and made you think.'
- 'It was different and interesting and made a change from the usual boring topics like "Myself", "Tudors", "Transport".'
- 'I enjoyed pretending to be someone else like the Minister of the Environment and having to work out the answers myself from reading something.'
- 'It made a change from just answering questions because you really had to work out what it meant.'
- 'At first I thought it was really hard but when I realised that it was quite easy, just different and not boring.'
- 'I liked working at the sheets by myself because then I didn't have to wait for others to finish or understand something.'
- 'It was nice to be allowed to talk about the work you're doing with someone else like your partner or friend.'

These particular 10-year-olds all had a tested IQ of between 120 and 140, but they did not produce as good work as one would have hoped. They enjoyed the pack and benefited from it in many respects – language, initiative, independence, discussion, thinking, etc. The topic itself interested them and they realized that the approach was different. Perhaps the poor quality of the written work was due to:

- inexperience with problem-solving techniques;
- lack of adequate study skills;
- poor guidance;
- their age – only just 10;
- not being able or gifted enough;
- lack of experience with different forms of writing.

(Christine Hale)

By way of contrast, I give some extracts from the Manchester Curriculum Group evaluation of 'Provision for Able and Talented Children', Merlin (Manchester Enrichment Resources for Learning and Interest). Merlin was formed in 1982 as the result of a 1981 conference on reviewing the secondary curriculum in 1980, and began producing newsletters and written materials for enrichment. There were three Merlin Packs for secondary-school-children. The designers tried to keep a balance between closed material with one answer and openended exercises with many possible responses.

The materials in this pack were described by the compilers as 'not conforming to a particular model but each one had one or more features involving problem solving, information processing, word play, decision making, role play, synthesis, communication, logical thought, organisation of material, creative and imaginative work'.

Each pack contains 14/15 items and appears to be aimed at teaching thinking skills. The packages seem to be good examples of the process approach to teaching and learning, demanding the use of cognitive skills at the higher level in Bloom's hierarchy.

(Pollard, 1989, p. 181).

Teare, who was the prime motivator, has continued to co-ordinate and develop the Merlin packs production with the same principles in mind.

Report on Middle Ages Project

I enjoyed the project very much and hardly used the answer book.

But I think it would take a long time to complete the whole project.

The parts I liked best in the project were clothing, travel, pastimes and food.

I think there ought to be more information in the reading book so that you do not have to cheat by looking in the answer book: for example, 13a which is virtually impossible for any ten year old however gifted to answer without outside help (my father said it looked like an O level question and he used to mark O level papers!).

(Sarah, aged 8 years)

The report shown in the box was kindly written by Sarah after she had worked through a substantial proportion of the package. It illustrates, often by omission, the points already made. The project was content acceleration material and as such was thoroughly enjoyed. Able pupils mop up facts and information like sponges. Sarah does not refer to challenge and being made to think as those working on 'The Motorway Project' did. The fact that answers could be specified in the answer book reinforces the content approach and convergent nature of any thinking abilities required. The highest level of challenge of this pack was the applications level in Bloom's taxonomy.

The bulk of the literature on enrichment appears to be descriptive. In the main, it describes activities that accelerate or broaden student experiences (Gallagher, 1985; Renzulli, 1977). Because of the varied definitions of the term and the lack of clarity of the enrichment process, in practice research has concentrated mainly on acceleration with enrichment more or less included. The tendency for enrichment to be associated with broadening experiences if not with acceleration leads to difficulty, for it is then an add-on experience. Add-on as opposed to no add-on will produce the expected positive results. It is therefore not surprising that Callahan and Hunsaker (1991) found mixed results when reviewing programmes described as enriching.

The vast majority of enrichment materials produced in this country have been for added value or have been 'bolted on' to the usual curriculum as extra-curricular activities. American and Canadian literature shows a range of substantial curriculum 'programmes' which students may enter full-time or part-time. The programmes are research-project-funded or privately funded, and many millions of dollars have been invested in gifted education over the last seventy years; thus much of the research on 'programming' has a North American bias. Results are beginning to emerge from Eastern Europe and the Far East on their specialist provision for the highly able. This too, however, concentrates upon segregation, acceleration and content enrichment approaches. Do they really meet the needs of the able, and do they help the society which wants to make the most of individual talent and ability?

Another issue emerges when one examines the programmes from the American studies, and educational processes in the USA, Germany, Japan, the Far East and Eastern Europe. Much of it is highly specified content with a text-based formal education, didactic in nature. Science education, even in the 1990s, is still largely text-based in the USA. The investigative-empirical approach adopted in most classrooms in the UK is quite the opposite of this, as a result of many innovative influences over the last twenty-five years, not least the Nuffield Science programmes. Thus what might be regarded in the USA as gifted education programming and curriculum is part of mainstream education theory and practice in the UK. Design problem solving in technology education and the 'Clues' approach to history have all become embedded in mainstream as process approaches with content curricular.

DIFFERENTIATION

The concept of differentiation emerged as a high-profile issue in the UK in 1981 at the DES conference on special educational needs.

There, the concern was particularly about the needs of children with learning difficulties. In previous decades, the issue was expressed as a need for mixed-ability teaching methods. The strategy was to persuade teachers to stop teaching only to the middle-ability group of twenty out of the thirty children to be found in streamed as well as unstreamed classes, and to provide materials or methods such as collaborative learning which would enable the slower learners to accomplish the main task and learn the main content and concepts of the lesson. Able pupils needed to be given extension material, or application and problem-solving methods and materials, related to the main content once they had covered it. It was difficult even for experienced teachers to do this in every lesson and required a great deal of extra preparation, for textbooks and programmes did not cater for this level of sophistication. Many, none the less, did successfully develop materials and strategies of their own or with colleagues for mixed-ability teaching. However, even in 1981, Hegarty and Pocklington recorded that the major strategy which teachers used was to teach to the middle and give extra time to helping the child with learning difficulties. The able pupils were either left to their own devices or given more of the same.

Following on from this period, there was a major trend towards individualization of provision. Again, this was most evident in provision for children with special needs. Each child was put on an individual programme to take account of learning need. This often required many hours of working alone on worksheets restricted to basic skills activities and was seen as a narrowing of the child's entitlement. The National Curriculum specified all children's entitlement to a broad, balanced and differentiated curriculum and has refocused attention on differentiation, this time in the main stream.

Able pupils were more often than not put in larger groups in the main stream and given segregated education in 'streamed' classes, as has already been noted. This was seen as differentiated education. Differentiation within a class group seems to be rather a British concept of education, although group work and collaborative studies in classrooms are much more widespread.

While acceleration and enrichment strategies can all be regarded as differentiation techniques, there are only a few different types of *within class* differentiation *per se*.

When students of different abilities and needs are integrated into the ordinary classroom, it is recommended that the work which is provided for them should offer differentiation. This can mean:

- the setting of different tasks at different levels of difficulty suitable for different levels of achievement: differentiation by inputs;
- the setting of common tasks which can be responded to in a positive way by all pupils: differentiation by outcomes.

Either of these responses would prove somewhat better than the traditional way of teaching to the middle, which can leave a third of the class unmotivated and uninvolved, but there are problems with both.

If teachers adopt the first system, where they provide different work at different levels, they will be creating a socially stigmatizing situation in which students doing work of an easier nature can begin to feel lower in ability and value than the rest, for they are doing recognizably easier work. This can in the long run prove academically handicapping, for these students come to expect that they can never achieve a high standard in any sphere of activity and cease to try, so that they compound their difficulties and begin to fall further and further behind. The able students in this system begin to feel special, for they are doing the 'clever' work; they can develop inflated opinions of themselves and their abilities and begin to look down on the other children, even poking fun at them. All of these attitudes are destructive and wasteful, so that none of the groups is motivated to develop its abilities and talents to the full. Only those with great strength of character or individualism can survive these social pressures and develop freely, and these pupils are few. In the arts, talented people are often reported as very overbearing and self-opinionated. They presumably have the 'bigheadedness' to continue to believe in themselves and their art when everyone else does not, and so they survive. It is sad to think of all those talented people who do not have such pigheadedness and self-confidence and who succumb to the education system. A second major problem is that teachers select who is to do the advanced work, and we already know that without training this is unreliable.

Education must enable the individual to feel justifiably confident, to feel of value and valued whatever level of skills and abilities s/he has, and to learn to value all levels of skills in others and show respect for other persons. In order to achieve this, teachers have to become appropriate models for the students, showing the tiniest, youngest students respect for their views and understandings rather than dominating or ridiculing them for their perceived shortcomings. Learners learn best from having their strengths emphasized rather than from having their weaknesses shown up and concentrated upon.

The second view of differentiation, where all students can participate in the same task, is advocated as one of the ways in which all students can have access to the full curriculum without being academically and socially downgraded during the teaching process. However, at the assessment stage or during continuous assessment processes the differences may become clear to the students and their peers, and thus this is becoming a less-favoured option. It too can be discriminatory in an unhelpful way. When able students are set the same task as all the rest, unless the task is itself demanding but not demoralizing for the pupils, the able are quite capable of regularly underfunctioning; they need to be stimulated and challenged to use their abilities and talents. Differentiation by outcomes thus often gives very disappointing results. Once again, teachers decide at certain stages which types of assessment are to be applied, and route 'sheep and goats' differently. Untrained as they now are to meet the needs of able students and in the identification procedures, we can expect substantial failure.

Differentiation in either of these forms is thus too simple a view. Each brings further handicaps and thus the concept needs to be further developed. Research evidence in controlled studies comparing the different methods is not yet available, although there are descriptive studies. In the research in the Learning Difficulties Project, a third definition of differentiation was developed:

- the setting of common tasks to which all students can contribute their own knowledge and experience in collaborative activities and so raise the level of output of all the learners.

In order to attain this form of differentiation, it was found necessary to adapt the teaching methods. Rather than change inputs and output mechanisms, the *process* between input and output created the differentiation. This avoided the problems of selection and stigmatization prevalent with the other methods. The official HMI (1992) definition of differentiation at this time was listed as follows:

- *by outcome:* different levels of response elicited;
- *by rate of progress:* at own speed;
- *by enrichment:* supplementary tasks;
- *by input:* different tasks within a common theme.

One of the central problems in the education of 'gifted' students was still the lack of proper curriculum materials, according to Poorthuis *et al.* (1990). They argued that enrichment materials for gifted students should meet the following criteria:

- they should be beneficial to the development and use of higher order thinking abilities.
- they ought to provide the possibility to explore continually new knowledge and new information.
- they should teach and encourage students to select and use sources of information.
- the content should aim at a complex, enriching and in-depth study of important ideas, problems and subjects, and at integrating knowledge between and within subject areas.
- they should offer the opportunity to increasingly autonomous learning activities.

(Poorthuis *et al.*, 1990)

The group have produced a curriculum analysis tool based upon these criteria for evaluating curriculum materials. What is of most interest is their definition of what 'good curriculum'materials for the able should consist. As can be seen, these are higher-order thinking skills as curriculum objectives running through curriculum contents or products.

SUMMARY AND CONCLUSIONS

Two types of curriculum have been outlined: the product and the process models. It was concluded that neither type on its own is a suitable vehicle for promoting the learning opportunities of able pupils. A judicious mixture of the two is required, geared to the development of higher-order thinking and metacognitive abilities. Nevertheless, the vast majority of the provision studied, although it purported to offer cognitive stretch, was much more focused upon accelerated content. Curriculum provision also needs to be more flexible, particularly in England and Wales, where age cohorts proceed in step whatever the needs of individuals. The content methods appear to be universal and are particularly unsuited to meeting the needs of the able. Even in Japan, where education is at its most formal and rote memorization of large masses of curriculum content is required, the system is beginning to free up (Amano, 1992).

Three main curriculum strategies were reviewed – acceleration, enrichment and differentiation – and it was concluded that each option should always be considered and left available. If we could train all teachers to teach the mainstream curriculum using methods which help develop and use higher-order cognitive components or abilities, then the tasks themselves would provide sufficient differentiation for most able children's needs. Where children have exceptionally advanced knowledge and special talents, then the schooling should be sufficiently flexible to permit acceleration so that the pupil can work with groups of the same level, or to arrange that mentoring is provided from a local pool of talent, such as from a nearby university, or through distance learning materials and special study packs from gifted education resource centres locally or nationally. It is quite clear that every region of the country needs to organize such facilities and to network with the NACE/DFE Project.

It has already been recognized by the DFE that the current systems of training are making no provision for the needs of the able, and training the student teachers in the schools will only compound this problem.

It is apparent that what is being offered as enrichment has got to cease to be a bolt-on provision and become part of the main stream. How this can be done will be considered in the next chapter. The nature of the enrichment has been clearly defined by Sternberg (1986) in his triarchic theory of intelligence, outlined in Chapter 1 and reinforced in application in the curriculum evaluation instrument design of Poorthuis *et al.* (1990).

The definition of an appropriate curriculum centres upon the development and use of higher-order thinking skills; exploration; complex in-depth and integrated studies; and the development of self-managed and autonomous learning.

Teaching for critical thinking and metacognitive processes

INTRODUCTION

In a report prepared for the Organization of Economic Co-operation and Development (OECD), Skilbeck (1989) wrote that although many innovations had taken place in recent years, education had not adapted to the structural changes of the last decades. The changes included a move from selective schools to a general school model and a refocus from education for a minority of academically able learners to mass education. More progress had been made at primary than at secondary level. He concluded that there had been little adaptation to individual differences, with an estimated 80 to 90 per cent of classroom instruction presented in the formal lecture style. The general goal was the acquisition of a body of knowledge. Very few schools had connected knowledge and skills to actual human problems such as ecological and environmental issues, war and peace, human values, culture and consumer awareness. There had been little willingness to move away from traditional 'basics' at the secondary level. What changes were to be found happened locally and were not systematically planned or centrally controlled, so progress was meagre.

In Eastern Europe, Asia, Africa, the Far East and the Caribbean, these formal methods of teaching also prevail, and thus the models of good practice which are needed are difficult to come by and have to be developed *ab initio*.

In this chapter, one such development will be described. The development took place over a 15-year span. The basic principles of the system will be described, with links to theory and research, and then practical examples will be given. Without the theoretical framework, it is difficult to design a practical teaching methodology.

To show how critical theory and cognitive process methodology are different from formal teaching methods, it is first necessary to take a brief look at the latter, for often teachers think that their methods are informal because they use 'discussion' methods and intersperse these with the lecture.

The lecture is the typical form which traditional teaching methods take in secondary schools and colleges. This is an exposition lasting 20 to 30 minutes, interspersed with practical or book work. In higher education, a straightforward 60-minute monologue may be the norm, with 2–3-hour lectures in some faculties. On visits to Eastern European countries, infants have not uncommonly been observed in receipt of these formal lectures all day long. Students may be invited to ask questions at the end of a lecture, or raise an occasional issue during the session. Seminars and tutorials are a feature mainly of British and North American systems.

A watered-down version of this may be observed in the upper grades and years of schooling, in which extended expositions by the teacher are coupled with questions to the students, usually requiring one-word answers. These are repeated by the teacher (reinforcement) and then the exposition continues:

Teacher	The human brain is made up of some 10 billion brain cells called 'grey matter' and a mass of nerve fibres called 'white matter'. The 'grey' and 'white' labels were first given by the ancient Greeks because when they poked into the skulls of the dead the deteriorating brain appeared to consist of these two types of material. Adrian. What was the grey matter?
Adrian	Brain cells.
Teacher	Brain cells. Brain cells are called neurons ...

When working with younger pupils, the teachers' monologues are shorter and more pupils are encouraged to participate.

Teacher	Our brains are made up of millions of brain cells. We think with our brain cells.
Stephen	He hasn't got any, Miss. (*Points to Harry.*)
Teacher	We all have them. We have the same number. How many have we got?
Tracy	Millions.
Teacher	Good, yes, we have millions and millions. In fact we have 10 billion. What is a billion, Stephen?
Peter	I've got trillions. (*Class laugh.*)
Teacher	You've got 10 billion like the rest of us. What is a billion, Peter?

Stephen's and Peter's responses are not required and to the authoritarian traditionalist would seem cheeky and undisciplined.

The boys would be admonished. Most experienced teachers know that such responses are typical of lively youngsters and need to be used, not suppressed. Instead of admonishing Stephen and Peter for talking out of turn, the teacher mildly corrects them and then asks them the question by name, so orienting them back to the lesson in hand.

Whilst there is a place in any lesson for some teaching of this kind, what is questionable is that it should be used as the only method. It is highly directive and does not require reflection or the extended use of language by pupils to explain their ideas. However, in a class of thirty the teacher would find extended answers difficult to cope with and other pupils could find them boring. Nevertheless, teachers are placed in a difficult position by research which shows that open questions are more effective in developing critical thinking and promoting learning and motivation in learners of all ages.

The teaching methods that were to be designed had therefore to enable the teacher to use open questions but not in the process lose control of the class. It had to be possible for multiple responses to be made to the open questions at the same time, and someone had to be listening to each one.

At primary- or elementary-school levels, education has been more geared to the young learners' needs since the earlier decades of this century. It became more child-centred, based upon some *learning by doing*, influenced by Froebel's methods and those of other early educators such as de Lissa and the MacMillans. These methods were originally termed *progressive* but have recently been used as models for development of teaching techniques in both further and higher education, where problem solving and independent and collaborative learning have been introduced. Their influence has been less pervasive in the secondary-school sector. In general, where examples of poor teaching have been identified in recent years, these have been labelled 'progressive' and used to pillory progressive methods and those who promulgated them. Research has shown, however, that 'good' teaching is not the prerogative of one method and examples of it can be seen throughout a range of style mixtures from traditional to progressive (Bennett and Jordan, 1975).

Traditional or formal methods are also referred to as expository teaching or *didactics* on the world stage. In schools and colleges around the world, instructional practice presupposes a didactic theory of knowledge, learning and literacy. Teachers lecture and drill, students listen, recall and reiterate. The curriculum is fragmented into subject domains, each with a large technical vocabulary and content: students are not required to integrate their personal knowledge with the curriculum content or apply it to new and different situations. They are expected to believe what is written in the textbooks and what the teacher says.

Despite the fact that we now know these methods are particularly unsuitable for able pupils, 90 per cent of education in Europe still takes place in them, according to Rogers and Span (1993). This is despite the fact that employers and the developed nations now realize that they must increasingly generate workers who can think critically, reason and work in a flexible and creative manner (Stonier, 1986). In 1987, thirty-six college principals in the USA co-signed a letter sent to all the other colleges warning of a national emergency which was rooted in the expectations of what schools had to accomplish. It ran in part as follows:

> It simply will not do for our schools to produce a small élite to power our scientific establishment and a larger cadre of workers with basic skills to do routine work... Millions of people around the world now have these same basic skills and are willing to work twice as long for as little as one-tenth our basic wages... To maintain and enhance our quality of life, we must develop a leading edge economy based on workers who can think for a living... If skills are equal, in the long run wages will be too. This means we have to educate a vast mass of people capable of thinking critically, creatively and imaginatively.
>
> (drafted by Donald Kennedy, 1987)

Similarly we can argue that on the social and political fronts both developed and underdeveloped countries face the need to solve complex problems. To do this would require major conceptual shifts by large masses of people in relation to overpopulation, environment, religious and political differences, territorial conflict, global competition and economics. This is unlikely to be achieved by those trained in fragmented, disciplinary and school-subject-centred, reductive thinking and simplistic views of the world. These issues and problems are interdisciplinary and multidimensional and can only be resolved by increased capacity worldwide for reflective and critical appreciation and some creative and inductive thought. It would be irresponsible to rely on those whose native abilities lead them in this direction, for they are reckoned to be too few in number. What the college principals required was *an education for all* which opened up these areas. In Britain this movement had been under way for some time, particularly in primary schools.

Paul (1990) has contributed in a major way to the analysis of theory in this area, explaining that critical thinking is the art of thinking about your thinking so as to make it more precise, accurate and relevant, consistent and fair. This had been expressed as *metacognition* by Flavell in 1979. He argued that thinking about how we are thinking and learning whilst we are doing so contributes in a major way to intelligence. If we can promote metacognitive activities, especially in those who would not normally use them, we will in these terms be likely to promote and enhance people's intelligence, or at least their intelligent action.

Apparently, most education worldwide is geared to inducing monological thinking, which is single-track and context-defined, because of the overuse of didactic teaching methods. Critical thinking, on the other hand, is:

- the art of constructive scepticism
- the art of identifying and reversing bias, prejudice and one-sidedness of thought
- the art of self directed, in-depth, rational thinking
- thinking which rationally certifies what we know and makes clear where we are ignorant

(Paul, 1990, p. 32)

One of the major goals is to cause learners to be self-starters, self-regulating and self-motivated. Research by Wang and Lindvall (1984) showed that self-monitoring and self-regulatory activities contributed not only to improved acquisition of subject content but also to improved generalization and transfer of knowledge and skills. They also gave students a sense of personal agency – a feeling of being in control of their own learning. Self-regulatory activities were defined by Brown *et al.* (1983) as including planning, predicting outcomes and scheduling time and resources. Monitoring included testing, revising and rescheduling, with checking to evaluate outcomes using criteria developed by the individual and also those which were externally defined.

Failure to develop higher-order cognitive or thinking skills in schools and colleges was, according to Resnick (1989), not surprising, for it had never been the goal of mass education. We can see even now education for the masses being driven to becoming lower-order didactics, leading to lower-order thinking and incapability in the twenty-first century, whilst the political 'speak' is of raising standards and instilling the disciplines of subjects, thoughts and actions. Paul has given a seventeen-section analysis of the differences between these types of education. Extracts from three of them here will serve to clarify some of the key differences, according to Paul's theory of knowledge, learning and literacy:

Didactic theory	*Critical theory*

The fundamental needs of students

To be taught more or less what to think not how to think; to be given details, definitions, explanations, rules, guidelines and reasons to learn.	To be taught how not what to think, and that it is important to focus on significant content; but accompanied by live issues that stimulate students to gather, analyse and assess that content.

The nature of knowledge

Knowledge is independent of thinking that generates, organizes and applies it. Students are said to know when they can repeat what has been covered. Students are given the finished products of someone else's thought.	Knowledge of content is generated, organized, applied and analysed, synthesized and assessed by thinking; gaining knowledge is unintelligible without such thought. Students are given opportunities to puzzle their way through to knowledge and explore its justification as part of the process of learning.

Model of the educated person

An educated, literate person is fundamentally a repository of content analogous to an encyclopedia or a databank, directly comparing situations in the world with facts in storage. This is a true believer. Texts, assessments, lectures and discussions are content-dense and detail-orientated.	An educated, literate person is fundamentally a repository of strategies, principles, concepts and insights embedded in processes of thought. Much of what is known is constructed as needed, not prefabricated. This is a seeker and a questioner rather than a true believer. Teachers model insightful consideration of questions and problems, and facilitate fruitful discussions.

Paul's conclusions were as follows:

> The pace of change in the world is accelerating, yet educational institutions have not kept up. Indeed, schools have historically been the most static of social institutions, uncritically passing down from generation to generation outmoded didactic, lecture-and-drill-based, models of instruction. Predictable results follow. Students, on the whole, do not learn how to work by, or think for, themselves.

They do not learn how to gather, analyze, synthesize, and assess information. They do not learn how to analyze the diverse logics of questions and problems they face and hence how to adjust their thinking to them. They do not learn how to enter sympathetically into the thinking of others, nor how to deal rationally with conflicting points of view. They do not learn to become critical readers, writers, speakers or listeners. They do not learn to use their native languages clearly, precisely, or persuasively. They therefore do not become literate in the proper sense of the word. Neither do they gain much genuine knowledge since, for the most part, they could not explain the basis for their beliefs. They would be hard pressed to explain, for example, which of their beliefs were based on rational assent or which on simple conformity to what they have heard. They do not see how they might critically analyze their own experience or identify rational or group bias in their thought. They are much more apt to learn on the basis of irrational rather than rational modes of thought. They lack the traits of mind of a genuinely educated person: intellectual humility, courage, integrity, perseverance, and faith in reason.

(Paul, 1990, p. 40)

Fortunately he identified a means of overcoming these problems in the application of what he called *critical theory*. This had arisen from an emerging theory of knowledge, learning and literacy which rcognized the importance of critical thought to all substantial learning and the relevance of higher-order, multilogical thinking in childhood as well as in adulthood. Paul emphasized that normal individuals do not naturally think critically and are not naturally inspired by rationality. They do not engage in reflective thinking automatically.

In the pursuit of critical thinking, teachers routinely require students to relate knowledge from various fields, and thinking is interdisciplinary. Students compare analogous events or situations, propose examples and apply new concepts to other situations. Students must have opportunities to express their ideas, however misconceived, and then must reason their way out of the prejudices, biases and misconceptions. Their learning starts from where they are and they must learn to learn through a process of reflective and critical questioning.

Critical theory must be applied, according to Paul, at all levels of education: it is applicable to *how* people learn, with the teacher as a model of the investigator seeking truth and fairness, the reflective questioner, the opener of minds. People are apparently happy to adopt biases, prejudices, stereotypes and short cuts to thinking and will state these authoritatively, quite genuinely believing them to be truths. As societies become less isolated and more complex, lack of rationality at both global and local level becomes increasingly dangerous for the maintenance of human existence. It is therefore essential for education to change to move all members of societies to multilogical and critical thinking – not just a small élite but the population at large.

Paul's analysis of critical theory is an important one. It is the essence of the approach which was developed in the cognitive process pedagogies, the so-called 'brain engage' strategies. It states the position more clearly, succinctly and fundamentally, and at its roots one can see the epistemological and rational–logical model of teaching fleshed out in psychological terms. If the critical theory of teaching is adopted as the principle, then some of the practices could be regarded as cognitive process pedagogies.

COGNITIVE PROCESS PEDAGOGIES

The early model promoted examples of *problem solving* and *communication skills* across all curriculum areas. By a process of grounded research over a period of years following this initial definition, a set of six *Cognitive Process Pedagogies* were defined, by which students' thinking processes could be engaged during learning:

- *investigative and problem-solving and resolving strategies*, particularly in real problem-solving situations;
- *cognitive study skills* requiring higher-order reading and study skills;
- *games and simulations;*
- *experiential learning* – experience-based action learning;
- *collaborative learning*, in which pair and small-group discussion was an integral part of the student learning activity;
- *language experience methods*, in which students' own experience is used as a major part of the study and resource material for learning.

An iconic representation of the cognitive process model was produced to reinforce the main ideas behind the developments (Figure 4.1). The theme of this model was that there were *two central objectives in teaching*, defined as:

- to enable pupils to think efficiently;
- to communicate those thoughts succinctly through a variety of modes and media.

This was in direct opposition to the expressed views of those classroom teachers who regarded their central objective as being

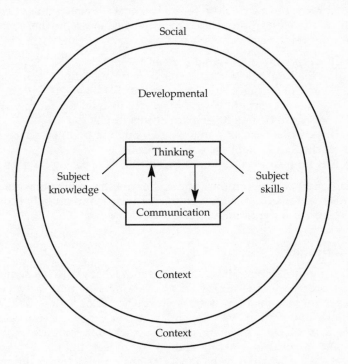

Figure 4.1 *A modern model of teaching*
Source: Montgomery, 1981

to 'cover the subject'. Those who regarded the aim as being 'to develop each individual to his or her full potential' as central found those of the model too narrow and too specific, and this was its intention. If these central objectives could be achieved, affective development would be encouraged as well as the wider potential and talent. The collaborative strategies introduced were in addition designed to facilitate socioemotional development.

It was argued that learning subject content and skills was subordinate to these two central objectives. All must take place in the context of the students' intellectual development in Piagetian terms, with a sensitivity to their profiles of development in other areas such as linguistic, emotional, social and so on. This learning had to be set within the developmental context of the modern age of technology.

Central to the cognitive process approach was that it should be integral to the curriculum for all learners. To contrast with enrichment curriculum provision it was termed *developmental provision*, and its principles were outlined thus:

- It *matches* the intellectual level of the pupil:
  - the bright 5-year-old is in concrete operational thinking not pre-operations and so is taught at that level *and beyond*;
  - the very bright 5-year-old is in abstract operations and so needs to be taught to learn at this level.
- It is *cross-curricular* – an approach and methodology used by *all* teachers in *all* subjects with *all* pupils.
- It is for *mixed-ability teaching* and thus is *enriching* for all pupils.

Enrichment programmes and materials, by contrast, were for a pre-selected group, were a bolt-on provision and initially provided breadth and depth of subject content.

Motivation

During the analysis, it was realized that what was most significant for promoting the ability of able learners in particarly and all learners in general was to capture their motivation. Whilst extrinsic motivation was dependent upon external reinforcement, such as teacher's pleasure, rewards, prizes or avoidance of punishment, intrinsic motivation and the joy of learning for its own sake were what was felt to be most desirable and self-sustaining. The materials and strategies had to induce *intrinsic motivation* so that the student would continue to learn when the teacher and the rewards were no longer present. A frequently used phrase had been 'Good teaching motivates students to Learn' but the processes by which this occurred had seldom been defined. Indications were that students would need to be 'ego-involved', feeling that the outcomes were dependent to some extent on their own efforts and contributions. Motivation was generated by materials which stimulated curiosity and interest and used the students' previous knowledge and experience.

As can be seen, this falls short of a set of teaching prescriptions by which these motivational results can be achieved. In the end it became essential to grasp the nettle and try to define 'good teaching' in terms which class teachers could test by adopting the practices and principles and then observing the 'good' effects or otherwise. Developing theory and practice, then testing these in the realities of classrooms in the hands of class teachers, was the method.

Differentiation

Because of the subject emphasis of much curriculum, it was evident that the development of the intellect was secondary to the educative process rather than central to it. The cognitive process approach attempted to reverse this, but it was very much more difficult to achieve and demonstrate than a knowledge of X and/or Y. It was during this phase that differentiation was redefined in terms of the process model as follows:

> The setting of common tasks to which all pupils can contribute their own knowledge and understanding individually and collaboratively to the inputs, and so structure their experience and raise the standard of output of all the pupils and enable them to progress to higher-order learning.

The definition of 'good' teaching incorporated this form of differentiation, and the result which would be observed would be an enhancement of intrinsic motivation. Good teaching was occurring where: 'Students wanted to learn rather than had to be made to, where they continued discussing and thinking about the subject long after the lesson ended.' This form of motivation was demonstrable when lessons and materials were designed applying the cognitive process principles and strategies.

By these means it was intended to avoid the 'Robin Hood effect', where lower-ability groups gained more from the mixed-ability setting and the able lost out. The children would be able to choose with whom they would work, and this allowed for cluster grouping of homogeneous groups within the class.

A range of examples was provided for the overall style of the approach and for the different pedagogies. Some examples were specific to the project, others were drawn from enrichment materials produced by other groups where they fitted with the model. It was not enough for them just to be called 'enrichment' materials. The main emphasis throughout was upon the class or subject teachers modifying the presentation of their standard curriculum tasks to fit the cognitive process model. Problems would be identified by careful observation of the pupils on-task and the quality of the intermediate and final outputs. During the process, the teacher would offer formative and supportive feedback to ensure a good 'match'. Any loss of motivation would be used as a prime indicator that the task needed adjusting to gain a better match.

In developing pedagogies suitable for critical thinking, a checklist of principles was established to guide the development and use of the materials:

1 If we teach, *the learner by implication is learning.* Teaching is thus an intentional activity and is not taking place in the absence of learning. The learner may not learn all the teacher intends and may learn much more that was not intended. Lecturing carries with it no such implications; the students did not automatically learn by this process. *Telling* information is not teaching.'

2 Teachers did not teach subjects, they *taught students to learn subjects.* This meant that education should be *learning-centred* not child- or subject-centred.

3 As the children set about the learning task, the class teachers, using well-defined observational strategies, would note the developmental levels of cognitive processing elicited by the tasks. This would enable them to prepare further material and strategies. It would also reveal the students' abilities and talents. This process was called *curriculum identification and assessment of ability* (CIA). It would replace test identification and obviate the need to spend time and money on pre-screening. It would also avoid the attendant dangers of checklists, teacher nomination and tests of ability missing many of the most able.

4 Teachers would treat all children as being potentially able. They would use the CBC ('Catch them being clever') strategy to help enhance self-esteem and give the children the confidence and the motivation to work even harder.

5 The task would offer cognitive challenge, often referred to as 'engage brain' strategies.

6 The tasks would harness and induce intrinsic motivation in the learner and galvanize the want to learn.

7 The tasks would help develop broader skills and abilities such as social and communication skills in real problem situations.

8 The tasks should help pupils develop metacognitive skills of reflection and meta-analysis.

9 Self-regulation and autonomous learning would be developed.

10 The learning should take place within the normal school curriculum content, not as extension or 'bolt-on' material but as part of the developmental curriculum.

11 The methods should provide opportunities for heterogeneous and homogeneous ability grouping in a flexible and appropriate manner.

INVESTIGATIVE AND PROBLEM-SOLVING STRATEGIES

A range of problem-solving approaches was presented across curriculum areas within subject disciplines and as examples of integrated topics and projects. One example was a study of homes: this often included studies of people living in houses, igloos, teepees, boats and homes on stilts. Instead of being shown pictures of homes on stilts and discussing various aspects and attributes of their owners' lives, the environment was described – monsoon rains, the terrain, the flora and fauna, the availability of tools. The pupils were then set to design in collaborative small groups the most appropriate form of dwelling. The discussions which ensued were lively, and detailed analysis of available materials and sites was evoked before the final plans – boats and stilt homes – were evolved.

Characteristic of the approach was that there needed to be plenty of content material to study. In the process of searching this for clues and ideas, much of it was committed to memory incidentally to the task in hand, the problem which had to be resolved. The didactic approach would treat the content as the main focus of the learning, and the development and use of intellectual skills would be incidental to the process.

- Design problem solving was just beginning to be taught at primary level, and examples were as follows:
- Using one broadsheet newspaper and half a metre of sticky tape, design a house big enough to sit in.
- In PE: using four different parts of your body in turn, move from one side of the room to the other. Then with a partner use four parts between you to move back again.
- In history: you are the master builder in the area. The local merchant would like a new house built on the main street but it is prior to the widespread use of bricks. Examine the descriptions of the area during this period and the ways in which people liked to live then. Design a house suitable for the merchant and her family. Research the costs of such materials today and compare these with the costs of her building materials.
- Small groups of twos and threes were set to produce a holiday brochure for their own or a selected suburb, town or village. This would begin with an analysis of typical holiday brochures and advertisements.

Now such problem-based approaches are common. Figure 4.2 shows an example.

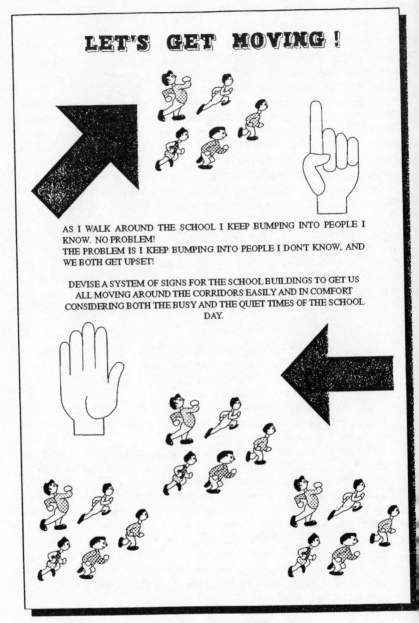

Figure 4.2 *Problem-based primary work*
Source: Chris Berry (Whitehall School)

The investigative style of approach to learning was encouraged by ensuring that as much first-hand experience of data as possible was provided. The studies of fresh water included visiting a pond or river, pond dipping and careful drawing of the contents. Microscopes were used at the earliest possible age to reveal the mysteries in drops of water and encourage descriptive, narrative and imaginative writings. Collections of drawings, photographs and magazine studies were made as data upon which to draw for creative and imaginative work in a range of areas.

According to Fisher (1994), the problems with which children are presented in schools are most often closed, with one definitive solution. He proposed a range of strategies to develop and support problem solving, similar to the following protocol:

1 Understand the problem:
   – Find the knowns and the unknowns.
   – Decide what kind of solution you need.
   – Investigate what is preventing a solution.
2 Planning the action:
   – Consider all the factors.
   – Think of a similar problem.
   – Simplify the problem.
   – Model the problem with real items if possible.
   – Consider a number of solutions.
   – Record the plan.
3 Select a best-fit method or most promising solution.
4 Try out your solution:
   – Try out a series of solutions or partial solutions.
   – Record the outcomes.
   – Modify your plan.
5 Put your plan into operation.
6 Review the situation and modify your solution if necessary.

The teacher can support the child in the following ways:

• Describe with interest what the child is doing.
• Ask the child what s/he is doing.
• Support the process when necessary.

COGNITIVE STUDY SKILLS

Study skills are a form of *self-directed learning*. When we read a chapter in a book in order to find and use the information in some way, we use study skills of some kind. Searching for information

– researching text – is different from the processes we use when reading a novel or a newspaper for pleasure. In schools and colleges, students need and use many different levels of study skills for different tasks:

• reading for general or specific information;
• preparing for a seminar discussion of a paper or article;
• preparing for writing an essay;
• preparing for writing in an examination;
• undertaking research for a topic, project or dissertation;
• note taking from lectures and talks;
• observation and recording by drawing and diagramming;
• making detailed or broad-brush sketches for painting;
• noting and rehearsing seqences in voice or movement in the performing arts;
• diagramming forms, relationships and ideas.

Critical processes in this variety of activities for different purposes appear to be careful and detailed *observation* – looking, listening and reading and *recording* – writing, modelling, imaging, drawing and painting, making, diagramming.

When reading for informtion, or for any of the above purposes, the first thing that most people do is try to *survey* the information. Surveying is not entirely straightforward. Readers are first advised to *scan* the information, e.g.:

• Read the title.
• Read the sub-titles.
• Look at the pictures.
• Read the summary.
• Rapidly flip through each page.
• Use the index to locate more specific survey areas.

Anderson (1980) found that so-called surveying was really very complex. He found that whilst nearly all students scanned for information, they were actualy trying to answer the following three more complicated 'How' questions, e.g.:

• How much do I already know about this topic and text? (Uses previous knowledge, experience and lecture/lessons to act as Advance Organisers (Ausubel, 1961).)
• How interested am I in it?
• How difficult or time-consuming will it be for me to learn what I need to know from it?

Students engaged in level 1 survey (called scanning by others) to answer all 3 'How' questions. It took about two minutes and included non-sentence, information-rich parts of text e.g. titles, subtitles, marked words, highlighted sectors, pictures, charts, etc. If they could not answer all 3 'How' questions by this method they then went on to levels II and III. Level II took about 10–15 minutes and consisted of reading introductory and summary paragraphs, and first sentences of each paragraph. Level III consisted of selected readings of larger parts of the text. Students moved from level III to I and II if they could answer the question or if the text became less interesting. If the text was too poorly formatted to use levels I and II, then surveying broke down and the students started to read each section carefully from the beginning.

In the context where there is free choice, such as the home or library, experience suggests the book is put down or returned if it is difficult or dull, and another book is taken up. If again the surveying breaks down, the study session is given up. Only if external pressure demands that the learner demonstrates the results of study in seminar, essay or examination will the search be taken up again. In the meantime, advice needs to be given on more suitable reading for that individual, or a better strategy needs to be developed. If interest is low and the topic difficult, study time will be short, and may also be mechanical – the eyes run over the text but meaning is not attached to it. If the students know that they are going to have to explain what they have read to others, then their efforts assume significance and they will work over a text again and again until they have mastered it. This new purpose heightens the attention to the task and maintains the motivation.

During reading we engage in a number of complicated cognitive activities:

- In reading for specific facts, we use locational and reference skills.
- In reading for the main point to understand the logic of the text, we interpret meanings, tables, graphs, ideas.
- In reading to understand the overall structure, we organize information, summarize, outline and label.
- In reading for critical comprehension, we use thinking strategies at literal, interpretive, critical and creative levels. We reflect on ideas presented, tap into the writer's organizational plan, and relate new ideas to old using mental imagery.

Many activities which increase the probability that what has been read will be retained are suggested by various writers. These are all very much in relation to *memorizing* in post-reading activities.

SQ3R

SQ3R is a higher-level study skill based upon the experimental work of Johnson (1964) and detailed by Robinson (1967). Survey (S) refers to glancing over the headings in a chapter to note the main points which are going to be developed. Question (Q) means turning each heading into a question, and 3R refers to reading, reciting and reviewing. You read in order to answer the questions derived from the heading, and then recite, meaning that you should turn away from the book and try to recite the answers to those questions. When the chapter has been completed in this manner, you should then review your notes for the main points and their relationships. You may even try to recite the main points under each heading. Robinson advised that the technique was not easy to master and gave detailed instructions for practice. The technique involves a fair amount of rote memorizing, which can be very tedious, and most students quickly lose motivation to continue after one or two sessions.

It would seem that it is in the pauses between reciting, reading and notetaking that the most valuable processes of all are taking place; that is, the mental activity engaged in trying to retrieve and reactivate old memories and structures to make sense of the bits of the new which are in the process of being stored. This seems to be what learners are very resistant to doing; they prefer to keep reading, keep note taking and keep on reciting. They seem to prefer not to allow the thinking time in between to organize the information in ways meaningful to them; they would rather learn the pattern imposed from without. They feel safer if they know what the book says in the words in which it says it rather than what it means in their own words. Deeper understanding and making meaning relate very much to the process defined by Piaget (1952) as 'accommodation'.

Outlining

Barton (Robinson, 1967) taught ninety-six high-school students from two schools the fundamentals of outlining; that is, he taught students to find main, subordinate, co-ordinate and irrelevant points in each paragraph in geography, American history and ancient history. These students performed significantly better in examinations than a matched group of students who had the same instructional programme without the outlining techniques.

Mnemonics

This is a memorizing technique in which the initials of key words are used to make a familiar name or acronym to reduce memory strain by chunking items. Making and designing a mnemonic is different and can involve higher-order cognitive skills. Borrowing someone else's mnemonics does not. An example of a cognitive approach is given later.

Mapping (Hanf Buckley, 1971)

This technique means writing the main idea in the centre of the page and attaching the rest to it after the style of Tony Buzan's work (1974a and b). Concept mapping is becoming a valuable learning tool in various aspects of learning, and an example of its use in higher education is given in Chapter 6. When it is used only as a memorizing device, it is less useful.

PQRST

This stands for 'preview – survey the text; question – ask yourself a number of questions that need answers from the text; read intensively to find out the answers to the questions and so that you understand the text as a whole; summarize the main points made in the text; test yourself to see if the summary can be recalled as well as all the main aspects of factual information' (Gibbs, 1980).

Table 4.1 *Average reading rates, fixations and spans*

	1st grade	2nd grade	3rd grade	4th grade	5th grade	6th grade	Junior high school	High school	College students
Average span of recognition in words	0.42	0.50	0.59	0.73	0.89	0.95	1.05	1.21	1.33
Average rate of comprehension per minute	75	100	138	180	216	235	255	298	340
Average fixation per 100 words	240	200	170	136	118	105	95	83	75

Source: Taylor, 1960

NIRT or NIT

This stands for 'Note-take, transfer to index cards, rehearse and test. (Originated by a group of students in the Learning Difficulties Project).

Reading rates

Good readers have various reading rates which they use as appropriate to the material:

- *skimming rate;*
- *rapid reading,* missing no sections of material;
- *intensive reading*: read and re-read at a slow rate;
- *recreational rate*: 350+ words per minute.

Study skills and reading to learn: DARTS

The Schools Council (1980) project explored this aspect in relation to reading for learning in the secondary school. The writers defined two types of reading:

- receptive
- reflective.

When reading a newspaper or a novel, one is engaged in receptive reading, which is straight-through, fluent reading with understanding. This type of reading is wholly inadequate for study purposes (reading school textbooks). What one needs to encourage is *reflective reading.* This is the type in which you stop, pause, think, work back over the text, go back and check points, etc. The writers called this the *broken read,* finding it was only through this method that the learners had time to bring their own understanding to bear on the new material. As a result of their studies, they devised a number of very useful strategies for 'engaging the brain', involving study skills using a variety of what they called *DARTs* – 'directed activities related to texts'. Most students were found to use receptive rather than reflective reading strategies in the Learning Difficulties Project studies, and so a purposive search was made to develop and extend the DARTs approach with a view to incorporating this into the mainstream curriculum of schools and colleges.

Between observation and recording, few or many cognitive processes may take place. Students frequently use note taking as an aid to memory and may 'shadow' the speaker, trying to write down all that is said, with no cognitive processes taking place.

This is seldom possible for long periods and the note taking is disconnected and incomplete. Others may try to listen and taken down key points and a scattering of detail, producing a coherent structure or *scaffold* of the talk, which it is much easier to reconstruct or use at a later stage. In this method, cognitive processing is involved.

In many classrooms, students can be observed copying sections of text from books into their own books or folders whilst talking about something else to a partner. Little is learnt or committed to memory in these circumstances.

Learning involves the memorizing of material in a form in which it may be available for use at a later stage. If the material is structured we may memorize it as though it were not, it can take a considerable amount of time and effort, so much that it may become tedious to do and the learner loses interest. The loss of interest quickly appears where material seems to be of little relevance, and a lot of school work may seem to be like this. Able students often have very good memorizing abilities and read/ observe something once and remember it. They respond well to closed questions and thus appear 'bright', but they may well fail to achieve as more and more they are required to organize information and reconstruct it to seek deeper understanding. Concerns are frequently expressed that able students have failed to learn appropriate study skills. This is often because they have had little need or opportunity to learn and exercise them because of their good memories.

Teaching study skills as a separate programme has frequently been tried, but with little success in transfer (Meek and Thomson, 1987). The most profitable approach is an across-the-curriculum one in which all subject teachers employ strategies which cause the students to develop and use study skills.

They need to learn, on the one hand, how to 'observe' and approach the study task and, on the other, how to record or note take. Schools concentrate more on the basics such as using a dictionary and a library, reference skills, and skimming and scanning approaches to study rather than *how* to listen and read and look – the cognitive study skills. If they were to focus on these, then note-taking and recording strategies could be directly derived from these processes and would certainly be made easier. A distinction was made between study skills – searching for, locating and recording information – and cognitive study skills, in which 'brain engage' strategies were fully involved (Montgomery, 1983a). The term 'cognitive study skills' indicated that in the process of study the material was incorporated into the learners' own understandings without need for extensive rehearsal and memorizing techniques. This meant that the cognitive study skills had to be powerful and applicable across many curriculum areas, both verbal and spatial. Some illustrations of the cognitive approaches are shown below. The main strategies identified were:

- reading (or listening, etc.) for the main point;
- flow charting;
- sequencing;
- concept deletion;
- editing;
- marking, assessing and evaluating;
- critical comprehension (identification of bias, propaganda, opinion, intent, tone, etc.).

Higher-order reading/cognitive skills: making a mnemonic

Labels	Definitions	Mnemonic
	An important area within study skills is that of higher-order reading skills. These are called *language skills* by some and *cognitive skills* by others.	D
Stages	The first exercise is presented with the purpose of demonstrating that *you* are an inadequate reader! We are taught to read in the infant and first school but after about the age of 8 years, when the mechanical skill is relatively fluent and comprehension satisfactory, that is usually the end of 'learning to read'. Thereafter we use our skills for 'reading to learn'. A distinction is thus being made between the *acquisition* and the *development* of reading skills.	
	In the area of reading development, the definition of reading which seems to describe the process most succinctly is that of Neisser (1967): 'Reading is externally guided thinking.' This establishes quite clearly the overlap between higher-order reading and cognitive or thinking skills (cognition meaning knowing and understanding.	S

Labels	Definitions	Mnemonic
Approaches	American sources such as Royce-Adams (1977), from which some of these exercises are derived, emphasize the *reading skills approach*; sources in this country such as Edward de Bono (1975) concentrate upon *thinking skills*. An exception to this, however, is the work undertaken by Thomas and Harri-Augstein (1971) at Brunel University, in which Gipsy Hill psychology students participated for a week's intensive investigation. They used a reading event recorder to measure *reading behaviour* whilst presenting exercises such as the following [see next box] on Darwin's *Origin of Species*.	A Mnemonic = DSA DAS

It is not really the mnemonic which helps us recall the content of the passage; it is the work we have put into the tasks on this piece of text, searching and thinking about it. This is what facilitates *adaptation*. It is necessary of course for the passage to be within the reading age of the reader. Students find this is a more interesting way of revising material or coming to grips with difficult concepts in a text. If they are allowed to discuss their thoughts with a partner as they work and come to an agreed conclusion, they gain even more from this task. It promotes questioning and debate and helps students who might not otherwise have such a legitimate opportunity develop skills of self-expression.

Reading for the main point and flow charting

Laurie Thomas came to Gipsy Hill in 1971 and worked with our psychology students for a week studying their reading-to-learn strategies. The following is based upon one of the exercises the students were given, and it demonstrates that with certain difficult texts most of us are inadequate readers.

Study the following extract which is drawn from Darwin's *Origin of Species* (1872). The paragraph has been laid out with each sentence numbered in sequential order.

The first task is to find the *kernel* sentence, that is, find which sentence is the key one, the *main point*, the one from which all the rest follow and from which all the sense of the paragraph flows. Put the number of the *key* sentence in the box.

1 Again, it may be asked, how is it that varieties which I have called incipient species, become ultimately converted into good and distinct species, which in most cases obviously differ from each other far more than do the varieties of the same species?
2 How do those groups of species, which constitute what are called distinct genera and differ from each other more than do the species of the same genus, arise?
3 All these results, as we shall more fully see in the next chapter, follow from the struggle for life.
4 Owing to this struggle, variations, however slight, and from whatever cause proceeding, if they be in any degree profitable to the individuals of a species, in their infinitely complex relations to organic beings and to their physical conditions of life, will tend to the preservation of such individuals, and will generally be inherited by the offspring.
5 The offspring also, will thus have a better chance of surviving, for, of the many individuals of any species which are periodically born, but a small number can survive.
6 I have called this principle by which each slight variation, if useful, is preserved, by the term Natural Selection, in order to mark its relation to man's power of selection.
7 But the expression often used by Mr. Herbert Spencer of the Survival of the Fittest is more accurate, and is sometimes equally convenient.
8 We have seen that man by selection can certainly produce great results, and can adapt organic beings to his own uses, through the accumulation of slight but useful variations, given to him by the hand of Nature.
9 But Natural Selection, as we shall hereafter see, is as immeasurably superior to man's feeble efforts, as the works of nature are to those of Art.

Eye movements and cognitive search strategies

When you were reading the passage by Darwin for the main point, which of the following reading strategies did you adopt, or which mixture of approaches did you use? Tick as appropriate.
1 One straight read through, stop and re-read the sentence you decided upon on the read through. Followed by:
   a) confirmation

b) confusion
c) start reading through again
2 Quick skim through the passage, a rapid read through.
3 Eyes scanning backwards and forwards through the text reading sentences or phrases out of order in the search process.
4 Pause for thought.
5 Note-making pause or in this case marking the possibly important section or word.
6 A slow, systematic read through.

When Thomas and Augstein (1975) undertook their studies of college and university students, they found that more than 50 per cent of them were inadequate readers; that is, after studying a piece of text they were incapable of doing an objective test with any degree of accuracy based on facts presented in the text, and they failed to be able to summarize the main points and follow the sense of the passage. The exercise used is shown in the box overleaf.

GAMES AND SIMULATIONS

There has been a growing acceptance in the last twenty-five years of games as a teaching technique in educational circles. The increased use of educational games, according to Dukes and Seidner (1978), may be attributed to many factors, including the coincidence of three trends:

- the questioning of the traditional socialization function of our educational institutions and the decline in the utility of the fact-dispersing function of schools;
- the emphasis on the active learner and discovery learning in the 1970s;
- the appearance of a new medium – the simulation game – during this period.

Non-simulation games

Students work in groups and are actively involved in the learning process. Success, or winning, is related to the degree of subject-matter comprehension demonstrated during the game. Students have to know certain facts, show certain skills or demonstrate mastery of certain concepts in order to win. The participants agree upon certain objectives, and there is a set of rules which limit the

Following the logic of an argument

In this exercise you are asked to insert the correct kernel sentence in the box below and then draw in the positions of the boxes containing the number of the other sentences in a *flow* diagram to show the meaning of Darwin's paragraph.

If you have tried but just cannot get the 'hang of it', turn over for a lay-out *clue*. [The page ended here.]

There is never one perfect answer to a task such as this, for the boxes can be switched from right to left or up or down with one or more connections, but the following map will allow you to see what is meant by a flow diagram and limit the number of possibilities you can consider. It will structure or direct your thinking. Now try again.

(Montgomery, 1983a)

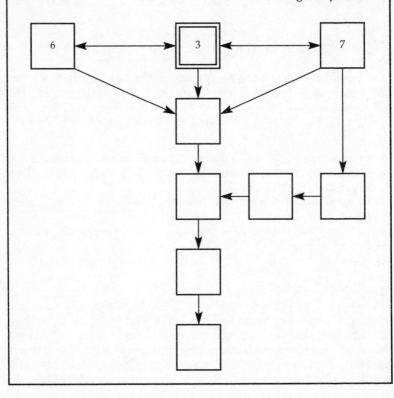

means whereby these objectives may be attained. Games are often competitive but may not be so.

The number of ways games can be used in education is limitless. Card games may be adapted to educational purposes by asking students to manipulate factual materials printed on to cards in order to reach some agreed or specific goal or objective. Teachers often construct their own games. A useful device is to use a game which permits the insertion of many different subject contents. An example of this is the 'Whole Book Game', a study skills game assignment using a text or story book as the basis. An example is given on p. 116–17.

Simulation games

'Simulation' refers to the abstraction of certain elements of social or physical reality in such a way that the student can interact with and become part of the simulated reality. Some types of simulation are as follows:

- *All-machine simulations*: completely computerized, these are most often used in research by planners and theoreticians but are becoming more frequently used in classrooms.
- *Person-machine simulations*: individuals interact with a computerized system for making decisions that affect the functioning of the system. Students may play the role of adviser and make decisions; the computer program uses these and shows their results – for example, planting crops and using fertilizers at particular times. The computer requests further information at intervals and recalculates the results. These programs are becoming more frequently used in classrooms.
- *All-person simulations*: a set of rules and specifications defines the roles and resources of the participants, who will experience some of the same kinds of pressure and influence that would occur in the real-life setting. Examples are the enrichment pack 'The Battle of Islandhlwana' mentioned in Chapter 3, and a communication 'game' used to explore issues and problems in child abuse cases between 'co-operating' services.

An example is given below:
This is an account of a conference for very able secondary pupils in conjunction with industry, which involved the pupils in simulations of 'real' industrial and community problem solving conducted in a naturalistic manner.

'It'

A Conference for the Most Able Youngsters in the Northampton area

Scott Hurd

The first simulation was introduced by Steve Robinson from Avon Cosmetics and Nicole Short from East Midlands Electricity. The five strong groups of students were given the task of creating their own sales campaign for an Avon Cosmetics product. To get a feel for the company they toured the factory and learned about Avon's policy.

Most searched for ways to reflect this in their campaign. When they returned to work they realised that time was flying, the client was in a hurry for results and only three groups were going to be asked to give a presentation.

Things began to hot up. The panel representing the client found themselves being shown many interesting ideas but, as it sunk home that this really was 'winner takes all', they also became the target of some very stiff sales talk. As in the real world it wasn't just the best idea which counted, it was the impression that the groups made. Three groups, with equally good ideas, emerged to give presentations, but the confident and dynamic performance given by one carried them through and earned prizes made even more interesting for being sealed in Avon Security bags!

The lunch break was kept as short as possible but this didn't stop those with cash to spare visiting the factory shop ... and when the time came to restart it wasn't the youngsters but their teachers who were missing – and it wasn't the organisers who told them off!

The afternoon revolved around the scenario 'Peninsula' in which an area of outstanding natural beauty was being choked to death, economically and socially, by traffic. The already established groups quickly got into their new roles which ranged from the Port Authority to the National Trust. The winning group from the morning's session were given the task of conducting the enquiry and the most vocal told to run a radio station while their neighbours operated a newspaper. Four construction companies decided upon the best route, worked out the costs and put their respective cases forward. Everyone acknowledged that a new road was needed but it was hard to agree on one solution.

At one point big business was in danger of steamrollering conservation issues and some of the quietest suddenly found their tongues. As the final meeting opened, the Press and Radio were silenced, rebellion seethed just below the surface and protests were made at the highest level. Many were very surprised at the Board of Inquiry's final decision and some realised, too late, that the arguments they had considered too obvious to mention might have swayed the day in their favour. Some did their best to prolong the session but they had had their chance! This was not the same shy and retiring group that had had to be coaxed, none too gently, into action at the start of the day!

An important part of an event such as this is the group review at the end ensuring that the skills learnt are reinforced. This session had an added advantage as the question sheet formed the basis of a statement for the student's Record of Achievement and was backed up by a certificate from Leicester University's Department of Citizenship. While everybody was working away on this exercise Scott relaxed. He was surprised, but very pleased, to be tapped on the shoulder and asked 'I'm dyslexic, any chance of some help?' This simple act showed how far schools have developed in the past few years. At one time this lad would never have been considered for a conference for the most able!

(Hurd, 1993, pp. 21–2)

Most simulation games involve interaction among a number of students. The student acts, and observes concrete events that result from the action. The games thus involve the students in experiential learning, and differ from the traditional information – processing mode. 'The Motorway Project' (Chapter 3) is an example.

A simulation becomes a simulation game when success is determined in terms of player goals and there is a prescribed criterion for winning. In simulations that are not games, there may be a final position but a winner is not explicitly determined.

Role-playing

It is difficult to isolate the educational efforts of simulations and games from other teaching techniques. This is particularly true of role-playing games and simulations.

A typical example is where the simulation game defines the roles of players within a given social context, specifies very broad goals, and then leaves the players largely on their own in determining how the role should be played out.

Post-game discussion

Nearly all designers and users of simulation games stress the usefulness of a post-game discussion in clarifying what has transpired during the gaming session. It is particularly useful in achieving educational objectives, and then the skill of the discussion leader can be crucial to the outcomes. It also brings about learning at a higher-order metacognitive level.

The following shows an example of a study skills game.

Shakoor is born

A game for two or three players
or to be played against the clock and scores ladder by one player

Kit:

• Game board
• One pack of study skills question cards (see pp. 118–19)
• Two or three different coloured counters or small objects
• Pot for shaking dice – hands can be used

Orange squares

1 Pick up another card.
2 Answer question correctly and you can *treble* your original score, e.g. move 9 places (3+6).

Green squares

1 Pick up another card.
2 Answer question correctly and you can *double* your original score, e.g. move 6 places.

Black squares

1 The player landing on a white square must make up a question for each of the other players.
2 One move is made forward for each question invented.
3 One additional square forward can be moved if the other player(s) cannot answer the question.

White squares

Move six places backward.

Joker card

Make up your own question and answer it. Move forward an extra three places if you are correct.

Rules

To play: Shuffle cards and place face down on the board.

Throw dice – highest score starts, next highest is second and so on.

1 Each player must throw a 6 to start.
2 The turn passes on and the next throw entitles player to move forward.
3 If player throws, e.g. a 3:
   a) Player takes top card from pack and reads it to players.
   b) If player answers question correctly to the satisfaction of the other players s/he can then move forward three places.
   c) Turn passes on.

If answer not satisfactory, player moves back three places or remains at *start*.

Partners may check answers in the book.

Classification of study skill questions (see pp. 118–19)

- Mime × 2
- Retell a sequences × 2
- Explaining × 2 (why)
- Factual comprehension:
  – Who × 6
  – How many, name, what is, etc. × 11
- Deletion × 1
- Main point × 1
- Problem solving?

EXPERIENTIAL LEARNING

Kolb in 1984 defined the experiential learning cycle, in which it was important that practical experience had to be reflected upon in order to achieve higher-order understanding and learning. The *learning spiral* shown in Figure 4.3 suggests that learning is not circular, returning the learner to the same point each time. It is suggested that at each turn the experience, the talking about experience and then the reflecting upon the learning and doing add to the sum of knowledge and change the processes and the under-

Cards

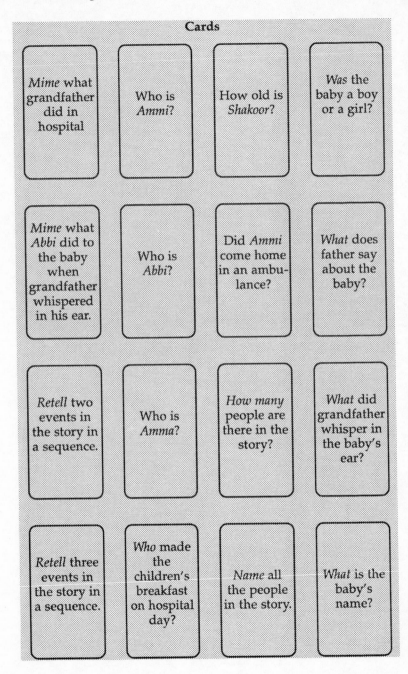

Mime what grandfather did in hospital	Who is *Ammi*?	How old is *Shakoor*?	*Was* the baby a boy or a girl?
Mime what *Abbi* did to the baby when grandfather whispered in his ear.	Who is *Abbi*?	Did *Ammi* come home in an ambulance?	*What* does father say about the baby?
Retell two events in the story in a sequence.	Who is *Amma*?	*How many* people are there in the story?	*What* did grandfather whisper in the baby's ear?
Retell three events in the story in a sequence.	*Who* made the children's breakfast on hospital day?	*Name* all the people in the story.	*What* is the baby's name?

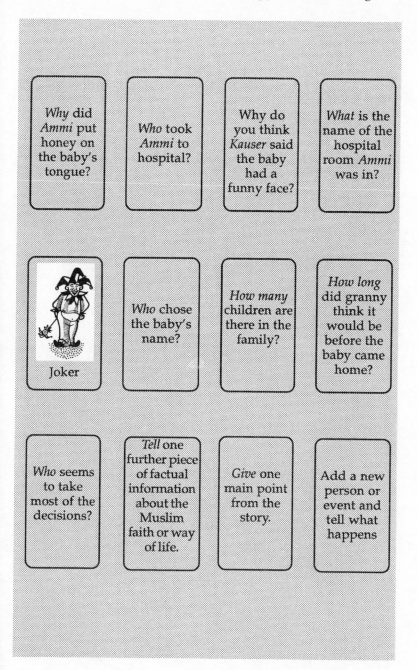

Why did *Ammi* put honey on the baby's tongue?

Who took *Ammi* to hospital?

Why do you think *Kauser* said the baby had a funny face?

What is the name of the hospital room *Ammi* was in?

Joker

Who chose the baby's name?

How many children are there in the family?

How long did granny think it would be before the baby came home?

Who seems to take most of the decisions?

Tell one further piece of factual information about the Muslim faith or way of life.

Give one main point from the story.

Add a new person or event and tell what happens

standing slightly in a cumulative way. 'Learning occurs not in the doing but in the reflection and conceptualisation that takes place during and after the event' (Kolb, 1984).

Experiential learning thus involves learning by doing or *action learning*. It is surprising how much students in schools and colleges remain passive in the learning process and yet how much more effective their learning could be if they were direct participants. This has long been recognized in early-years education and primary (elementary) education in Britain. Kolb (1984) has shown, and experience dictates, that unless the learner reflects upon the learning during and after the event it is not as effective and meaningful.

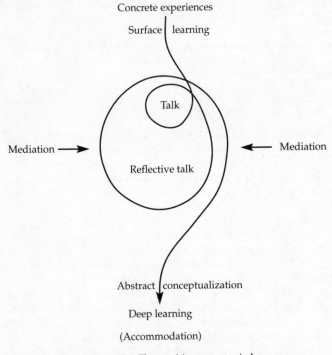

Figure 4.3 *The cognitive process spiral*
Source: Montgomery, 1994

Although learners may learn without direct experience by observing and modelling others, and able learners can be particularly adept at this, this does not mean that direct experience is not useful. The experience does, however, have to be cognitively challenging, otherwise it is no more than other mundane activities. Simply manipulating clay to make farmyard animals can be of value in exploratory activities with the material. This will soon pall for the able, and more advanced challenges in designs, goals and purposes need to be encouraged. This can be promoted by detailed observation of form and structure and by remodelling, redesigning and playing with the material. Creative persons emphasize the role of play in their work.

Similarly, no study of farming, the sea, transport, Victorian life, etc., is complete without visits to museums and sites of interest or films and videos. Whilst able pupils are often more knowledgeable and observant and so gain more from these experiences, the experiences can often be made more of by cognitive challenge. Visits need to be prepared in advance by the teacher. This can assist in the design of preliminary learning and problem solving sessions for the pupils.

For example, a visit to a farm can be prepared for by some investigative and hypothesis-forming collaborative work. Small groups of three or four people can be given three products or artifacts from a selection of the farm's produce, such as a carton of milk, a potato, an egg, a food packet, an egg box, sprouts, dried peas, onions, sugar, grain/bread roll. Each group has to collaborate to produce a flow chart or critical path analysis, working backwards from the object to its origin, through processing and processes to the raw source. The first attempt can be made without any example from the teacher, but with support for the groups as they puzzle out what the task means. Each group should present and explain one of their chains, charts or pathways to the rest. Further work should be undertaken after this to improve the charts to meet questions raised by others in the class. At this stage recourse to texts can be permitted. Each group should complete the session by raising a number of questions they need to have answered about their investigation ready for the visit.

The post-visit sessions can be supplemented with wider research about the general topic and a selected process, and the work can be mounted later as an exhibition or presented as a book. A few more enterprising individuals armed with cameras, videos or tape recorders could produce a radio or TV programme for others in the year group or for younger children. All of this activity cannot of course be encompassed within the timetable, but this usually proves little object once children's interest is engaged and they feel involved with the methods and outcomes; they will continue working on the project during breaks and in their own time, organizing their own study groups.

Where schools have developed 'homework clubs' and facilities outside school hours for children to return or study in a more relaxed environment and atmosphere, collaborative projects stemming from experiential learning such as this can thrive. When pupils themselves are introduced to the concepts in Bloom's taxonomy about levels of intellectual or cognitive operation, they will be able to reflect upon their own thought processses during learning and seek higher levels.

In addition to more open learning examples such as this, experiential learning methods include the use of games, simulations, role-plays, visits and work experience. What is crucial is that discussion, critical thinking and reflection are made a consistent part of this process, otherwise learning can remain at a superficial, unconnected level.

COLLABORATIVE LEARNING

'Collaborative' means students work with each other towards the framing and design of problems and strategies as well as in their resolution or solution. Each contributes some part to the whole. Quite often this process is called co-operative learning. Either term is appropriate, but frequently what is meant to be co-operative or group work is more often observed as students sitting together doing individual work. In Britain, it is common to find students in groups of four to six working at tables in both primary (elementary) and secondary schools. In the United States, classroom grouping is less common and research funding is directed to studying the effects of it.

An HMI survey (HMI, 1979) showed that most teachers grouped students for some aspects of their work. In maths, reading and writing, the grouping was most often homogeneous (setting by ability); in sciences, arts and crafts, groups were usually mixed-ability. The Plowden Report (1967) had encouraged grouping so that the teacher's time might be used more economically and children would help each other and develop their social and interpersonal skills. A range of HMI reports (1983, 1985) had encouraged more group work, and yet research studies showed that interactions within the groups were mainly between children of the same sex and not related to the task in hand (Galton *et al.*, 1985; Bennett, 1986). Students in groups on average spent two-thirds of their time on individual work, interacting with no one. Only 5 per cent of the time was spent talking about the task, and then it was likely to be requests for information. It was in fact the exception rather than the rule to find a 'group' working as a group.

Bennett's studies, which recorded the task in detail, showed that little talk which did take place was task-enhancing. When Wheldall *et al.* (1981) looked at the effect of placing pupils in rows as opposed to 'groups', the major finding was that this increased the quantity of output and the quality was maintained. The influence of peer tutoring and constructive collaboration in classrooms can thus be said to be negligible. This does not devaluate collaborative group work. What is at fault is the method or pedagogy used by the teacher which does not induce or create a need for group problem solving or group work. The examples given in the earlier sections on problem solving, games and simulations incorporate collaboration. The study skills work should all preferably be done in pairs, and some tasks by triads where a greater brain input is required in complex tasks. Sometimes it is appropriate for the group goal to be the overriding purpose, but at other times it is necessary for the individual's work to be assessed so that at the end of the group process individual as well as group products can be evaluated.

Research studies on the effectiveness of group work have been relatively limited, not only in number but in design and preparation of the appropriate content and process. Examples of types of heterogeneous American-style (race, gender, ability) study groups include the following:

- *the jigsaw classroom.* Students prepare segments of a task in teams, then return to a 'home' team to teach their segment to the rest (Aronson, 1978).
- *team games and tournaments.* The students study in teams and then take part in quizzes or a final tournament on the subject content (Slavin, 1977).
- *group and team investigation.* Groups divide the topic into individual tasks, which are studied and then presented by the group to the whole class; or team members mark each other's work, and scores at the end of the week are computed (Johnson and Johnson, 1975; Slavin, 1987).

As can be seen, the style of these activities was individual work brought together at intervals as a group presentation. It was usually content- or product-based in mathematics, and would have proved more time-consuming than our National Curriculum would permit. It was not the same in nature as the collaborative interactive work in the problem-solving, simulation and games approaches already described. The interactive aspects of these are designed to:

- model real problem solving which we need to do in adult life and in job or career;
- occupy a small period of time in an individual lesson, or small slots in a series of lessons;
- take no more time than traditional or didactic methods would take when all inputs, rehearsal and recording time is taken into account;
- offer opportunities for more creative and original contributions from individuals, sparked off by their interactions;
- use and link new material to students' prior experience and knowledge.

Where the collaborative approach is designed to take longer, then the gains in terms of higher-order learning and the strength of that learning should be sufficient to merit this. This will often be the point where a new subject area or topic is to be introduced.

Bennett and Cass (1986), using a computer program to provide decision-making tasks, observed triads of children in homogeneous and heterogeneous groups, and found that high-attaining children understood decisions and attained a 95 per cent success rate whichever type of group they worked in. Thus, working with average and low attainers did not damage their capacity for achievement, a concern which has frequently been raised:

> In this co-operative decision-making mode on-task behaviour was very high, and instructional talk was very high in relation to procedural or management talk. There was an indication of a link between the amount of talk, particularly amount of instructional talk (by the children), and pupil understanding.
>
> (Bennett and Cass, 1986, p. 16)

One of the strongest influences on the design of the Learning Difficulties Project work on collaborative learning was the work of Bowers and Wells (1985) in the Kingston Friends Workshop Group. This work of the Quakers' originated in the riots and violence in America in the 1960s. It was based on the view that the seeds of conflict were sown at an early age and that it was important to help adults and children to develop constructive solutions to conflict and violence. Bowers and Wells developed a structure and three main themes as a basis for problem solving in conflict resolution and bridge building between people. These ideas are expressed in the iceberg principle (see Figure 4.4 on p. 126).

The examples from their handbook given in the box illustrate the relatively content-free process methodology of some of the activities and the possibilities of briefing sheets and scenarios in others.

Examples of collaborative learning work from Bowers and Wells (1985)

The Liver Transplant List

A set of six role cards, varying according to the age and interests of the groups, is provided. Each card describes a person's role, such as pop singer (age 19), unemployed man with wife and three children (age 45), one of two children of a single parent (age 13). The groups are asked to imagine these people are patients waiting for a liver transplant. A donor has become available, and the liver is suitable for any of them. They are asked to put forward the case for the role they have been given and then agree among themselves which one is to be selected for the operation.

Notes on managing the progress of the discussions are given to help the teacher; for example:

- Emphasize there are no 'right' answers, as well as further stages.
- Ask them to repeat the process, but this time argue the case for themselves.
- Next, argue the case for the person on your left (or right).
- New roles can be developed by those who complete these stages.

Circle time: affirming

This is a technique for closing a workshop where friendship and trust have been established. Each person in turn is affirmed by members of the group: two or three positive statements are given about each, such as 'He kept us all cheerful' or 'She gave us the questions at just the right moment.' Circle time has become extremely popular in all types of school and is used to help counteract bullying and behaviour management problems.

Who is Mrs Brown?

Mrs Brown is described by several people she cares for; she is seen in the role of a mother, a hospital nurse, a nagger by her son, and a good cook by her husband. The children discuss the problem of who Mrs Brown really is and what is she like herself, and then are asked to draw or describe themselves as seen by four different people.

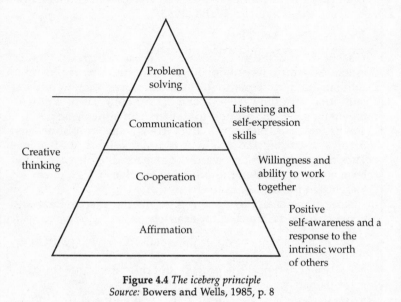

Figure 4.4 *The iceberg principle*
Source: Bowers and Wells, 1985, p. 8

These activities lead towards working with the pupils on the total process of problem solving. Each stage is followed through with suggested strategies:

* definition
* expressing feelings
* creating options
* goal setting

Brainstorming, role-play and a wide range of action learning strategies are used to promote co-operative learning.

The group received many commissions to train teachers in a number of LEAs in the techniques, and demonstrated them in classrooms. Research funding was obtained and showed that the collaborative learning methods were successful in decreasing bullying, misbehaviour and conflict in classrooms (Saunders, 1989).

The techniques were also taught to students on inservice and initial teacher education programmes in the higher education institution and were found to be highly valued by the students and the teachers. It was clear that a more substantial programme of such work was required rather than the day-long input if the techniques were to be fully internalized. It was decided to design and develop a full inservice module in conflict management, which became extremely popular.

Pyramiding, targeting and brainstorming

Techniques which were also introduced into the mixed-ability classrooms and the segregated teams of able students were *pyramiding* and *targeting*. There are also commonly used variants of these in business education and management courses, termed 'Snowballing' and 'Focusing'. There was also the ubiquitous *brainstorming* or 'synectics', used to draw ideas together, pool them on a display board and then classify, order, redevelop and research them as part of a range of topic introductions.

Pyramiding involved every member of the class jotting down his or her own ideas about the subject in hand for three minutes. The members were then formed into threes to discuss and prepare a composite list. Next they were formed into sixes, then twelves, to present their group's main points. Able students often found these strategies more difficult than other students; they were not used to having their ideas challenged and having to justify themselves or be proved wrong. Less able groups benefited from the repetitions through to groups of twelves, whilst the able worked best up to sixes.

Targeting was used in situations where there was a complex phenomenon to deal with, such as what the essence of the king's/leader's economic policy is; what the main idea is behind deciding which area to settle; what the essence of democracy is; what you should do if bullied or threatened; what lies behind racism; what causes conflict; what are the qualities of leadership; and so on.

As already indicated, collaborative learning when it is properly organized and targeted can have a constructive effect on learning. It helps develop language skills and social control and is an effective outlet for emotional tensions, for it provides legitimate channels for its expression and release. Collaborative strategies provide the experience in listening, speaking skills and interpersonal skills which the lone teacher with a class of thirty cannot do to the extent that is required. This is particularly important, for even the most able do not know what they think until they have to explain it to someone else. Collaborative work of this specific kind encourages the development of peer tutoring and teaching skills. It also provides the environment in which other learners can challenge and ask questions of their peers, when they do not understand, without being diminished or devalued. This improves the quality of the peer tutoring and interpersonal skills over a period of time.

Learning to listen and communicate one's own ideas and feelings to others is a valuable part of the educative process, but it is too often overlooked in an overfilled content curriculum to the detriment of an individual's life chances.

LANGUAGE EXPERIENCE METHODS

These were first described in relation to the teaching of language and literacy skills. Where students were having problems in acquiring the basic skills because of motivational and learning difficulties and disadvantaging environments, their own words and their own stories were used as the texts for them to read and write. The students, having enjoyed a visit, for example, sit down with a scribe, who makes notes as the student tells the story about the events of the day. The scribe types up the story and presents it as reading material to the learner, and perhaps a book is made of it all, 'Written by ...' with a proper title and pictures and photographs throughout. Frequently the word processor is used for shared events. Two students compose a story or write a narrative account of their experience together. This is then printed out and used as reading material in their story file. Teachers have found these strategies particularly effective and motivating for students with a range of abilities and learning difficulties.

One very powerful motivation is for the students to prepare their stories to read to and with younger children, who may also have some literacy difficulties. It is common in British classrooms for class books such as this to be prepared on a range of topics, and these are regularly read by peers. Gardner (1990) showed how able children's creative abilities could be developed and extended by a mixture of study skills and language experience approaches.

The newspaper project

Making a class newspaper has for many years been a popular primary- or middle-school project. It quite often features in some measure in secondary-school language work too. As a project for able pupils, it has many advantages: it can be used with any age group from 4 or 5 onwards; it can be designed as a full process approach to teaching and learning; it can be repeated often without losing its impact; it results in a unified product, which may become a commercial enterprise and so develop a whole new set of learning experiences, possibly involving setting up a small business as part of the project. This is an example of a class project.

Once the principles of news collection and dissemination have been understood and practised, they can be applied to many different contexts. Historical news methods can also be researched, and these may be used to represent historical evidence in order to clarify old issues and concepts and provide motivation to study and research original sources.

Pupils will not usually have worked in a way which conforms to process principles and may not have made their own newspaper before. It is therefore important to run a series of teaching sessions which allow them to learn about the nature and structure of newspapers in as interesting a way as possible. Too often, unfortunately, the introductory sessions consist of first a discussion – really only a question-and-answer activity – with the teacher asking closed questions and gaining one-word answers. The result of this is the compilation of a list on the blackboard of types of reporter contribution, such as news, fashion, entertainment, sport. The children choose or are then assigned a role such as fashion editor/reporter for the girls, and sport for the boys. They are then given newspapers to look at, if they are lucky, and are asked to write news stories of their own and draw pictures to illustrate them. More forward-thinking classrooms actually centre the newspaper lessons on real situations in and outside school, with pupils devising questionnaires and obtaining interviews with local people, taking photographs and collecting information. Where this approach has been adopted with groups of alienated adolescents in a Newham schools' study skills lesson, considerable success in motivating these pupils has been reported. Significant improvement was also found in the pupils' attention to detail, presentation and general basic skills work. Their general self-esteem also improved, and with it their attitude to school and school work.

The following box details a series of lessons which it has been found help pupils understand some of the nature of newspapers, and how and why they are constructed as they are. The sessions also show how the process approach to teaching and learning can be applied to a specific situation and subject. At the end of the series of lessons and workshops, there is a unified product which can be evaluated, enjoyed and even sold if necessary – the newspaper itself. In the process of its development and construction, basic skills in number and language can be taught and practised, and specific skills and knowledge will be learnt in as many subject areas as considered necessary.

There will also be many opportunities for self-initiated and self-directed learning, as well as for decision-making, leadership and negotiation. It is an opportunity for pupils to experience real group work, often for the first time. The work can be used as a series of lessons and projects for a whole class (Montgomery, 1991).

Newspaper project: 1.15–3.15 p.m. on two afternoons per week.

For a class project, divide the class into small *leaderless* groups of three to five pupils. (Groups of more than five tend to split into sub-groups. A group of three will allow the maximum detailed talking time to each one in the group. A group of two provides too little stimulus.) The introductory lessons work best when the groups are made up of three pupils only, or for a special project for one or two very able pupils. If there is only one very able pupil, select preferably two or three other pupils to work with him or her. Find children who are above average ability or have some special ability, such as creative flair, to join the group. If there are two very able pupils, let them work together without any others, unless they choose another friend to work with them. Getting the social mix right is an important consideration.

Do not appoint a leader, for the leader in this group will emerge and may change with the task as necessary. In some groups, a task leader and a socioemotional leader will emerge (Bales, 1950). When leaders are appointed, it can seriously demotivate the other pupils and lead to overload on the leader, who is then given all the information to handle and the decisions to make whilst the others abdicate their responsibilities. The pupils may decide to appoint a leader themselves as they progress to undertake a specific task.

N.B. The real-life work of making a newspaper is only distantly related to the tasks presented here. They have been remodelled to conform to the process approach.

The examples from tabloid newspapers had been selected specifically to conform to the reading-age level of young able pupils. With very able or older pupils, the *Financial Times, Independent, Guardian, Telegraph* and *Times* would be appropriate.

Introductory lesson: 1.15–3.15 p.m., twenty-seven pupils

Presenting the news: Introduction – Teacher talk

Explain briefly to the pupils that they are going to learn how a newspaper is put together, and that it is more than just gathering and presenting information. The pupils are going to be put in a series of problem-solving situations such as those in which newspaper people often find themselves, and they are going to try not only to resolve the problems but also to learn about the things which lie under the surface – the pressures and issues. These latter they will be able to work out as they go along and can share their thoughts on at the end of the session. They will work in groups.

Each group will be given a brown envelope which contains three news assignments for the 'day'. On the envelope will be written what the editor wishes them to do and the deadline which they must meet.

Stage One: Organizing groups, moving furniture, etc.

1 Organize pupils in friendship groups of three (or four if they wish). Separate groups as far as is possible so that they do not disturb each other.
2 Explain that there will be a lot of talking to be done, so that shouting is out. Anyone trying to make a point by bellowing will be removed and put in the 'time-out area' to cool down. Too much noise from everyone will have to be stopped and the task tried at another time when they can be calmer. You may have great noise on the first occasion because of the novelty effect and the great enjoyment that they are having, and so it is worth taking these precautions in advance by laying down rules so that you do not have to nag continually. For example, warn once and then remove the culprit for one minute to the 'time-out' area. This will have a calming effect on the others – the ripple effect. A time-out area can be simply a chair in a vacant space by or at the teacher's desk. The pupil is made to sit with his or her back towards the groups, close his or her eyes and sit still for exactly one minute to calm down.
3 Give out the brown envelopes with the three assignments in them, one to each group (nine envelopes). Ask the pupils to read the instructions carefully and begin as soon as they can in whatever way they wish.

Stage Two: Children working on assignments – pupil talk

Each envelope contains:

1 a news headline (without a story);
2 a news picture (without a headline or story);
3 a news story (without a picture or a headline);

N.B. All the headlines should actually have a story and/or picture, which is kept by the teacher and either put in another group's envelope or pasted into one of three scrapbooks. These scrapbooks are used for later research:

- No. I contains all the stories and/or pictures belonging to the headlines.
- No. II contains all the headlines belonging to stories.
- No. III contains all the headlines and captions belonging to the pictures.

The following instructions are written on the envelopes in large freehand with felt tip – 'Editor's hand', which the pupils learn to recognize.

On the brown envelope (6½ × 9" size) should be handwritten the following, in approximately this area of space:

INSIDE
1) One headline   –   write story.
2) One picture   –   write headline and caption.
3) One story   –   write headline and outline type of picture
                       you want photographer to get for you.

DEADLINES
2.00–2.15 p.m. *News Conference*
All groups show picture, describe to class and give suggested headline(s).
2.45–3.15 p.m. *News Conference*
All groups give outline of their story.
Give headline and describe picture wanted.
3.15 p.m. File stories for headline.

During the 1.30–2.00 period, the pupils will need to sort out their order of priorities and discuss their headlines, pictures and stories. Allowing them to do this is part of the learning experience, even if they get it wrong! They will learn from this too. The reason for stopping at 2.00 p.m. and changing the activity is twofold: their attention span demands a change in activity, and also they need to learn how to deal with interruption and be businesslike in switching from one thing to the next and back again. It allows them as well to share their first efforts and see how the injection of humour by some groups can make some interesting points.

Lesson Two: 1.15–3.15 p.m.

Investigating layout: Introduction: 15 minutes – Teacher explanation of the task

The class should reorganize itself as before in groups of three, ready to begin the task this time. The teacher explains the purpose of the initial task, which is to look at the way the front page of a newspaper is laid out to attract attention. First ask pupils to count the columns and divide their A4 page into the number of newsprint columns. The next thing to do is to transfer the rest of the layout of the tabloid and reproduce it on the sheet of A4 paper over the columns, with all headlines represented by red sticky paper and all pictures by green sticky paper; the writing area can be left white.

Very young children can, if given an A4 copy of the front page, trace over the picture area, etc. on tracing paper, and then cut paper or colour in the areas. Older subjects can calculate the areas and scale down exactly; the less able and those without the specific number skills can work by eye and rule of thumb or string. Decide according to ability and knowledge whether you want them to scale down, estimate or trace.

Each group should have at least one if not two front pages or copies to work on. (For the intellectually younger children, it will also be wise to give one task at a time, for example, first trace/draw and cut out/paint the picture areas and put them where they should go. Check this has been done and understood, then go on to the headlines in red.) Recording individual paper stories could be done as follows:

	Daily Mail	Daily Express	Daily Mirror	Sun
Stories 1				
2				
3				
4				
5				

N.B. On days when there is a definite disaster or storyline, all the papers carry the story to some degree. When there is 'no' news, each paper contains a different set of stories and headlines, which indicate editorial policy and preference. The examples which were given showed, for example, 'Prince Philip's near miss'; 'A girl's bottom' and 'A sports star's relationship'. (For further examples see Montgomery, 1991.)

Extracts from a report on school-based research into differentiation for able pupils using cognitive-process methodology

Introduction and background

This piece of research into differentiation using cognitive process methodology was part of a larger project investigating differentiation of the curriculum across three separate phases of education and involving teachers and schools from three local education authorities.

The Project was funded by the National Primary Centre and endorsed by Buckinghamshire local education authority. The National Primary Centre supports primary education in England and Wales through publications that bring together the views of teachers and other professionals to give an overview of the current thinking on a specific issue. There is also support for school-based research. The practical results for this work are presented in a format useful for teachers, and for those concerned with staff development and with the in-service training of teachers.

The research was based on the work of Diane Montgomery at the Middlesex University as published in her book *The Special Needs of Able Pupils in Ordinary Classrooms*. She states that:

> Differentiation is achieved by the setting of common tasks in a manner by which pupils can contribute individually and collaboratively to the inputs and so raise the standard of output of all the pupils in the group.

Our aim was to use cognitive process methodology to differentiate the curriculum for able children in ordinary, mixed ability classrooms. The research was school-based and used teachers as researchers.

Conclusions

The benefits of approaching differentiation of the curriculum for able children through cognitive process methodology were demonstrated to be manifold: for the able children; the rest of the class; the teachers; and the school.

It became apparent how essential it is to start using activities designed to train children to be active thinkers from a very early age. There was an obvious need to practise divergent thinking and to start such activities in the nursery. As the children grew older their enthusiasm to approach a new and untried activity became noticeably jaded and they became more reluctant to participate. In part this may have been due to the relative inexperience of the teachers themselves in working in this way using open-ended questioning.

They have rarely had the luxury of pursuing a child's ideas or interest beyond a superficial level.

Moreover, it became evident that where the teacher shared the focus and purpose of the lesson with the group, the children's enthusiasm was greatly enhanced, and the children were able to take positive control over their own learning with the teacher more of a facilitator than an instructor.

The most successful activities were those:

* that were part of the ongoing classroom work.
* where the children were involved in the setting of the learning task,
* which contained built-in levels of progression.

The teachers made some interesting observations both during and after the sessions. They found that once the children's interests had been captured, the children, even the youngest in the nursery class, would stay on the task for a considerable length of time. The teachers realised that they had often underestimated the capacity of the children to explore a subject in depth and to support and generate their own learning. When the children were enthused they often continued the activities back in the classroom in their spare time. The knock-on effect was that the rest of the class also then became involved in the activities, each child working at their own level of interest and understanding. Back in the classroom, some of the unselected children demonstrated qualities previously unrecognised when they became involved in the continuing activity of the selected group, e.g. leadership, organisational skills.

Changes within the school resulting from the research have been noticeable. The observations will influence our future in-service training for the staff. The teachers need training in the development of open-ended questioning and divergent thinking. Also, the teachers need to adapt their time-planning to give able children the time to pursue and develop their own learning.

Teachers now reflect the influence of the research in their planning of classroom work by mapping out at least three levels all centred around a common theme:

* a core activity for the main stream,
* an activity with more clearly designed steps for the less able,
* and an extension and enrichment activity for the more able.

As a result of the teachers' heightened awareness of the cognitive process methodology, there have been activities that clearly reflect the influence the research has had on the whole school and the way we now approach the organisation of the curriculum. For example, two direct consequences are:

- The children now run a school newspaper, involving mixing across classroom and age boundaries as well as ability groups.
- One class formed its own plant company complete with corporate identity logo, a finance team, a marketing team, a sales team and a general work force. The whole class was involved with the more able children taking the initiative and organising the other children. The finance team even visited the local bank to negotiate a loan.

We at Iver Heath First School and Nursery are of the opinion that the research showed that the provision for able children can be met within a mixed ability classroom without necessarily accelerating the children through the levels of the National Curriculum. Extension and enrichment can be offered to able children through cognitive process methodology, which also benefits the whole group by raising the standard of output for all pupils.

(Mary E. Malyon, head-teacher, Iver Heath First School)

DRAMA IN EDUCATION

In many primary and secondary schools, drama teaching is a mainstay of the curriculum. It is a powerful medium for the learning and development of a range of problem-solving, interpersonal and communication skills. It has proved to be an excellent route to the development of imaginative writing in a range of classrooms. Experience or imaginative situations are reconstructed and reconstrued in dramatic work, followed by the realization of this experience in written form. The writing, following such a series of lessons, has proved to be much more imaginative, detailed and interesting than traditional methods of inducing writing.

This does not mean that every drama session should be followed by writing; this would be counterproductive. Similarly, attempts to write for later dramatic production can easily founder before coming to realization. Drama teachers have a wide range of teaching and learning strategies of trust building, team building, communication skills, role-plays and simulations, all in collaborative groups which strengthen and underpin educational development in a wide range of areas.

There is now a strong and developing literature of handbooks and guides to methodology and research. Examples are Fulleylove (1984) and Taylor (1991).

TECHNOLOGY EDUCATION

It is perhaps worth mentioning the strength of technology education in designing and making. The new approaches in this field use a range of problem-posing, problem-solving, decision-making and thinking skills. Much of the work is based on collaborative learning in product design and development, and excellent examples are to be found in Shipley and Webster (1988). These new developments in technology far remove it from the old ideas and attitudes of 'boys' craft'.

CONCLUSIONS

Throughout this chapter, the argument has been made that thinking and communication skills work should be integrated and incorporated into a *whole-school approach* and an *across-the-curriculum policy* if we are to serve the education of children well for the twenty-first century. The emphasis has been to take ordinary and traditional curriculum programmes as specified in the National Curriculum documents but elicit higher-order thinking and communication skills by changing the pedagogies used. In Britain, we are closer to being able to do this than in the more formal teaching environments observed in other countries.

In a sense, we are at a crucial point. Do we turn back to basic, traditional teaching methods, which have failed to change our creative populace into active innovators, or do we move forwards in the directions proposed? Moving forwards has its problems; we have case examples, grounded research and professional experience, none of which is valued sufficiently. Nevertheless, even if we had definitive proof that eight tons of this produced sixteen caravans of that, this has never been sufficient to change educational fashion or public opinion. Teachers must work hard in the current climate not to have their skills devalued and not to be deskilled.

Cognitive process specialist programmes

INTRODUCTION

Chapter 4 described the development of a theory and practice for making provision for able pupils in the ordinary classroom. Although in itself it represents a multidimensional approach to the problem, other researchers and practitioners have approached it in different ways. However, they all have the same focus upon process objectives and cognitive and metacognitive activities. These developments have arisen both in different countries and within the same country at roughly the same period. Clearly the time was ripe for such changes. The special programmes described are frequently pull-out programmes, although their originators would like their work to be mainstreamed. They are also more often more carefully prescribed and a progression is clearly laid down for teachers to follow.

In Canada and the United States of America, it has been common for sums of money of the order of billions of dollars to be put into special withdrawal programmes for part- and even full-time study. Similar sums have been gifted to centres for research and teaching especially geared to the needs of the able and talented. Most recently, however, there have been large cuts in the education budgets, and these have fallen heavily on the gifted education areas. The money has been switched to the 'gifted handicapped', and the learning disabilities fields and specialist teachers are having to learn about the needs of these different groups. Another strategy which is also being used is to develop the provision for the gifted in mainstream education and to promote mixed-ability teaching and differentiation within it. The first signs of these changes have been in the alterations to the study visit programmes of the teachers from across the Atlantic; they now wish to study examples of good practice in these areas in the UK. Integration of the gifted is now their theme.

In certain countries of Western and Eastern Europe, it is common for national olympiads or competitions to be held to identify children for special places on fast-tracking programmes, particularly in science, mathematics, music and chess. Details and reports of these can be found in the *European Journal of High Ability* and in Heller *et al.* (1993). This latter is an account of ways in which mainstream provision may be developed to meet the needs of the able, to which can be added flexible options for those with specific talents.

In this chapter, three examples of interesting and well-developed programmes from Canada and the USA are described in detail, followed by a review of some recent and some more longstanding programmes developed in Israel, the USA and the UK.

THE DISCOVERY CENTRE, HALTON, ONTARIO

> Children need time to question, to explore, to wonder and to ponder in order to develop their curiosity and imagination.
> (Edna McMillan, Consultant to the Gifted, 1990)

Organization

A Discovery Centre operates in each area of Halton. Small groups of highly able young students attend the programme for blocks of time, usually seven consecutive days. It serves as a resource for classroom teachers to acquire additional knowledge and skills in meeting the needs of highly able students; these skills are readily transferable to a regular classroom setting.

Once selected, full attendance at the programme is expected. Homework should not be given for what is missed in the regular classroom.

Description of candidate

The Discovery Centre Program provides for the student who:

- is an able primary learner from kindergarten to grade 4;
- is curious, questioning and motivated to discover;
- has been selected by the school resource team.

Description of the programme

Learning outcomes

The programme:

- allows for independent study;
- is based on the needs and interests of the individual students;
- presents a variety of activities within the cognitive and affective domain;
- focuses on broad-based issues, themes or problems;
- emphasizes structured learning processes rather than content;
- encourages development of new and exciting products;
- reflects a variety of materials and forms in the products created.

Knowledge

The programme will differ from the regular school programme in the following ways:

- The content is broad in scope.
- The content is organized around a major theme.
- The content allows for the integration of many disciplines.
- The content allows for a wide diversification of interests that the child may pursue individually or in small groups.
- The activities emphasize the learning processes in addition to content and product.

Skills

The programme includes the following:

- *Basic skills:* the reinforcement and extension of basic skills, and on to more abstract applications.
- *Research skills:* the planning for and research of information pertaining to their topic.
- *Thinking skills:* using the technique of brainstorming and evaluating according to the steps of established process.
- *Interactive skills:* encouraging leadership and co-operative skills.

Affective

The programme encourages:

- development of a recognition of a self-worth;
- understanding of the differences of self and others;

- development of responsibility for learning;
- valuing own ideas;
- communication and co-operation with others;
- development of the ability to make decisions;
- working to completion of tasks;
- the social graces.

SISK PLANNING AND TEACHING MODEL FOR FUTURES STUDIES

This second example is based on the leadership development programmes run by Sisk (1991), which are independently funded. The diagram of the Sisk model in Figure 5.1 is based upon the three-dimensional model of intellect by Guilford (1959), and shows the interaction between curriculum content and process methods and what students will be able to do as a result of the course.

Sisk (1988) defines in the following list what curriculum activities should provide for the able:

- add breadth and depth to present knowledge;
- utilize many instructional media, especially those which free students from limited content bounds;
- develop efficient reading and writing skills;
- raise conceptual levels on which they function and do conceptual thinking;
- utilize problem solving techniques;
- develop and use critical thinking skills;
- develop and utilize creative abilities;
- do independent work;
- explore, independently and under guidance, many fields of interest;
- deal with high-level abstractions;
- converse with students of like abilities;
- participate in planning their learning experiences – both active and passive roles;
- apply theory and principle to solving life problems;
- develop leadership abilities and ability to become followers and good listeners;
- develop a personal set of values;
- set and reach immediate and ultimate goals;
- develop self-discipline and a sense of social responsibility.

Sisk's interest in leadership programmes for the highly able developed because of her concern that so many able individuals achieved high office without necessarily ever developing the qualities which they needed to carry out their functions of leadership. Over the years, she has promoted and developed them to a high level of sophistication and, with research funding, has been able to demonstrate the efficacy of them (Sisk, 1988, 1993).

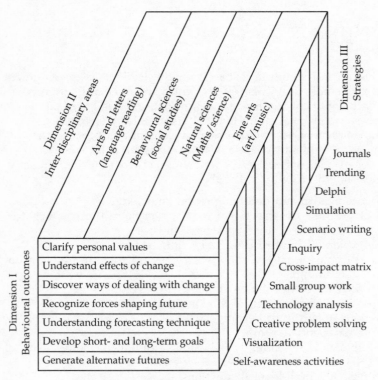

Figure 5.1 *The Sisk planning model for futures studies*
Source: Sisk, 1988

CoRT (COGNITIVE RESEARCH TRUST PROGRAMMES)

The CoRT Thinking Skills Programme was first developed in 1973 by Edward de Bono (1976, 1983), famous for his 'lateral thinking' approaches to problem solving and creativity.

His view was that much of Western culture was based upon the adversary system, where each side takes up a position and then sets out to prove the other side is wrong. The Cognitive Research

Trust materials were republished (de Bono, 1983) and are designed to take a constructive approach to problem solving. They were taken up by a number of schools to enhance their pupils' thinking, communication and decision-making skills.

There are now three packs, with a teachers' handbook and pupils materials set out as lessons, each of about 35 minutes' duration. The packs are:

- CoRT I: Breadth
- CoRT II: Organization
- CoRT III: Interaction

De Bono illustrates one of the problems of defining and undertaking research in this area as follows:

> With more able groups (grammar school, sixth form, etc.) at first sight there may be little difference in the essays from CoRT pupils and control group pupils. The essays all seem articulate, reasonable and well argued. It does require some experience in looking at thinking as distinct from its expression to note the difference and then it can be very obvious. For instance, the control group tend to take up a position and then use their thinking to defend that position, whereas the CoRT group tend to explore the situation *before* taking up a position. Finally there are aspects of thinking behaviour (like listening to others and being prepared to think about something) which cannot be examined by a simple point-count of ideas.
>
> (De Bono, 1983, p. 3)

The CoRT Thinking Skills lessons are designed to be taught as a specific and separate subject on the curriculum and are aimed primarily at the 11–12-age range and upwards. The programme was designed to improve practical thinking, and it provides a framework in which students can do this. Some of the lessons, especially in CoRT II, do apply to other subjects, but in the main could only be used in English and personal and social education in the current National Curriculum, where time would not permit the introduction of a 'new subject' for the year for which the programme is now designed, without considerable difficulties.

In order to help children remember the strategies, a series of acronyms was developed (which are more popular with students than teachers!), including:

- *PISCO:* purpose, input, solutions, choice, operation;
- *CAF:* consider all factors;
- *EBS:* examine both sides;
- *PMI:* plus, minus and interesting;
- *OPV:* other people's views.

Whilst during the 1980s the CoRT programmes had many particip-
ating schools and advocates, the long-term benefits were not
sufficiently obvious for the competition for curriculum time to be
won. With the institution of the National Curriculum, this would,
regrettably, currently be impossible. De Bono has published results
of his researches (1983) which show quite clearly the beneficial
effects on thinking of the programme, but the examination system
is set to test content and end products of thinking rather than to
value and validate the process of arriving at solutions.

Other countries with greater foresight have, however, adopted
the programmes, and so in Venezuela two hours per week on
CoRT is compulsory for all students. Thinking skills lessons based
on the programmes are already compulsory in Malaysia and
Pakistan, and teachers are trained in the programme in Singapore.

INSTRUMENTAL ENRICHMENT

This programme was originally designed by Reuven Feuerstein
(1980) to promote the educational development of disadvantaged
children whose families had been destroyed in the Holocaust.
More recently, it has been used with a range of disadvantaged
groups, such as refugees and other traumatized individuals. The
programme of learning is *mediated* by the teacher and provides a
curriculum and a methodology designed to promote and develop
thinking and decision-making processes. Foundations adopting its
principles and practices for a wide range of learners are being
established in a range of countries, and the Cognitive Mediation
Foundation held its first International Conference in late 1993 to
promote its aims and objectives. The BINOH ('Understanding')
Centre of the Jewish Educational Needs Service is the London link
to the international network.

Many of the children in the original programmes demonstrated
intellectual performance which was so low on psychological tests
that they were classified as having moderate or even severe learning difficulties. It was Feuerstein's (1980) belief that these pupils
were 'low achievers' because of cultural breakdown, rather than as
a result of genetic impairment. He described intelligence as
the ability to learn from experience and argued that, when there
was cultural breakdown as after the Holocaust, parents and grand-
parents were unable to pass on the basic thinking skills which
enabled the children to make sense of their world. He suggested
that this breakdown was common amongst immigrant groups
moving from underdeveloped to highly sophisticated technolo-

gical societies, and where such groups and cultures were fragmented by poverty and war, or social and geographical upheaval.
As can be seen, this could include vast areas and many peoples of
the world, for there have been more than two hundred and fifty
wars recorded since 1945, some approaching their second decade.
There have also been vast famines, earthquakes, and transloca-
tions of peoples from one country to another. One might also
include in this equation not only the social and cultural problems
of battle, famine and earthquake, but also the emotional shock of
abuse, which can bring with it severe emotional trauma which
may be a barrier to learning (Herbert, 1975).

In Israel, some 40,000 children were reported as receiving instrumental enrichment in state schools; in Canada, the prison system
has claimed success with its use; and Venezuela has incorporated
it into state education just as it did de Bono's (1976) CoRT thinking skills programme. In Britain, the system has had a mixed
reception, but trials at three Somerset comprehensive schools were
reported by Blagg (1987). He found good results and confirmed
the predictions of Feuerstein. He has since produced a programme
based on this research, entitled the Somerset Thinking Skills
Programme.

The instrumental enrichment programme is made up of over
five hundred pages of paper-and-pencil exercises, divided into
twenty 'instruments'. Each instrument purports to focus upon a
specific cognitive deficiency, but enables other prerequisites of
learning to be acquired as well. Fourteen of the instruments are
regularly used in any classroom implementation, and provide
material for a one-hour session on three to five days per week for
a period of two years. When using the materials in a diagnostic-
prescriptive remedial programme, the 'instruments' are selected to
match the pupil's need.

As Blagg (1987) noted in the Somerset study, there were draw-
backs. The method required a high degree of theoretical
understanding of how flaws may develop in children's thinking
and how these can be corrected. It also required 200–300 hours'
teaching for two years; but schools in this country are unable to
devote any time for seemingly abstract thinking skills work.

The techniques of Feuerstein at the basic perceptual and spatial
orientation levels very much resemble those of Frostig and Horn
(1964). They are also derivative of *Gestalt* psychology. The first
instrument is the organization of dots, which is said to require: the
projection of virtual relationships, discrimination of form and size;
constancy of form and size across relationships; size across changes
in orientation; use of relevant information; restraint of impulsivity;

precision planning; and systematic search and comparison to the model. The thickened dots aid in the projection of the square, but also serve as a distractor, preventing the perception of similarities between the dots in the frames of the last row of the page.

In the instrumental enrichment (IE) programme, it can be seen how tasks of graded difficulty which enable the learner to achieve success can be highly motivating and involving, and how, over time, such a programme could induce reflectivity and reduce impulsivity; but it is nevertheless mechanistic and highly time-consuming. It approaches more complex cognitive levels and achieves broader educational objectives only in the later stages, and it is mainly curriculum-content-free, although it itself has a sequentially ordered curriculum of skills.

If we could structure the learning of all children so that they achieved in an incremental and motivating fashion, in a content-filled or content-enriched curriculum according to their individual needs, and in a co-operative, supportive environment, perhaps even better results could be achieved than Feuerstein claims for his work. They might also prove useful within the curriculum for the purposes of differentiation.

Feuerstein explained that the organization of dots in the first instrument was presented in this form because the tasks in it were remote from classroom subjects and would not remind the pupils of previous failures. He recommended it also for pupils with perceptuo-motor impairment and suggested that the tutor drew the lines for them to their instruction. He described several classes set to decorate their classroom: one had been on the IE programme for three months, the others had not. The pupils were asked to work without help from their teachers. Those on the programme sketched plans, measured windows and walls, and calculated materials needed. They assigned tasks to members and made a schedule of the order in which things were to be done. The other classes proceeded impulsively without prior planning in their groups There were quarrels, acrimony and blame-casting.

What was not explained in this example is why the particular teacher was selected or selected him or herself for the programme. It is intellectually demanding and requires a very systematic and ordered approach from the teacher to get the best from it. The system and order seen in the class's approach to the problem might result as much from the teacher as from the programme. It is a common observation, for example, that a class of children working with one teacher are quite reasonable whilst with another they may be noisy, disruptive and quarrelsome. Another factor which may have influenced the Feuerstein class was that they were on a 'special' programme, which the others were not, and so they saw themselves as special, deriving more meaning and significance from the process than they ordinarily might.

The programme, even at the dots level, involves some acquisition of vocabulary, concepts and operations. The pupil labels not only the figures but also the operations and the strategies used to construct them, and these can transfer to other subject areas. As part of the strategy they tend to talk themselves into a problem: 'Now, what do we do when we are given a problem? First we have to find out what the problem is.' Nevertheless, the encouragement of verbalization in IE transferred to the wider context and provided structure, organization and system for tackling other tasks.

As can be seen, this is very valuable learning, but again it could be suggested that this is what good teachers do anyway and it is what all should do – teach pupils to organize their responses to problems and to 'learn how to learn'. Perhaps it is a good programme for those who do not know how to teach or for those who are unable to move beyond rote approaches to subject contents. It seems a very roundabout and time-consuming method of achieving cognitive and learning objectives when there are more direct ways available. It assumes transfer will take place from the abstract to the educational contexts, but this is not assured. Able children are likely to benefit most, for they will transfer their learning more easily. Slower children will find this much more difficult, for transfer of learning from one situation to another is what they have difficulty doing. Lower attainers and children with learning blocks could well profit from a structured and systematically rewarding approach to help them overcome their difficulties.

IE is probably one of the best examples we have at the moment of the psychological classroom – individuals work on their own learning programmes defined by their performance upon psychological tests, their behaviour directed towards goals defined by psychological theory. This proceeds in parallel with normal school curriculum, and positive transfer to it is expected. Such an approach, which is apparently so mechanistic, would find less support in Britain, where teachers like to construct their own programmes in pursuit of their learning objectives for the children. There are, however, over a hundred reported studies into the effects of IE in several countries and with a variety of different groups. A number of them show that performance on IQ tests is significantly improved by exposure to an IE programme. The teaching and learning experiences seem to have an even more profound effect upon the teachers, and so most thinking skills training programmes include an introduction to IE.

Interest in the UK in IE began with an exploratory Schools Council project by a consortium of five LEAs in the early 1980s. The results appeared to have positive effects on the pupils, particularly their confidence and behaviour. In 1983, Oxfordshire successfully bid to take part in Sir Keith Joseph's Lower Attaining Pupils Project (14–16), electing to join with Somerset to pilot IE amongst other activities. The project ran for three years. There was little evidence gained of transfer to academic abilities, although there was a rise in the self-esteem and confidence of the lower attainers, which the teachers valued highly. From these experiences, both groups developed their own methods and strategies, which were more contextually related and appropriate. These became the Oxfordshire Skills Programme and the Somerset Thinking Skills Course. In both, the Feuerstein's thinking remained central, although the Oxfordshire group have drawn upon the American experience and in particular on the work of Paul at the Sonoma State University. They have also extended their programmes and materials to primary schools and incorporated the strategies of Lipman (1991), described in the next section. The programme now aims to bring about effective thinking in the 5–18 curriculum. The Somerset Thinking Skills Course, developed with lower attainers, has become popular in adult work-linked training programmes and in dyslexia institutes and dyslexia schools. In some LEAs, it has been made a mandatory part of the training for those working with pupils with specific learning difficulties of a dyslexic nature.

Both have in fact by their very nature moved a significant step from Feuerstein's work and thinking. They teach contextually related thinking strategies and skills whereas he is concerned with 'structural cognitive modifiability'. By this he means that even the cognitive structures of the brain can be changed by enabling people to learn how to learn. Learning becomes cumulative and in turn affects performance over the life span. This is in direct contrast to much current thinking, which holds that we become less effective as learners as we grow older.

For Feuerstein, the key to learning to learn lies in the notion of the *mediated learning experience* (MLE). MLE is the way in which stimuli emitted by the environment are transferred by a mediating agent, usually a parent, sibling, care giver or teacher. The mediator, guided by intentions, culture and emotional investment, selects and organizes the world of stimuli for the child. Through this process of mediation, the cognitive structures of the child are affected. This is a more fundamental change than developing a new thinking skill, for the structural alteration can result in the transferability of learning from one situation to another. Without mediation, IE becomes just another thinking skills programme. Feuerstein (1993) used the example of a child who cannot read initially, but can after intervention, to illustrate a non-structural change – although this would undoubtably be a great step forward, it would not be a structural change because it is limited to reading. If, however, the mediator has helped the child to acquire the ability to compare, analyse whole to part and reconstitute the picture, and the child has been helped to use these skills in other contexts, then this would exemplify structural change. (Teachers of reading might well argue that this is indeed the nature of reading teaching in the UK.)

The mediator needs to match what the child brings to a situation with what is required, so that there can be a sharing of concepts of the local and personal culture and that of the classroom. The denial of cultural sharing, according to Feuerstein, is what causes learning difficulties. Mediation in this form must become a 'way of life' for the teacher/mediator, and all is dependent upon the quality of this rather than the instruments. This is why Feuerstein insists that IE should not become a freely available package but must be accompanied by intensive training and ongoing teacher support.

The construction of LPAD (Learning Potential Assessment Device) and IE are directly related to the notion of the cognitive map. This identifies the crucial elements in the completion of any mental act, and Feuerstein listed these seven key features:

- the content on which the act is centred;
- the modality or language in which it is expressed;
- the power of cognitive functions required by the mental act;
- the cognitive operations required by the mental act;
- the level of complexity (including novelty and familiarity);
- the level of abstraction;
- the level of efficiency with which the mental act is performed.

In his keynote address to the European Council for High Ability in 1990 in Budapest, Feuerstein was at great pains to stress that, although IE had been developed for disadvantaged groups, it was nevertheless a powerful method for developing the abilities and intellectual skills of able individuals too. He stressed the need for quality in the mediation experience if the learner's potential was to be realized. The model he presented was based upon an elaboration of the early stimulus–response (S–R) framework of the behaviourists, extended by the later cognitivists to (S–O–R) or stimulus–organism– response, the mediation model, as in Figure 5.2.

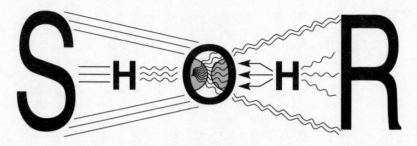

Figure 5.2 *The mediated learning experience (MLE) model*
Source: Feuerstein, 1990

In order for a change to become structural, there are three criteria which must be fulfilled: intentionality and reciprocity, investment of meaning, and transcendence. To meet these requirements, the mediator must be aware of, and make known and ensure that the learner has understood, what s/he is going to do (intentionality and reciprocity). The mediator should explain why s/he is going to do it (investment of meaning) and the act should be conveyed as having value beyond the here and now (transcendence).

The characteristics of structural cognitive change are as follows:

- a strong relationship between the part and the whole;
- a propensity to become involved in processes of change (transformism);
- the self-perpetuating, self-regulating nature of the process of change.

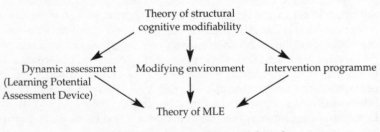

Figure 5.3 *The structure of Feuerstein's work*
Source: Feuerstein, 1993

Figure 5.3 shows the structure of Feuerstein's work.

The mediator's overall functions in a mediated learning inter-action are described as follows:

- *filtering* and *selecting* the stimuli/experiences;
- *organizing* and *framing* the stimulus/experience in time and space;
- *isolating* selected stimuli and ensuring their sufficient reappear-ance;
- *regulating* the intensity, frequency and order of appearance (sequence) of various stimuli;
- *relating* new stimuli/experiences to previous events and events that will/may occur in the future;
- *establishing relationships* (cause–effect, means–goal, identity, similarity, difference, exclusivity ...) between perceived stimuli;
- *regulating* and adapting the child's responses to the stimuli to which s/he is exposed;
- fostering *representation* and *anticipation* as to different possible effects of various responses to given stimuli;
- *interpreting* and *attributing meaning* and value (affective, social, cultural ...) to various stimuli/experiences;
- eliciting *motivation*, interest, curiosity in relating and responding to various stimuli.

(after Feuerstein, 1993)

Despite the seeming isolation of this approach, it is based upon the work of Piaget and the Geneva school, and in particular to the influence of Rey (1930), to whom Feuerstein acknowledges his indebtedness; although he was always concerned that there was insufficient emphasis by the school on the contribution of social factors to intellectual development. Rey's work on the assessment of learning potential was introduced in Chapter 2 (see p. 54).

Feuerstein's work also seems to link very well with what has already been discussed in relation to metacognition. The constant guidance and intervention of the mediator could act to develop the metacognitive skills in the learner which makes that learning transferable. This might well be a way of establishing 'learning conversations' such as those described by Thomas and Harri-Augstein (1985) and later used to improve teacher's performance (Montgomery, 1984, 1988). These were also described as metacog-nitive strategies.

The following shows extracts on guidance to teachers from the London MLE Conference (1993), presented by the BINOH Centre as examples of training papers. These raise questions for teachers to ask of themselves during their teaching, and illustrate how checklists may become internalized and be used to frame thinking and further actions and changes to teaching methods. They encourage the teacher to become a more reflective practitioner, and this is presumably what the transferable content is when used in the other thinking skills training programmes.

Sample behaviours in teacher–pupil interactions reflecting various aspects of MLE

Intentionality and reciprocity

- Was there a conscious prior selection by the teacher of the subject and content of the activity?
- In the event that these were imposed upon him [sic], was the teacher aware of the reasoning that preceded and determined the selected subject matter and content?
- In the course of his presentation of the activity in the classroom, does the teacher convey this reasoning to his students?

Transcendence

1 Does the teacher indicate the relationship between the current activity and those previously experienced by the student?
2 Does the teacher indicate how an element or elements of the current activity could be applied in other future circumstances?
3 Does the teacher extract essential elements of an activity and formulate them into a principle or generalization?
4 Does the teacher equip the students with criteria so that they can distinguish between the essential and non-essential elements of the activity?

Mediation of Meaning

1 When the teacher refers to a concept, an object, or an event in an activity, does s/he take care to add a meaning to them in addition to their inherent significance?
2 Does the teacher tend to make the students differentiate between the meanings of the same concepts, objects, or events in a variety of contexts?
3 Does the teacher refer to new situations or new contexts that require the development and attribution of new meanings to elements of the activity that transcend the familiar ones?

Mediation of a feeling of competence

- In the tasks selected by the teacher for the students, is there a balance between elements that are familiar and have been mastered and new elements which require further investment?

- Is the teacher in the habit of referring to all of the students' reactions, interpreting and evaluating their responses?

Mediation for regulation and control of behaviour

1 In this presentation of the task, does the teacher indicate its level of complexity and difficulty?
2 Does the teacher direct the students' attention to the relationship between the complexity of the task and their capacity to deal with it adequately?
3 Does the teacher tend to delay and orient the students' responses when s/he anticipates an impulsive and/or inadequate reaction?

To appreciate how all this is to be achieved it is necessary to see Feuerstein work with children as he did at the MLE London Conference (1995). He is gifted and the experience is inspirational.

PHILOSOPHY FOR CHILDREN

Matthew Lipman is a professor of philosophy at Columbia University who, during the student unrest of the late 1960s, became concerned at the low level of thinking skills that students brought to college. He decided that this had to be attacked early – as soon as they entered school. In his programme (1991), he lists over thirty separate thinking skills, and first in the list is 'formulating concepts precisely'. Improving thinking was to be the aim which permeated every way of learning. In addition to this, the children would be offered a course in the study of thinking itself. (This would increase their metacognitive awareness.) The course is based on discussion plans and judicious questioning. The classic question is rather like that of Professor Joad's 'What do you mean by ...?' The aim is for the children to become more thoughtful and reflective. This, Lipman states, is best learned through language, by creating a 'community of enquiry' in which children engage in dialogue as a co-operative venture.

Lipman decided that the best way to teach children was through stories. To this end he wrote a short novel for children, which he called *Harry Stotdemeier's Discovery* (the name is a play on 'Aristotle'). Because Harry does not listen in class, he misses out on part of an explanation about the solar system. Therefore when he is asked what has a tail and revolves round the sun every seventy years, he says it must be a planet and is laughed at by the rest of the class. This later leads him to reason that all planets revolve round the sun, but not everything which revolves round the sun can be a planet. In other words, the sentences are not reversible. He practises this on other objects – all oaks are trees but not all trees are oaks, and so on. He develops this line of thinking with his friend Lisa, and she responds by showing that it does not always work; for example, 'No eagles are lions' is also true when it is reversed. They pursue this line of thinking and discover a new rule: 'If a true sentence begins with "no" then the reverse is always true but if it begins with "all" then the reverse is false.' They then go off to apply their knowledge to some real situations with interesting consequences.

The programme's success, according to Lipman, depends upon having a thoughtful and animated discussion, often on subjects and in ways which were traditionally not thought possible for young children. The teacher needs to be skilled in generating the discussion by prompting in the Socratic manner, with openended questions. The discussions, Lipman reports, frequently revolve round the questions of interest to young people of any age: 'But is it fair?', 'Is it true?', 'Is it real?', 'Who are friends?' and 'Why are things so?'

The points that Lipman makes are as follows:

- Productive thinking does not just happen. It has to be planned and orchestrated by the teacher. Children find it difficult to listen to each other. This is part of the discipline of the approach and is good for discipline in general.
- Children often find it difficult to understand at first that right and wrong will not be given and in fact may not exist.
- In the Socratic discussion, the teacher becomes the facilitator of the investigation, encouraging listening, justifying, clarifying, summarizing and moving the discussion onwards.
- To encourage critical thinking, teachers develop rules with the children such as these:

  - Listen carefully and follow the story or argument line.
  - Ask if something is not clear.
  - Think of one or two relevant things to say.
  - Make suggestions to carry the argument further.
  - Say things in a positive way so that others do not get upset.
  - Take turns.
  - Share ideas.

It may not at first be apparent from the title, but the origins of this programme and its concerns are the same as those in the collaborative learning project, Ways and Means, already described (Bowers and Wells, 1985). Their methods of discussion, valuing and procedural rules are almost exactly the same. Their overall goal is to help children develop self-management skills through discussion.

Lipman has developed a comprehensive programme of material, published by the Institute for the Advancement of Philosophy for Children (IAPC) at Montclair College. Each session is in the form of an enquiry into issues raised from reading a particular story. A list of his material is give in Table 5.1.

Table 5.1 *Philosophy for Children Programme (IAPC)*

Age (years)	Children's novel	Instructional manual	Philosophical area	Educational area
5/7	*Elfie*	Getting our thoughts together	Reasoning and thinking	Exploring experience
7/8	*Kio and Gus*	Wondering at the world	Philosophy of nature	Environmental education
8/9	*Pixie*	Looking for meaning	Philosophy of language	Language and arts
10/11	*Harry*	Philosophical inquiry	Epistemology and logic	Thinking skills
12/13	*Lisa*	Ethical inquiry	Philosophy of value	Moral education
14/15	*Suki*	Writing: how and why	Philosophy of art	Writing and literature
16+	*Mark*	Social inquiry	Social philosophy	Social studies

Each session begins by reading or re-reading part of the story, usually from half a page to three pages long. This allows for choice of topic. The group take it in turns to read aloud, and those who do not wish to do so say 'Pass.' The teacher may also read sections, and asks, 'What did you find interesting or puzzling?' Each response is written on the board with the name of the child who made it. Others may help to express these ideas. Then they choose one of the topics to discuss.

Of course, it is not necessary to use this philosophy programme. Many children's texts contain useful discussion material and many teachers, particularly in English, social studies and personal and social education programmes, use them for discussion purposes. They are not, however, used to calling it 'philosophy' or teaching about thinking skills in the process. Where these different methods could be united, the benefit for the children would be even greater. Perhaps it would be helpful to suggest that in a mainstream and mixed-ability setting, where there are a number of difficult children, the problem-solving and collaborative learning materials of the Kingston Workshop Group would be a first recourse. Their 'Circle Time', discussed in Chapter 4, has become widely used to discuss issues of fairness, friendship, discipline and bullying in schools throughout the country. Later, the Lipman programme could be introduced.

PHILOSOPHY AT MANCHESTER GRAMMAR SCHOOL

Manchester Grammar School has apparently the largest school philosophy department in the country. Two hundred boys study the subject compulsorily in the lower sixth, and over half continue it in the upper sixth. In a questionnaire designed by the pupils, 86 per cent said that they found it to be 'a welcome diversion from the grind of other A-level subjects'. They also thought it allowed science students in particular to stay in touch with debating, analysing and argument. It enabled them to understand better the reasons behind laws and how society operated.

Palmer (1989) concluded that it had certainly proved more popular than the religious studies course it had replaced. He suggested two possible methods for learning philosophy:

- learning it by doing it;
- learning it by seeing it done.

He gave the example of teaching the concept of 'justice'. In the first method, puzzles for the pupils would be set so that they could begin from the outset to think philosophically. In the second, a debate would be introduced, say between Socrates and Crito, on 'civil disobedience', and then the pupils would have to decide between the two arguments. He reported that both methods were successful, but that he preferred the second because something of cultural importance is learnt and it is less taxing on the teacher to prepare. It also gives the pupils ground rules before they begin the debate. In 1995, civil disobedience, following on the legislation to outlaw large spontaneous protest demonstrations, would be highly topical. The transport of live animals to other European countries, the movement to ban blood 'sports' such as fox hunting, hare coursing and deer chasing, and the fight against vivisection in the cosmetics industry are all current.

According to Palmer, his pupils, a highly able group of 16–18-year-olds, are certainly capable of conceptual thinking, but it becomes significantly easier when related to situations they actually know. However, in the book he is writing he tries to show how pupils throughout the range of ability can benefit from philosophy. He first developed his ideas when he was Humboldt Fellow in Philosophy at Marburg University in 1978.

HEURISTICS

Heuristics and problem solving are an important area in cognitive psychology (Anderson, 1980). Heuristics has developed in importance and significance in a range of studies in association with the development of logic boxes and computer programming. In a heuristic, it is possible to specify all the moves to the solution of a problem, and it is thus not quite a model of problem solving in the real world, with the interplay of the sequential, analogous and inductive processing which goes on in the human brain.

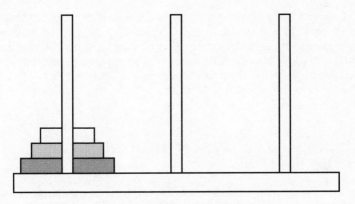

Figure 5.4 *The Hanoi Tower problem*

A famous example of a heuristics problem is called the 'Hanoi Tower' (Figure 5.4), which can be made simpler or more complex by adding on or taking away single disks. The problem is that the three coloured disks on the left-hand spindle have to be moved one at a time so that they are restacked on the right-hand spindle in exactly the same order. At no stage may a larger disk be placed upon a smaller disk, though smaller ones may of course be placed upon larger ones. This has to be completed in the smallest possible number of moves. To make the task simpler, only two disks can be used, to make it harder, four or more disks can be stacked. Try to do all the moves in your head.

It is possible to use such problems to assess the Zone of Proximal Development (ZPD). In a study of ZPD in able children and controls, Kanevsky, (1992) came up with some most interesting but not surprising findings. He found that some pupils of average ability consistently outperformed their highly able peers on heuristic problem solving. They were presented with a series of analogous problem-solving tasks, based on the Hanoi Tower model and adapted for children, and could not at first do them without adult help. Each task could be solved with the flexible use of the same strategy, but each was progressively more difficult. The learner was given multiple trials on each task, and as much assistance as necessary until mastery was achieved. The poor performance of the able group appeared to be because the tasks did not seem to provide sufficient challenge and motivation for them, given their IQs of over 154. Presumably, once they had trained on simpler examples and knew what to do to achieve the solution, they stopped being interested in pursuing the goal any further.

One can have some sympathy with this. It is probably unlikely that this group would find satisfying careers in computer programming. In fact, one of the problems of gifted individuals is often this low boredom threshold. A group of students in higher education referred to their studies as a 'psychic prison', and said that they were never free from the boring, mundane work which they had to do.

COGNITIVE ACCELERATION THROUGH SCIENCE EDUCATION PROJECT

Adey (1991), with his colleague Shayer, has been working since the 1980s on a problem which they had identified during the 1970s. They use high-ability children in their work in order to set a standard which would raise the ability of all children. They had found that only about 30 per cent of 16-year-olds were capable of demonstrating formal operational thinking (Shayer and Adey, 1981).

They based their operational definitions on descriptions of Piaget's levels of information-processing capability at the various stages of cognitive development. In formal operations, a person is able to handle a number of variables at once, to use hypotheses as a basis for planning, and to classify and organize material flexibly in different ways for different purposes. Individuals are able to make use of any learning experience – they are capable of learning to learn from their own experiences.

The Cognitive Acceleration through Science Education (CASE) project's aim was to make more children able. In their review of the literature, Adey and Shayer had found that particular features were necessary and had to be built into an intervention programme to maximize the chances of bringing about long-term effects on the subjects' general ability. These features included:

- The preparation of students to a state of perceptual readiness through concrete experiences which provided the necessary vocabulary and familiarised them with the terms of reference of the problem.
- A focus on the schemata of formal thinking – control and exclusion of variables, ratio and proportionality, probabilistic thinking, correlation, combinations, compensation, classification, equilibrium, and the use of formal models.
- The presentation of problems which induce cognitive conflict.
- The transfer of thinking strategies developed within the context of the special lesson to other areas of science, to other parts of the curriculum and to everyday life.

(Adey, 1991, p. 29)

Adey also emphasized the importance of metacognition in learning, quoting the work of Sternberg (1985).

The CASE subjects were aged 11+ to 12+, in nine classes in eight ordinary secondary comprehensive schools. A set of thirty activities was designed to develop metacognitive abilities, and this was introduced to teachers through a series of one-day workshops, followed up by school visits and discussions with the teachers. The CASE lessons occupied one science period every two weeks, in place of the normal lesson, over a period of two years.

The particular features of the programme were to ask pupils to reflect on the difficulties and successes they had had with problems, to discuss with each other how they had solved or failed to solve them, and to accrue understanding of the vocabulary of reasoning, so that they could more easily transfer reasoning patterns from one context to another. In a classification activity, for example, they were asked to reflect on their thinking processes after they had sorted animals into groups according to their own criteria, arranged a variety of foodstuffs on the shelves of a larder, sorted chemicals two ways by colour and solubility, and so on.

They were asked what was the easiest, what was the most difficult, and why, as well as their feelings about the tasks. They compared these with those of other groups. A classroom atmosphere was encouraged which facilitated pupil talk about how they had solved the problems, and they became familiar with the appropriate terminology of problem solving. The researchers described this as a specialist application of what Vygotsky (1978) discussed as the use of language as a mediator of learning.

As a result of the programme, they did not find any immediate gains in the experimental groups over matched controls in post-tests of cognitive development or delayed post-tests of scientific achievement, but they did find significant gains over controls two years later in GCSE science, mathematics and English. From this they argued that there had been a far more general beneficial effect of the programme.

CONCLUSIONS

The emphasis in the selection of programmes has been upon those that have sought to develop cognitive and metacognitive processes. All the developers have claimed some success for their particular methods, and a number have produced data from controlled studies to back their claims. The time has therefore come for this work to be taken seriously by all educational establishments in countries throughout the world, not just the enlightened few.

The researchers also claim that their methods will benefit not just an able élite but all children, and will raise their levels of performance in a wide range of school and real-world activities. They would all welcome their programmes being adopted by the mainstream. Some are more clearly adaptable than others to this.

The objective of training in metacognition is to make one a skilful user of knowledge. Nickerson *et al.* (1985) concluded that if training in metacognitive skills is done effectively it should have considerable pay-off: 'in particular inasmuch as these skills are very general, a successful effort to improve them should beneficially affect performance on a wide range of tasks.' (p. 104). It is clear that training in metacognitive activities can have beneficial results, but the work is as yet in its infancy. It is not easy to become an expert problem solver because of the semantic knowledge load involved (Larkin *et al.*, 1980).

6

Teaching the able in higher education: teaching the teachers

INTRODUCTION

In the last half decade of the twentieth century the whole of higher education (HE) in Britain is faced with the challenge of large increases in the number of students but with the number of teaching staff held at former levels or in decline. One of the results of extreme pressures on staffing such as these can be retreat to traditional methods or didactics, such as large-scale lectures, the doubling in size of seminar groups, and a decline in individual tutorials. Pressures also arise in the assessment areas, decreasing more interpretive activity and increasing the numbers of formal summative examination assessment papers, increasing machine-marked factual recall and recognition test items and decreasing double marking, formative assignments, comments, and interpretive and real problem-solving activities.

One of the most valued aspects of higher education, and a prime indicator of quality, is the 'production of knowledge' through research and development of its professional élite. Surveys by Shore *et al.* (1991), examining the relationship between professors' research methods and teaching methods, showed that few undergraduates engaged in knowledge production as part of their studies. In the UK, the final-year dissertation presentation has some elements of knowledge production built into it, but the thesis is based upon independent studies. It would be rare to find a coherent programme for knowledge development overlaying the content programme which students have to memorize and recall at examination times.

A turning point in the development of our teacher training programmes came when it became clear that few students could learn to develop real problem-solving and collaborative learning methods and materials with their classes if they did not learn in the same way in their HE progamme. For most of their years of schooling they had only been exposed to traditional methods, and they found it difficult to adapt their plans to problem- and learner-orientated studies. Lectures and seminars explaining the techniques, videos and visits to see good examples, and design activities and even structured and guided teaching practice did little to pass on the new methodology. Even the child-centred methodologies proved difficult to transmit, except to the most insightful and able, by the HE teaching methods then in use. They mostly led to highly variable implementations, ranging from good child-centred education to child-minding.

Students themselves criticized courses for preaching what to do but not following the advice in relation to student needs for active learning. Tutors, whilst recognizing these needs, allowed their overriding concern 'to cover the syllabus' – an old refrain – to justify their adherence to expository methods. However, a programme teaching about special needs and learning difficulties could not but respond to the students' needs. The sudden cuts made in Teacher Education in 1976 put target entries down by 50 per cent in some institutions. The resulting contraction provided both the opportunity and the stimulation for a major rethink and redesign to implement *theory and practice* in education. This provided a training experience for the slower cycle of change produced by funding cuts in the late 1980s and early 1990s.

It has to be stated, however, that students' needs are not always the same as *wants*. This was borne out continuously in the process of meeting 'inservice needs'. Teachers expressed to their LEA advisers their wants. These were self-identified, and they expressed needs (wants) to know more about science, art and design technology, for example; but after working with them, we identified the need for them to know more about *method* as well as content areas. They *needed* to know about more fundamental issues such as teaching handwriting and spelling, when the *want* was to learn more about reading teaching and so on. Balancing and meeting wants and needs is part of the design and implementation of successful inservice postgraduate training programmes, or any programme. The most articulate expression of success indicators in inservice education is the opportunity for the students to 'vote with their feet'. 'Good' programmes came to be only those which after the first session demonstrated the same or increased numbers of participants.

Perhaps the most powerful criterion of teacher effectiveness is 'student growth', a difficult set of variables to measure or evaluate but probably worth the attempt. Interestingly, Burkhardt (1969) found that out of 1,000 studies of teacher effectiveness only twenty used student learning as a criterion. Judgements by superiors, researchers and principals were used to define 'good' teaching, and teacher behaviours were analysed in the classroom in order to find the 'good' teacher.

Pupils, teachers and observers often have different conceptions of teacher role and good teaching, valuing didactics, for example, even when the results in terms of learning outcomes were lower than with other, more open methods.

Bannister et al. (1961) and Rayder (1968) found that, when carefully and properly handled, student evaluations provided the best criterion of the quality of instruction and were not substantially related to age, sex or achievement grades. They gave the opportunity to view the tutor in day-to-day teaching activities at both micro and macro levels. A synthesis of a range of research studies of student evaluations by Trent and Cohen (1973) elicited five major attributes of good teachers, which students in our studies during the 1980s and 1990s confirmed:

• clarity of organization, interpretation and explanation;
• encouragement of class discussion and the presentation of diverse points of view;
• stimulation of students' interests, motivation and thinking;
• manifestation of attentiveness to and interest in students;
• manifestation of enthusiasm.

The students' preferred 'types' of tutor, in rank order, were teacher, researcher, socialite and administrator. The 'researcher' type increased in popularity through higher education (Yamamoto and Dizney, 1966). The ghost of teaching versus research re-emerged during this period, as it has again in the 1990s. The findings then showed clearly that research productivity was not responsible for poor teaching. Xenos-Whiston (1989) studied teachers of the gifted as a group over an eight-year period. They found that teachers were engaged in publishing, artistic productions, programme development and materials design, and they expected similar efforts from their students. Bruner (1960) had first identified and recommended knowledge production as an element of curriculum. He insisted that students should be taught not conclusions to a field but the processes by which an expert learns.

These concepts and principles were incorporated into our courses. Students would be expected to design materials and programmes, including their own learning and study programmes, and to design and make, produce, perform and publish not only for their pupils but for themselves at their own level within and outside the course framework:

Bright children (and adult students) need, especially need to be introduced to learning from the point of view of an enquirer, an explorer, a question asker. Bright learners should experience the kind of thinking that leads to new discovery, at every opportunity. There is also little doubt that all children (students) can benefit from such a diet.

(Shore and Kanevsky, 1993, p. 142).

To achieve this, we have to produce the sort of teachers who can facilitate learning and critical thinking. We have 'to ensure that they are independent learners, have experienced and experience making a contribution to knowledge in any valued field of human endeavour be it artistic or cultural, social, academic or professional' (Shore and Kanevsky, 1993, p. 142).

Higher education ostensibly 'values' the ability to think efficiently, to use this knowledge to gain more information to solve real problems, and to communicate these ideas – often until students raise fundamental questions about their course. The ability to think flexibly and creatively had been shown in various surveys to be what employers needed and valued. This ability can be found in a range of highly successful individuals both in and outside higher education, but they may never be directly assessed and only indirectly 'taught'. Most often these attributes are acquired incidentally in the learning process. Strangely, they have been observed in programmes where no attempt is made to teach the students at all and the students, becoming concerned, have though it wise to do something about it themselves. Poor lecturers, absentee professors and self-help educational groups often illustrate the fact that the results obtained are no worse whatever is done to the students. If, however, we regard not much of anything we do in HE, whether we work hard at it or not, as enough of the 'right sorts of education' then these results, although hard to take, are not so surprising. The 'basics' seem to be an appropriate environment or context in which to learn.

These conclusions have not been arrived at easily, and are confirmed when academic results after three years in higher education demonstrate the pattern of the normal distribution curve – that which might have been achieved by different individuals by a process deriving marks whose sum results from a random distribution of errors. If we were to teach in order for students to learn, then the distribution should be heavily skewed or bulged at the top end. We should take them on to the programmes and bring many more to a higher order of operation. The effectiveness or otherwise of the programmes would be assessed by student evaluation of them and the processes, and by the gains or otherwise in learning outcomes. If the programmes were 'good', the student results ought to show a 'negative skew' with more grades in first class and upper twos in the traditional examinations.

As a result of putting the cognitive process methodology into practice in the initial teacher education courses, a gradual transformation of the learning outcomes was seen. There was improved curriculum provision by the students in the classroom, an enhanced ability to identify a wide range of able pupils, an increased sensitivity to their needs, a greater flexibility and willingness to make provision for them, and improved quality in the formative and summative assignments of the students themselves. In the final degree results, the programme contributed greatly increased numbers of grades in the first-class and upper second-class honours. For example, from an average of 2 or 3 per cent, first-class grades went up to 17 per cent, showing that improving students' metacognitive and cognitive skills was having a beneficial effect on their studies as well as their pupils. On teaching practice, increasing numbers were being offered jobs, often well before the end of their courses. The students also reported using their new-found skills in other content areas. Their increased interest and motivation led to questioning and argument, which were not, however, always appreciated by their other tutors. Details of these methods and results have been described elsewhere (Montgomery, 1993, 1994). In the rest of this chapter, a new development in teaching and learning using cognitive process methodology will be described. This is the conversion of critical thinking theory and cognitive process pedagogies into inservice distance learning materials. This was done so that a wider group could have access to them than just those who were local to Middlesex University in London. It proved to be an interesting challenge, for the learners this time were mainly individuals working on their own at home. How could these learners be caused to engage in critical thinking without the teacher's direct input and judicious questioning? How could they be caused to develop communication and team-building skills?

They key to the answers was, of course, through the assessment activities. The programme would be assessment-led but with the fewest possible essays, those backstops of the formal degree programmes. The assignments would be process-orientated and geared to developing cognitive and metacognitive skills and abilities. The ways in which these goals were achieved are explained in the following pages.

PRINCIPLES AND PRACTICES IN GUIDING THE SELECTION OF APPROPRIATE LEARNING AND ASSESSMENT PROGRAMMES

The students on our programmes were learning to teach. The curriculum was not to be subject-centred or child-centred but *learning-orientated* and *learner-centred*.

The critical concept of motivation had to be addressed directly. Where pupils and students did not have it, then it had to be engendered, and not extrinsically, in a means–end, mechanistic way. Somehow we had to promote and foster intrinsic motivation. The goal to be achieved was that the learners – the teacher education student and the pupils – had to come to a position where what they did became intrinsically interesting to them although it had not originally been so. The means by which this could be achieved had come to be described as cognitive process strategies (Montgomery, 1984) and was bound up with views of good teaching which we had to make explicit in many ways.

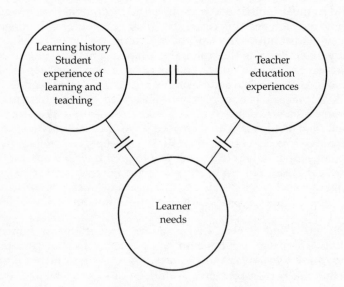

Figure 6.1 *A Cycle of Disconnections*
Source: Montgomery, 1993, p. 61

The methods had to be appropriate for mixed-ability teaching in ordinary schools and for teaching in higher education, bearing in mind different learning needs and with sensitivity to different learning preferences, styles and abilities. Particularly anxious students, for example, needed the security of structure and order in learning, with the opportunity to discuss problems with peers and to have a mentor readily available to offer structured support, leading them towards independence and self-regulation. Part of this was done through counselling and building the self-concept rather than reteaching and subject guidance. During these mentoring and counselling sessions, we found that often the learning experiences of the student were in a cycle of disconnections from the earliest years in school into higher education (see Fig. 6.1).

As early as 1975, Thomas and Harri-Augstein had found that more than 50 per cent of students in a range of degree programmes did not have the necessary higher-order reading skills to deal with the demands of the subjects and the texts which they were reading for their degrees. Students arrived from a wide range of schools without these skills (Meek and Thomson, 1987), and later study skills programmes and the pursuit of their subject studies for their degrees did not necessarily inculcate them.

According to Flavell (1979), metacognition is a highly important contribution to higher-order learning: 'Metacognition is the process by which we think about our cognitive machinery and processing mechanisms' (Flavell, 1979). These metacognitive activities contribute to the development of the self-regulatory and self-management skills as well as to the sense of personal agency. The failure to develop higher-order cognitive skills in schools and now in colleges was, according to Resnick (1989), not surprising. It has, he postulated, never been a goal of mass education to do more than develop basic schools and core subject knowledge. He defined higher-order cognitive skills as follows:

- non-algorithmic;
- complex;
- involving multiple solutions;
- needing nuanced judgement;
- involving multiple criteria;
- involving uncertainty;
- needing self-regulation;
- imposing meaning;
- effortful.

LINKING ASSESSMENT AND COGNITIVE PROCESS STRATEGIES

The cuts in teacher education faced us with a set of problems or dilemmas. On the one hand, we had an increased number of students per member of staff. The students typically had insufficiently developed cognitive skills and skills for independent learning, all of which they needed if 'education' in the mass was to be undertaken. Small group work and more open systems of assessment, which we had found developed higher-order cognitive skills, were in retreat.

Table 6.1 *Extent of undergraduate learning through different methods and materials*

Method/material	%
Lecture	5
Books	10
Audiovisual (AV) presentation	20
Dramatic lecture with AV presentation	30
Discussing	50
Explaining	75
Teaching	90
Assessing	95

Source: Race, 1992

The research reported by Race (1992) now supports what we knew we needed to introduce to student learning programmes if we were to achieve higher-order learning. For example, Table 6.1 shows an estimate of the extent of undergraduate learning through different methods and materials. We found a programme of 'dramatic' lecture followed by discussing and explaining had enabled students to move from surface to deep learning (Gibbs, 1990). When we set up situations where they taught us and assessed various models of work and learning outcomes, we found new material was fully accommodated or achieved deep levels. These processes of explaining, teaching and assessing involved the students in higher-order cognitive processing activities of planning and self-regulation.

It was at first difficult but not an insuperable problem to achieve similar results with large groups and lower tutor input. This tutor input still relied to some extent upon 'judicious questioning', which HMI (1992) had found crucial to the needs of able and highly able students in schools. The model which had been developed was the *cognitive process learning spiral* (see Figure 4.3). This was used as a model for teacher education in schools and on degree programmes. Material to be learned was presented through a variety of what were called cognitive process strategies or pedagogies, as detailed in Chapter 4 for students in schools. The same pedagogies were used with students in HE to deliver their training programmes on the theory and practice of teaching and in special educational needs and learning difficulties:

- investigative learning and real problem solving;
- cognitive study skills;
- games and simulations;
- experiential learning;
- collaborative learning;
- language experience methods.

These strategies had been found through grounded research to be effective in moving HE students from surface to deep learning.

In the first cycle, the students most frequently discussed subject, content, skills and applications, and explained them in ways which fostered understanding, by which they ordered and tried to make structured patterns and sense of the incoming information. The second cycle of talk was reflective thought and talk, induced to enable them to examine the process by which they planned and executed the learning and then evaluated the outcomes, thus tapping into their metacognitive processes. This was often 'mediated' by the judicious questioning from the tutor. It was this which needed to be supplemented in our new system for large group and distance teaching, and it seemed that the assessment process held the key.

Many students then as now (Terrell, 1993), despite what tutors would believe, will only do what is the basic minimum and 'go through the motions' in modules which they regard as peripheral to their main programme of studies – their majors. Many students adopt this attitude to all their studies. Thus it is the assessment tool that is a prime extrinsic motivator and, regrettably, often the only one students experience. We wanted commitment and *intrinsic motivation* set up by the learning strategies used and supported – preferably reinforced – by the assessment system.

What had been learnt from the other programmes was that students do not learn at all unless they are motivated to do so, and the vast majority seemed to have little intrinsic desire to pursue study for the lengthy periods needed to achieve mastery of concepts and skills. Teaching practice suddenly drew from that majority amazing volumes of work into the early hours. Examinations drove most to engage in several weeks' revision, and attempts at mastery and course assignments drew extra effort from many. Once they had invested the time and effort, many would say after finals 'Now I know what I don't know I really wish I was just starting on the course again, I would really get the best out of it and work properly.'

The MA Special Educational Needs – MA (SEN) – and MA Specific Learning Difficulties, both offered only by distance learning at Middlesex, have been designed to bring about the sorts of change described. They also form the basis of a research project which investigates ways of improving pupils' learning through pedagogical and assessment strategies which seek to enhance learning in their teachers. Thus far the results have proved particularly promising (Montgomery, 1994a, 1995). The programmes have been kept on track by the learners themselves, from the early days of the full-time courses through to the present. This was done by holding regular feedback sessions on tasks, questionnaire returns, formal course committee meetings with students representatives and staff, nominal group techniques as part of annual formal feedback, and weekly staff team meetings. The distance programmes use similar evaluation techniques adapted to the distance mode.

In designing the new programmes, it was decided that at first they must be assessment-led in order to draw the maximum amount of effort from the students. However, traditional essay-type assessments could only play a small part in the process if the students were not to lapse into a bored state. The assignments had to be designed to achieve the cognitive and professional objectives whilst evoking the maximum cognitive input from the students.

In the model used, evaluation was to be a part of teaching and learning, and:

- improve quality continuously as an everyday activity;
- help individual students learn better;
- focus on process as well as product;
- be collaborative;
- engage brain rather than rely on memory recall;
- operate in the main at the three higher levels of Bloom's taxonomy – analysis, synthesis and evaluation against external or internal criteria.

THE NATURE OF ONE OF THE PROGRAMMES: MA (SEN)

A programme was devised which had the central theme of improving the learning opportunities of all pupils in mainstream school through the education and training of their teachers. All teachers were regarded as teachers of pupils with special needs, and every teacher was expected to be dealing with at least 50 per cent of the pupils in every classroom who had learning difficulties, (SED, 1978; Montgomery, 1990), as well as many exhibiting behavioural difficulties, and the much smaller numbers with sensory and physical difficulties. Special needs co-ordinators and classroom and subject teachers alike were welcomed onto the programme. They were permitted to import credit for prior learning and experience into the programme through an accreditation process, and to negotiate assignments within the programme which best matched their needs and work situations. Although there was a set route through the programme, it was possible for students to negotiate different pathways and take extra modules. A special route for teachers of able children was also available.

The programme was 180 credits long, 120 pursued in the taught distance mode and 60 by research preparation and dissertation. The taught modules, each of 90 hours' learning time, were as follows:

- M1 Introduction to SEN: learning difficulties: case study method
- M2 Study skills; language difficulties
- M3 Teaching and learning strategies
- M4 The needs of able and underfunctioning learners
- M5 Reading and spelling difficulties
- M6 Curriculum assessment (handwriting and number difficulties) and testing
- M7 Managing behavioural difficulties
- M8 Managing emotional difficulties
- M9 Sensory and physical difficulties
- M10 Appraisal and staff development
- M11 Management and institutional development in SEN
- M12 International study (independent study).

At any point deemed appropriate in consultation with the tutor, the student could substitute any of the above modules for an independent study module as long as the proposed study made a cognate course and contributed to the whole. After 120 credits, students could obtain an advanced diploma in SEN or proceed to the research module and dissertation. (The majority of credits are at level 4, and level-3 modules can be converted to level 4.)

Assessment strategies: general and specific capabilities

Traditional forms of assessment tend to require the reproduction of factual material in short answer papers, which can often be computer marked, or require the student to select an essay to write from a list of subjects. The larger the class sizes in higher education the more tutors seem pressurized to return to these assessment modes, and the more they have had to give up the more time-consuming continuous assessment modes and more flexible real problem-solving forms. Thus the assessment designs of the distance programmes needed to preserve the best features of the formative and summative methods without increasing unduly the length of time spent by the markers, who might have twice as many students as before. An illustration of how this was achieved follows:

Module 1: *introduction to SEN*

The first set of tasks was as follows:

- students were asked to draw a concept map of their thinking about SEN. Examples and explanation of concept maps were given.
- Several readings and book references were presented.
- At least two days after doing the readings, the students were asked to draw another concept map to show the current thinking.
- Then ten differences between the pre- and post-readings maps were asked for, together with reflections upon these.
- The next task was to look at the two maps and evaluate them against the SOLO taxonomy (Structure of Observed Learning Outcomes: Biggs, 1992).

Having done the readings and focused upon the main types of SEN, the next set of tasks was to write four 500-word summaries to explain to a group of colleagues the nature of the following special needs and what can be done to help the pupil:

- general learning difficulties;
- specific learning difficulties;
- emotional and behavioural difficulties;
- sensory and physical difficulties.

In the third set of tasks, readings were presented on general learning difficulties, observational techniques and case-study methods. The teachers were asked to identify a pupil who might appear to have general learning difficulties, and then to make case notes based upon observation of the pupil on the curriculum task, under the following headings:

- Memory;
- Language;
- Thinking.

The rationale behind all this is that we often do not know what we think until we try to explain it to someone else. Drawing the concept maps enables the students to bring to the forefront of their minds the previous knowledge and experience, inspect it, and try to establish connecting links. Having heightened awareness in this way, there is a better chance that the information in the new readings will be integrated into the past structures. There is also the chance that further questions will be raised about the old structures, and changes implemented. Requiring a list of ten differences and reflections upon them causes the students to reflect once again upon what has been learned, and once again interrogate the sources. This completes the cognitive learning spiral (Montgomery, 1994b), and causes the students to think about their thinking, which is frequently not what the learner does willingly. The SOLO taxonomy enables students to examine the quality of that thinking, using an external frame of reference and externally defined criteria. The tutor can examine all these responses and determine the levels and status of the learning, how much resistance to new ideas is evidenced, and the learning ability.

The 500-word summaries enable the tutor to find out exactly what the students' basic understanding is in the four main areas of special need at the outset of the programme. It enables wrong assumptions to be challenged and areas of complete lack of knowledge to be identified and pointed out, with suggestions for further study and readings. A dialogue is established between tutor and learner. At this stage and throughout the programme, the comments written on the students' responses identify the strengths before suggesting further aspects for study – the CBG ('Catch them being good') and CBC ('Catch them being clever') principles which had already been found to be so powerful in promoting learning and motivation in both teachers and learners in the appraisal researches (Montgomery, 1984, 1988; Montgomery and Hadfield, 1989, 1990).

The second and third units present material on the nature of children with general learning difficulties, and on observational techniques. Students are then required to make the new knowledge operational by undertaking first observation exercises and evaluating them, and then a case study in the classroom. This could be at any school or college phase. From well-carried-out observational study, it is possible for the report writer and reader to evaluate the pupil's needs and begin to formulate an intervention policy. Teachers are seldom if ever required to observe in this close fashion, and they learn a surprising amount about the pupil and learning strategies as well as how learning is avoided and difficulties masked.

The assessment strategies, as can be seen, are designed to enhance students' thinking skills, drawing particularly on the higher levels of analysis, synthesis and evaluation, whilst giving new material to think about. They also exercise literacy skills of writing for different audiences and in different registers. All teachers need to have a knowledge of children's learning difficulties, and this is a complex and specialized area of knowledge not acquired easily. It is necessary to observe pupils closely with this knowledge before it is possible to identify ways in which to help them. Lack of this knowledge and these skills negates much of the learning which could take place in classrooms. Its lack also creates the learning difficulties seen in so many pupils. Teachers are required not only to have this specialist knowledge and skills but also to have presentational and communication skills for different audiences – pupil, expert and lay. Clearly, one module of a programme cannot deliver all of these capability outcomes, but the outline given below of some of the tasks in other modules will give an indication of how this is done.

It may also be becoming clear that a teacher education programme with 'all that irrelevant theory' expunged has thrown out the baby with the bathwater. The new training, using colleges to teach the subjects plus mentoring and 'sitting by Nellie' to effect the professional training, is hardly going to deliver the capabilities required. Nurse education has found this out after a hundred years. I wonder what hope we have for the future education and training of teachers. One of our problems is perhaps the lay view that 'We have all been to school, therefore we all know all there is to know about teaching.'

Cognitive study skills

Cognitive study skills were defined as those which 'engaged brain' and caused the reader or listener to interact with the material and grapple with its ideas and deeper meaning. They would break the reading process up and cause interaction with the text, bringing about reflective reading, which is often necessary for text other than novels and newspapers. As mentioned earlier, the Schools Council project (1980) referred to these activities as DARTs – directed activities related to texts.

In **Module 2**, a study skills work book is sent with the module book and the students are asked to complete specific exercises as a training run, as follows:

- to read for the main point a section of difficult text on Darwin's *Origin of Species* (Thomas and Harri-Augstein, 1971; see Chapter 4, pp. 109–11);
- to complete a flow chart of the meaning of the text;
- to identify which reading and scanning strategies were used;
- to complete similar but easier exercises from children's texts;
- to complete deletion exercises with pupils;
- to try to put texts which are out of sequence into logical order;
- to distinguish fact from opinion in newspapers;
- to mark two essays written by teacher education students on a behaviour problem with which they had to cope on teaching practice. The marking of the essays had to be set against a 12-point grading system which was criterion-referenced.

The final task was to design a piece of cognitive study skills material, use it with pupils and evaluate its effectiveness.

In another module, the student was required to read a book written by a person with special needs or by a carer, and then to write a critical review of 600 words. A framework for how to write a review was given as well as some example reviews and references. The student evaluation of this showed that it was an effective strategy for enabling them to empathize with a person with special needs (for example, Susan Hampshire on her dyslexia) and to see the education system from a different perspective. It also required summarizing, writing, drafting and editing skills, and the ability to become so familiar with the book so as to give an overview and critique. It was a very quick and easy assignment to mark, especially if all the books chosen were familiar – a good reason for providing a suggested reading list.

In a third module, the students were presented with readings on various aspects of teaching and learning strategies and then asked to:

- design a problem-solving lesson and evaluate it with the pupils' help;
- select a collaborative learning session, modify it to suit the pupils' ages and experiences, use it, and then evaluate it with them;
- design and make a whole book game based upon study skills principles and practices, and evaluate it in use with a group of pupils (see Chapter 4 for details).

In other modules students are required to do the following activities:

- Prepare a chronology of spelling teaching.
- Undertake a miscues analysis of reading, spelling and number, and suggest appropriate intervention and remedial strategies.
- Make a critical appraisal of a software remedial package and a remedial teaching programme.
- Compile a directory of special needs contacts.
- Tabulate the remedial programmes in use, with their main advantages and disadvantages.
- Write a short answer paper on dyslexia worth 100 marks and consisting of true-or-false, multiple-choice and sentence-completion items. The main bulk of the questions have to be based upon three recent research papers which indicate new directions in the research findings.
- Read a research paper and complete a flow chart of it which defines its main and subordinate points. The paper is on the value or otherwise of early screening techniques in school.
- Critically evaluate the construction and use of a common standardized test of reading, according to specific criteria governing test construction and use, preparing a short report for the head-teacher on its value.
- Compile an easy-to-use staff handbook on managing classroom behaviour problems.
- Write a new work pack which brings the material presented in the module up to date.
- Examine the neurological sections of the human brain (right and left hemispheres) and list three differences between them.
- Raise several hypotheses which might account for what you see in these brains.
- Write a pen portrait of your best and worst maths teacher.
- Imagine you are interviewed by Joan Freeman, as in her book Gifted Children Growing Up (1991), and give an account, real or imagined, of what you might say to her.
- Visit a special school or unit and write a report of the visit.
- Listen to or watch two programmes on special needs and write a summary of the main points.
- Prepare an annotated bibliography for staff.
- Negotiate and carry out a staff appraisal session of a colleague.
- Develop a team-building programme with colleagues and undertake it.
- Prepare, carry out and evaluate a staff inservice training session on a special need.
- Prepare or evaluate a school development plan for special needs.

These and many more activities are presented in the work packs to evoke both the general and specific capabilities required of an educated professional, and to match the real tasks of professional life. The tasks are also geared to challenge the thinking processes and to cause the learner to operate at the higher-order thinking level, where the skills can be considered to be core skills and transferable. None of the activities takes place in a vacuum. There is a large amount of course content presented and referred to which has to be followed up and researched. By the stage of the independent international study and the dissertation, the student has the required skills to engage successfully in studies at that level. There are also opportunities throughout to pursue independent learning.

Three examples of the students' work are given below:

Pen Portraits: Five able pupils in a class of 6- to 7-year-olds

Graham

Graham has a broad general knowledge and a more developed vocabulary than other pupils in his class. He learnt to read early and enjoys factual texts more than story books. He appears to regard some of the other children as 'silly' when they ask 'obvious' questions. He does not have one particular friend, neither is he part of a larger group.

Lorraine

Lorraine appears aloof and mature for her age. She hides her abilities as much as possible so that not too much is expected of her. She reads well but only does so in school as she says her parents never have time at home.

Rose

Rose is a conscientious child. She presents her work neatly and listens to and carries out complex instructions. She can work independently, concentrating on work and tackling problems. She reads fluently. Rose is quiet and shy, preferring to play with one particular friend.

Archie

Archie is regarded as odd by his fellow pupils. He has a great interest in the world generally, particularly the planet system. His general knowledge is extensive. He reads fluently but very slowly.

He rarely finishes any written work as he appears to be constantly 'daydreaming'.

Steve

Steve is very artistic. His drawings are considered and have a distinctive style to them. He is quiet and conscientious, paying meticulous attention to detail in his pictures and presenting other written work neatly. He doesn't contribute to class discussions and is very much an observer.

(Pamela Summers, 1995; Task 6: MA (SEN), MA (SpLD))

Task: Write a brief 50–100-word pen portrait of two mathematics teachers, one who helped you and one who hindered your progress.

The teacher who helped me most with mathematics was my first one. With her I was enthusiastic and responded well to her patience and help with counting, sorting, one to one correspondence. She provided me with farm animals, colourful cubes and counters. We had a shop and cardboard money and I remember the fun I had 'going shopping'. There were scales for weighing, sand and water. My books were full of simple addition and subtraction sums and I did well. The teacher made me feel good about mathematics. As soon as the next teacher came I began failing in maths and all the kindness and patience this teacher had shown me disappeared.

The teacher who hindered my progress most was one I had when I was 15 years old. She gave me very little support. I worked my way through pages and pages of class maths work and was unable to demonstrate that I had understood what I had been doing. She seemed oblivious to the fact that key concepts had been misunderstood through poor teaching. She presented her subject in such a way that I underfunctioned and became extremely anxious, fearing her and her lesson. The final unforgettable humiliation was when she called me up to the blackboard to show how I had proceeded with a homework assignment. I had received an unusually high mark and she probably guessed that I had been helped at home. She was right and I was unable to demonstrate how I had done the homework.

(Dawn Shindler, 1994; Module 4, Task 2: MA (SEN))

A brief history of reading instruction

Without exception the teaching of reading is viewed by society as the most important task of early schooling. Perhaps this is why theorists argue so passionately about how it should be taught. Despite considerable research into the teaching of reading, disagreements about the relative merits or different methods continue. The contentious issue is whether reading is decoding or comprehending words, and how readers actually process what they read.

Historically, reading instruction can be broken into four broad periods, however, there is considerable overlap as many teachers were slow to adopt new methods. The dates given are approximate, but swings against one method and another are clearly evident.

The Alphabetic method: classical times to the mid-nineteenth century (750 BC–1850)

The Alphabetic method is a simplistic way of teaching reading which starts with and emphasises the names of the letters of the alphabet. After learning letter names in the correct sequence, children learned the sounds of vowels and how punctuation worked. With these rudimentary skills, children then began combining letter names and vowel sounds which they practised until mastered. The Alphabetic method was a two step process; teach the code, then have children read. In reality learning letter names in isolation is of little value to the decoding process and children learned to read because the texts that accompanied this method, such as the Bible, were familiar to them.

The Phonic method: mid-nineteenth century to the First World War
(1850–1914)

The Phonic method is a way of teaching which starts with and emphasises the sounds of letters. A child who has been taught by this method will decipher each new word by sounding out letter by letter, or letter unit by letter unit. Phonics was criticised because it involved a lot of tedious drill and in some cases the English language was highly irregular. However, it is now acknowledged that without mastering the sound-symbol code children cannot recognise unknown words.

Whole Word methods: between the First and Second World War and beyond (1918–1979)

The Whole Word method of teaching reading was based on the principle that reading was more about understanding what real words meant than breaking words down into meaningless sounds and putting them back together into words again. The Word Patterns, Look and Say, Kinaesthetic method, Sentence Method and later developed Language Experience method of reading instruction are derivatives of the Whole Word approach which encourages children to use their knowledge of the visual patterns in words, their understanding of the sentence so far or any illustrations to recognise unknown words. Whole word theorists generally view sounding out as a last resort.

Eclectic approaches: since the Second World War (1945–)

As society now recognises that reading involves both decoding and understanding words, current research advocates an eclectic approach that teaches graphophonic alongside semantic and syntactic clues.

Whilst young children benefit from learning high frequency words that are often phonetically irregular via the Look and Say method, an understanding of the sound/symbol code is essential. Similarly, proficient readers use linguistic variables such as syntax and semantics to predict words and speed up the reading process. Thus readers use both text and experience, language background and prior information to read, understand and remember unfamiliar words.

> There is simply no one single way to teach reading successfully to every child because all children have preferred learning styles. So, whilst the Phonic method favoured auditory learners, the Whole Word method was easier for children with a strong visual memory. Taking the best parts of each method and combining them to provide children with a variety of ways of learning to read has resulted in teachers employing a number of techniques which are modern day adaptations of very old methods.
>
> (Lorraine Hammond, 1994; Module 7, Task: MA (SpLD))

CONCLUSIONS

Cognitive process pedagogies have been converted into distance teaching methods for evoking higher-order learning. In addition, a wide range of assessment strategies has been designed which would strengthen these links and result in students having both general and specific professional capabilities.

The systems for evaluating this type of programme are in place within the assessments themselves as well as in the summative assessments which students are asked to complete at the end of their programme. The programmes are thus in themselves a research project, which will produce hard data on their efficacy. So far, it is possible to track individual students' development from producing descriptive work at simple applications level through to an increasing command of the higher-order levels of operation. Grades and quality of work can be seen to improve steadily throughout the programme or leap suddenly to a consistent high standard. Students' comments on the work become more knowledgeable, sensitive and critical. One of the most encouraging features is that they say that it is fun and interesting but hard work. They also talk about their activities with colleagues, who join in too.

The general conclusions have been that the programmes are professionally relevant and academically challenging, and this has been confirmed by the external examiner. On the downside, of course, there are students who prefer a face-to-face course and find the independent pursuit of study too lonely. They need to find a different programme. Some have complained that it is not at all like the Open University courses they have previously followed, with summer schools and tutorials, and so we do offer some clinic tutorials each month and three seminars in the half-terms for local residents. But those at a distance in Hampshire, Kent, Essex, Australia, Cyprus and so on seem to manage perfectly well with the occasional telephone tutorial. The main initial complaint has been that it is not possible to go and copy the material out of books and rehash it for an essay or two. My response is 'Good, I am glad. At least it has been successful in that.' In a year or two, more substantial numbers should be completing the programme and it will be possible to complete a full-scale evaluation and review.

Many students in higher education are highly able and talented, but they often regard their education there as a 'Psychic prison', according to the researches of university tutors reported at the European Council for High Ability Conference at Nijmegen in October 1994. Students complained that their education was mundane, boring, unchallenging and repeated areas which they had already covered. It focused upon quantity to be learnt and subject knowledge, rather than on equipping them to meet the needs of modern life and future careers. These criticisms were particularly applied to the traditional so-called academic studies in the humanities, social sciences and sciences, rather than in the performing arts and the newer areas such as business studies and computing. It is a matter of grave concern that an education planned to suit an able élite should meet their perceived needs so badly, and this seemed to be a Europe-wide if not a worldwide problem.

In Britain, this has been realized for some years, and this was why the Higher Education for Capability movement was established by Stephenson and Weil in 1988 with the support of the Royal Society of Arts. At Oxford Brookes University, the team at the staff development centre under the leadership of Gibbs has been developing research, theory and practice on improving student learning for a number of years, culminating in a series of conferences and publications to help tutors improve the educative experience for their students (Gibbs, 1994, 1995). All of these activities have established an agenda for teaching in higher education in Britain which does appear to be chiming with what is concerning others in higher education on the world scale.

As yet, however, the studies and their results have not permeated all the deep and dark recesses of traditional university programmes. In some quarters it is argued that the highly able group of university students should not need to be taught; they should be able enough to read for their own degree, the purpose of the university is to undertake research, and undergraduate students are of little significance. If this attitude prevails, many uniquely able individuals will turn from academic studies and their potential will be lost. Perhaps no one with an IQ of more than 130 will ever be engaged in research and teaching as a result.

In his inaugural speech at the Royal Society of Arts, launching the challenge of Higher Education for Capability, Stephenson outlined the following agenda:

> employers of graduates ... had said that capability consisted of 40 per cent specialist knowledge and skill and 60 per cent personal qualities. Qualities of being continuously prepared to learn and adapt, being self critical, self starters, able to communicate in speech and writing, initiative, empathy, self awareness, commitment to what they are doing, teamworking, problem analysis and solution, ambition, and a sense of purpose. Higher education was not doing enough to foster these qualities.
>
> The theme of the new Higher Education for Capability project which we are launching today is to do just that: to encourage the development of the qualities of capability through the process by which students learn. (after Stephenson and Weil, 1988, p. 1).

It was the articulation of this challenge which gave encouragement to many of us working away in isolation to pick up the challenge and continue the development of this type of work.

7

Helping the underfunctioning able

INTRODUCTION

In many ways, the subject of the underachieving able pupil and student has been a neglected area by comparison with studies of high-ability and disadvantaged groups. Perhaps one of the reasons for this is the complexity of the interacting factors which predispose some individuals to underachieve and others not. In a family with two highly able children and one of average ability, one of the highly able may underfunction to a degree which takes his or her performance below that of the average member.

There have, however, been a number of important research contributions on the subject, beginning with that of Terman and Oden (1934), who compared 150 successful with 150 unsuccessful men, all with IQs over 140. They found that 90 per cent of the successful graduated whilst only 30 per cent of the unsuccessful had. The profile of these underachievers was defined by the researchers as poor motivation to succeed and lack of coping strategies for dealing with problems. This group had also come from families where there was less support and more marital breakdown. It could be argued that failing the degree or opting out from it or from their studies, and so obtaining lower qualifications, predisposed the unsuccessful group to lower career achievement. They might fail to overcome entry hurdles.

It is in the very nature of underachievement that it often defies definition. If underachievement is regarded as 'unfulfilled potential', then to recognize it there has to be some indication of the potential which for some reason is unfulfilled. The difficulty for the researcher and educator is that the underachiever is not demonstrating the potential. For a time after IQ tests became established and widely used, it was thought that the IQ alone could reveal this potential. Of course, it does so in a number of individuals – thus most identification processes begin with an abilities or IQ test of some kind. When a discrepancy is found between IQ and school attainment, such as an IQ of 140 at 10 years and school attainments test in reading, spelling and mathematics at a 10-year-old level, then some underfunctioning is evidenced. This may be borne out in all or some other areas of the curriculum when these are checked. To all intents and purposes, this pupil would appear to be of average attainment and might move through school being treated as such if the IQ score were not so startlingly discrepant. The school's response might be to try the 'carrot' and then the 'stick', but the pupil's performance might remain steadily average and the school reports read 'could do better', 'disappointing'. The pupil may be unaware of any high potential and be working steadily, but becoming depressed by the unhappy comments, not knowing how to do better. Another perspective may be to regard the pupil as 'lazy' or 'careless', particularly if the handwriting is untidy, and strong recommendations may be made to 'pull up socks', 'turn over a new leaf, 'start making an effort' and so on – all equally depressing.

As the definition of ability has broadened and the IQ has receded as the single means of identifying it, so the measures of underachievement have needed to be broadened. No single measure can suffice, nor can potential itself be defined adequately.

One of the most important ways of identifying underachievers is to ask teachers for their judgement. According to Fine (1967), teacher judgement yielded the greatest number of under-achievers. It is more sensitive, and sampled areas of behaviour not covered in IQ tests. An IQ test is after all only sampling a set of general problem-solving behaviours, usually verbal and spatial reasoning, which are two-dimensional and can be recorded in written form. All this sample is undertaken within a given time span of 30–60 minutes, depending on which test is used. It is hardly surprising that the test constructors left out some items. It *is* surprising that on such limited evidence we have seen large numbers of children selected for special education for the able, with cut-off points rigidly adhered to, when they have proved to be quite arbitrary.

Teacher judgement may yield more underachievers than IQ tests can find, but some teachers find identification of able pupils very difficult compared to identification of much less able under-achievers. Their judgements tend to be more stable if they see the pupils working across a number of curriculum areas, as in primary/elementary schools. Secondary and tertiary subject special-ists find identification of subject expertise and knowledge easy, but not of potential or underachievement. Learning Difficulties Project studies revealed this on a consistent basis. Painter (1982) found secondary teachers able to identify only one-third of the gifted in their schools, leaving out one-third who were gifted and including one-third who were not, by comparison with her range of tests and questionnaires.

Judgements by teachers may sample many more pupil behaviours than tests, but may be influenced by the teachers' attitudes and so subject to bias. The best results have of course been found after teachers have received courses of training on identification of ability and underachievement (Denton and Postlethwaite, 1985). Even so, it can be expected that some underachievement still escapes detection. It may only be revealed in later life when we learn of their achievements, or they may never achieve at all. Perhaps the classic underachiever in school of all time was Albert Einstein. His father was told by the headmaster that 'Albert would never make a success at anything.' Albert was later expelled from the Gymnasium with the admonition, 'Your presence in class is too disruptive and affects the other students.'

We still rely upon teacher judgement and the discrepancy method to identify able underachievers. More emphasis is, however, placed upon multiple criteria, and this will include the use of behavioural checklists which provide a 'clinical' (observational) pattern of behaviours, as well as the use of interest and personality inventories and checklists. Multiple cut-off points are also used to ensure inclusion rather than exclusion. Greater sensitivity and understanding by researchers have improved the situation for many underfunctioning students. It is, however, my experience that large numbers of able individuals underfunction in a systematic and serious way because the expectations of learners are too low and too limited, or too narrow and too stereotypic.

One further issue is raised by this focus on underachievers, and that is the question of teacher time. If researchers with all their tests cannot satisfactorily define who is underfunctioning and why, how can the teacher be expected to do more? In fact, many schools do not have data on IQ – most have only that from group tests of verbal reasoning for the majority of pupils, apart from those who have been statemented. Attainment test data and progress on levels of attainment in the subject target areas will now become available, but this by itself will not give an ability/discrepancy score warning. Discrepant profiles will be available, but none of this will necessarily address the problems of identification and provision for the underachievers – even those who are not of the stature of an Einstein.

ABLE UNDERACHIEVERS

Torrance (1965) was one of the first to awaken interest in able underachievers. His research led him to offer a set of criteria for identifying those who might be underachieving. These directed attention to the social context. He found some commonly associated conditions in underachieving able children as follows:

- unstimulating home background
- lack of early suitable training
- unhappy family relations
- an overambitious home
- schooling which failed to arouse and engage the child's interests.

(p. 122)

In her research on 'Able misfits', Kellmer Pringle (1970) came to some similar conclusions. She found her able underachievers had:

- a sense of inadequacy and limited ambitions
- a dislike of school and book learning
- poor work habits
- unsatisfactory relationships with peers
- a high incidence of emotional difficulties.

(p. 123)

Belle Wallace was appointed as adviser with a brief to develop provision for the able and gifted in Essex in the 1970s. From her initiatives and training course checklists, strategies and enrichment packages were developed (the Essex Enrichment Packs). According to one typical checklist (Wallace, 1983), the underachiever may be:

- Generally anti-school and very critical of its values. Often scathing in remarks about teachers and lacking in enthusiasm for most school activities.
- Frequently abrasively humorous with an ironic perception of other people's weaknesses.
- Orally good while written work is poor and incomplete. He/she is not really interested in seeking the teacher's approval by completing work.
- Apparently usually bored and lethargic, lacking energy and motivation.
- He/she watches the time and is anxious to finish the school day and leave.
- Restless, inattentive and easily distracted, often at the root of mischief and practical jokes.
- Absorbed in a private world, often wasting time by doing

nothing or distracting other pupils.
- Friendly with older pupils, deliberately seeking their company and often accepted by them.
- Impatient and critical, sometimes rude and insolent, finding difficulty in making relations with peers and teachers.
- Emotionally unstable, very prone to moodiness or bad temper, apparently easily frustrated and lacking in kindliness towards others.
- Outwardly self-sufficient and apparently careless or indifferent to school standards. Irregular in attendance but able to keep up with the other children.
- Defensive but very astute in argument and self-justification.
- Often the leader of the 'malcontents' and the anti-school group.
- Well endowed with 'low cunning' and survival skills.
- Able to manipulate others while not being personally committed or involved.

But the underachiever is also:

- When interested, inventive and original although impatient and reluctant to persevere with in between stages.
- Quick to learn new concepts and able to pose problems and to solve them ingeniously, especially those unrelated to school tasks or 'academic' subjects.
- Able to ask provocative, searching questions and very aware of problems about people and life generally.
- Persevering when motivated, sometimes performing at a high level in one or two areas only and particularly when the relationship with the teacher is very good.
- Inventive and responds to open-ended questions.
- Philosophical and wise about everyday problems and commonsense issues.
- Perceptive in discussions about people' motives, needs and frailties.

(pp. 39–40)

In an earlier study of giftedness, conflict and underachievement, Whitmore (1980) summarized some of the most important characteristics of able underachievers as follows:

- large gap between quality of oral and written work;
- failure to complete daily school work;
- poor execution of work;
- persistent dissatisfaction with accomplishments;
- avoidance of trying new activities;
- low self-image;
- aggressive behaviour;

- not functioning well in a group situation;
- lack of concentration;
- setting unrealistic goals – too high or too low;
- difficulty in peer relations;
- poor attitude to school;
- dislike of drill and memorization.

Whitmore suggested that if a pupil demonstrated ten or more of these thirteen characteristics, then the teacher should undertake an evaluation to determine whether the child was an able under-achiever.

Freeman's (1991) longitudinal study of gifted children growing up identified a group of underachievers she called the 'career gifted' (p. 31). These were young people who had been nominated as gifted at an early age by parents or identification procedures and who enjoyed the aura that the title could bring, but who feared they might be unworthy of it or were really not highly able, and so avoided any area of challenge in which they might be found wanting. They could always explain failure away by saying that they could not be bothered to try, that the work was too uninter-esting and beneath them, so they did not do it. The results of this consistent approach were that they fell further and further behind their peers and did not then have the requisite knowledge and skills when they did have to apply them. They could only succeed on tests and activities which did not require a significant degree of prior knowledge. They were regarded as 'having great promise' which they subsequently failed to fulfil.

One of the key early studies which linked theories of under-achievement with educational interventions was that by Raph *et al.* (1966). They reported on a programme which was part of the Talented Youth Project in the United States. The educational methods, used with underachieving secondary-school pupils in tenth grade, were derived from their analysis of current theory and research.

In the first method a *'special teacher'*, with a warm and flexible personality but capable of maintaining high scholastic standards, was the focus. The pupils were told they had high ability but needed to improve their standards of achievement. They were taught by their special teacher on educational aspects, followed by teaching of social studies in a two-hour session daily. At the end of the year, the group showed greater scholastic achievement, and better social behaviour and attitudes than matched controls. When the supportive provision and teacher was changed the next year, the progress was not maintained.

The second method was *modification in curriculum and teaching methods*, focused on mathematics, where all the group had failed. Many pupils enjoyed the special programme, which was in geometry with great emphasis on completion of assignments and correct form and content. Those with the most severe problems of underfunctioning did not improve, although they showed an interest in learning the new material.

The third method combined the roles of *special teacher and counsellor*. The underachievers were given special skills instruction in learning skills and received individual counselling.

The general conclusions were that at the end of the programme there were no differences between the experimental and the control groups. Sadly, the underachievement was so deeply rooted at this stage that it was unamenable to change. The researchers recommended that much earlier identification was needed, which might enable 'preventative rather than curative programmes' (p. 179). These would be likely to stabilize the gains which were found, but which proved transitory when the special teacher changed. It was interesting that the warm and flexible personality able to maintain high scholastic standards was the factor capable of making at least some change. In support of this, Kellmer Pringle's (1970) research showed it was teachers themselves who exerted the strongest and most lasting influence on their pupils, through their own personalities. This aspect was regarded as particularly important for those able children who lacked appropriate model figures in their own family. Underachievers were shown to perform better with supportive, encouraging teachers than with those who simply demanded high standards of work.

Among the remedies she suggested were improving the self-concept and morale of the underachiever and enlisting parental interest and support. Community, neighbourhood and peer-group attitudes towards intellectual achievement may also need modifying, but this was inevitably a long-term goal. In school, the opportunity to work independently, to explore individual interests in depth, to develop or perhaps rediscover a sense of commitment and excitement about learning, she concluded, were all prerequisites for rehabilitating the able misfit. Most of us can remember the teachers who supported us and the influence they had upon us, independent of what they taught us at the time.

One of the most important studies of underachievement in recent times was undertaken by Butler-Por (1987). It started from experiences in London primary schools and was followed up with a research project in schools in Haifa. It provides a model of good practice for those concerned about pupil underachievement, and is innovative in methods of identification and intervention. It is worth outlining its main strategies, beginning with a quotation which underlines the sensitivity and dedication of the teacher-researcher:

> My earliest insight into the problem of underachievement occurred many years ago, during my first job as a supply teacher in a South London primary school. I was told that 'the class was alright, but some children were pretty hopeless'. I was also told that the children were used to working through their arithmetic book and were tested at the end of each week. After receiving the first test papers in long division, which were disastrous, I did not know what to do ...
>
> I subsequently divided the papers into small groups according to the main errors they revealed, and spent my next lunch breaks working with the children on their own specific difficulties. I soon realized that some of the 'hopeless' children were pretty bright but for different reasons had lost confidence in their ability to cope with their school work. However, I found that when each child was helped to understand the specific problem in arithmetic that had been holding him back, his progress was not only remarkable, but also quite out of proportion to the effect I invested. As I gained more experience, I met children in every classroom whose performance and achievements gave no indication of their actual abilities.
>
> (Butler-Por, 1987, p. 3)

Underachievement is most apparent at secondary schooling stage, but the remediation is often too late and targeted at limited areas, as found by Raph et al. (1966). By this stage, the patterns can be entrenched, and in any case they have such complex origins that simple and single measures are hardly likely to prove effective. It was for these reasons Butler-Por targeted primary-age children, but the methods used could be applied throughout the educational range. She argued that since the underachiever's school record of poor achievement was not caused in the main by inability to do better, then it was the expression of conscious or unconscious *choice*. Roth and Meyersberg (1963) identified this as choice to invest effort in learning or not. When the choice made was not to invest, a syndrome or pattern of underachievement followed, which was characterized as depreciation, lack of clear personal goals and values, vulnerability to disparagement by others, immature relationships, lack of insight about self and others, depression and anxiety.

Butler-Por and Arnon (Butler-Por, 1987) compared successful children enjoying learning with unsuccessful ones, and proposed a model of prerequisites for 'joy in learning'. It had two aspects, the *emotional and social* and the *motivational*, in which the theories of need fulfilment of Maslow (1954) and Erikson (1963) played a significant part. If the emotional and social needs of the individual for affiliation and trust in self and others were not fulfilled, the autonomy, self-confidence and initiative of the child could be damaged and the motivation to achieve mastery and competence, respect others and respond to challenge and stimulus would be harmed. This damage would occur both in the home and later in the school in a self-defeating cycle of disadvantage to the able child, causing him or her to underachieve. As the underachievement manifested itself, so parents and teacher support would be likely to be withdrawn.

Butler-Por goes on from this basic model to give case examples of how each aspect contributes to an individual's pattern of normal and adequate functioning. She gives as examples of how these patterns could be distorted, leading to underfunctioning, the following main negative social and socialization factors:

• hostility in family relations;
• rejection of the value of that member of the family;
• parental expectations which were unreasoning and excessive;
• lack of support for emotional and social development and stability;
• lack of interest in the child.

These characteristics were also found by Rutter (1975) to predispose children to be disruptive in schools.

The personality characteristics which were identified with underachievement were as follows:

• low self-concept and negative self image;
• high self-concept but no motivation to achieve in school;
• locus of control which was external – blamed others and acts of chance;
• fear of failure;
• need affiliation, which the child found difficult to quantify;
• fear of success, particularly in girls.

These concepts were derived from the theories and research of McClelland *et al.* (1953), Atkinson and Raynor (1974) and Horner (1968). Butler-Por's view about what to do was summed up as follows: 'Since scholastic achievement is mainly a school problem, efforts to deal with the problem should relate to the school situation'. (p. 24). She identified three key variables in schools where there had to be change in order to combat underachievement. These were:

- attitudinal factors;
- curriculum and teaching methods;
- teacher variables.

The intervention programme was an attempt to implement Glasser's (1965, 1969) theory of reality therapy. He argued that significant improvement could only be achieved when both the teacher and the pupil were involved in planning the process of change. He said that to break the child's cycle of failure, the teacher must change the scholastic behaviour of the child through a process including three basic principles:

- acceptance of the child;
- recognition of the need for changing the child's school situation;
- undertaking personal responsibility for bringing about the desired change.

The evolving personal relationship between the teacher and the pupil set the stage for change by constructing new images and models of success, leading towards changes in attitude and performance in school.

Butler-Por's study took place in primary schools. There were three experimental groups each of twelve pupils and three matched control groups, comprising a total of seventy-two children aged 9–12 years, with twelve teachers, of whom three were special class tutors and nine were in mainstream classrooms. There were two able experimental groups with IQs over 130 and one average IQ group (102–10). All subjects were in the bottom quartile of their class on standardized achievement tests and on school grades in subject areas. During the first school week the class teachers initiated weekly meetings with each individual child in class for 15–20 minutes to gain insight into personality, interests and capabilities, whilst others in the class were engaged in independent work. This meeting was repeated on a weekly basis for a discussion of progress throughout the year.

The diagnostic/identification process was most significant and interesting:

1 The pupils were asked to read silently a short story, poem or description. Then they were asked to write the *three most important questions* that they would like to ask about what they had read.
2 (a) Next day they were given another passage to read and asked to write one *most important question*.
  (b) They were then asked to justify this question and explain why it was the most important question.

3 (a) The following day the teacher selected a problem behaviour within the pupil's experience, such as getting on with peers, an environmental issue or current affairs, and wrote it on the blackboard. Each pupil was asked to write down *three important problems* related to the topic.
　(b) The next day the pupils were asked to identify the *most important problem* relating to the topic and give as many alternative solutions as possible.
4 Pupils were asked to write a few lines of first positive and then negative evaluations of a given experience. They then had to write an alternative method if the teacher had:
　– introduced a new rule or concept;
　– read a poem;
　– presented a plan for a class project or outing.
5 They were asked to write a review of a book they had enjoyed or disliked and give the reasons for their evaluation.
6 They were asked to list their favourite interests and explain the reason for their choices.
7 They were asked to give personal learning priorities by stating what they would like to learn in school which was not being taught to them.

This method represented a *thinking skills approach* to identification.

These assignments were followed by new sequences. The purpose was to compare the responses on the creative thinking skills tasks with progress in curriculum areas. According to Butler-Por, these diagnostic activities also served as 'appropriate teaching methods for systematic development of thinking skills and abilities in the different subjects of the curriculum'. (1987, p. 75).

After the diagnostic period, the teachers explained to the pupils the purpose of the programme and invited them to join. When they accepted, an agreement was made about the urgent problems to be tackled. This was formalized as a contract by which the pupils set their tasks for the next week and chose the rewards which they would accept as reinforcers; for example, if the task of completing homework in subject x or checking spellings in y were completed, to be allowed to sit next to x, bring in their pet, spend time on model making, and so on. The tasks and rewards focused upon one of the three domains: learning, social and behavioural. The subsequent weekly meetings were spent on evaluation of how and how well the contract had been met, and on the contract to be established for the following week. The teachers met the researcher on a weekly basis to give feedback on the programmes, and to discuss individual pupils' progress and any problems encountered in dealing with them.

At the end of the three-month intervention period, the outcomes clearly showed that the programme had had positive effects on all the underachievers and their teachers, but that the pupils of lower ability had more negative attitudes and teachers found it more difficult to identify them and help them. The controls for this group, sadly, deteriorated; most left without the advantages of the programme just described.

A detailed analysis of the responses of teachers and pupils to the programme enabled Butler-Por to devise initial teacher education and inservice education programmes, which she then used effectively in Israel and London to help teachers identify and overcome the problems of their underfunctioning pupils. As a member of the Plowden Committee, she had become interested in investigating the possibility of creating educationally meaningful links between schools in which teacher education students did their teaching practice and the college programmes. These programmes of theory, problem-solving discussion, fieldwork and feedback are still in operation in Haifa, whereas 'theory' has almost been expunged from all teacher education courses in Britain and the training progressively handed over to teachers in schools. As can be envisaged, this strategy for on-the-job training for such complex professional concerns could prove seriously disadvantageous for many of our children.

Teacher educators are fundamentally expert teachers who have changed career from teaching to teaching about teaching. The two are different. The latter requires considerable research and scholarship to develop, and is enhanced by the opportunities to observe and research in classrooms to evaluate the results of theory and research on teaching effectively. Teachers in schools do not have these opportunities – they are teaching pupils on a daily basis and so one cannot expect them to be able to stand back, reflect, and undertake research and intervention to improve their teaching, except at the margins.

The crucial factors which emerged from these researches on educating underachievers is the importance of taking a detailed interest in the pupil. The 20-minute interview, and the work requiring main points to be articulated, explained and personally justified, enabled a *cognitive-counselling* type relationship to be developed by the child with a significant adult, the *mentor*. Study skills and thinking skills were modelled and developed in the diagnostic period and reinforced in later curriculum areas. As the pupils analysed content and issues, and then had to explain themselves and their ideas to peers and teachers who listened and discussed their responses, so individuals came to value themselves and take an interest in learning. We could summarize this as follows: When an interest is taken in us, then we can take an interest in things outside ourselves and in learning. This interest was repaid tenfold by the pupils.

In our appraisal research (Montgomery and Hadfield, 1989, 1990), it was noticeable that the observation followed by feedback created a rapport between teacher and researcher which was detailed and intense. This was highly beneficial when deputy head-teachers were trained in the technique and became mentors to their appraisees. The method proved significantly capable of improving the performance of underfunctioning teachers with benefits for their pupils. The studies of Raph et al. (1966) emphasized what was also found essential in all the studies: the need for the 'special' teacher to provide a warm, friendly, flexible and supportive classroom climate for the learning to take place. In fact, evidence from a range of studies shows that the presence of these factors creates a supportive classroom climate and school ethos, which benefits all pupils and is essential for those with learning difficulties and behaviour problems (Montgomery, 1989).

The following Learning Difficulties Project checklist provides a summary of the behavioural characteristics of many underfunctioning children. The presence of a cluster of five or more of these should lead teachers to suspect underfunctioning. The presence of any one of them is a cause for concern to the alert teacher, who will observe and analyse the pupil's performance and behaviour and seek ways of helping and fostering learning and development.

Able but underfunctioning: a teacher's checklist:
- inconsistent pattern of achievement in schoolwork subjects;
- inconsistent pattern of achievements within a subject area;
- discrepancy between ability and achievements, with ability much higher;
- lack of concentration;
- daydreaming;
- clowning and other work-avoidance strategies;
- poor study skills;
- poor study habits;
- non-completion or avoidance of assignments;
- refusal to write anything down;
- overactivity and restlessness;
- overassertive and aggressive or oversubmissive and timid social behaviour;
- inability to form and maintain social relationships with peers;

- inability to deal with failures;
- avoidance of success;
- lack of insight about self and others;
- poor literacy skills;
- endless talking, avoiding doing;
- membership of stereotyped 'minority' group (not caucasian, male, middle-class).

ABLE, UNDERFUNCTIONING AND LEARNING DISABLED

The problems of able and underfunctioning individuals may not have been widely researched, but there are a number of substantial studies which have sought to understand their difficulties and try to help them. There is, however, a vast literature on learning disabilities, but it is separate from that on ability. It tends to concern itself with analysing the nature, origins and remediation of the difficulties, and rarely examines the issues which arise when the learning disabled individual is highly able. To some, particularly the highly literate, able individual often researching the area of high ability, it almost seems a contradiction in terms. In this section, some of these dilemmas and issues will be explored in order to try to help identify further underfunctioning able.

The term 'learning disabilities' is used in most countries to refer to those who have problems and low performance in a particular area of learning that is surprising when other achievements and abilities are taken into account. In Britain, the term preferred for this group is specific learning difficulties.

The learning disability can appear in any area of educational performance: artistic, musical, number, co-ordination, handwriting, reading, spelling, language, design engineering and so on. It appears in the presence of otherwise superior intellectual performance. It is thus possible to find slow learners, average and able learners with much poorer performance – *performance decrement* – in, for example, reading and spelling in comparison with their measured IQ. There may be other learning disabilities present such as dressing difficulties, clumsiness, visuo-spatial difficulties and attentional problems, which may or may not impinge on educational progress.

The areas of learning disability which are fundamental to educational progress are language, reading, spelling and handwriting, and this section will concentrate on these difficulties in relation to ability. In Britain, these learning disabilities would be referred to as *specific learning difficulties in language* or *specific learning difficulties in reading and spelling,* and so on. For ease of communication, specific learning difficulties in the literacy area will be referred to as 'dyslexia', although developmental dyslexia is characterized by a wider pattern of difficulties (Miles, 1993) including in some saying the days of the week, months of the year, the alphabet, polysyllabic words, number difficulties and recalling random digits. Most children with specific learning difficulties in reading and spelling do show significant difficulties in some of these other areas, and so could be regarded as developmental dyslexics or 'dyslexics'.

Developmental dyscalculia

This is seen as difficulties in the understanding and manipulation of numbers and has a more equivocal research base. Kosc (1974) was a major researcher in this field, but much data since shows that number difficulties, particularly in reading problems, the language of number work, reciting tables, place value, and number processes such as addition and subtraction, are more a manifestation of an underlying verbal processing problem associated mostly with 'dyslexia' (Miles and Miles, 1991; Miles, 1983, 1993) than a distinct developmental difficulty.

Developmental dysphasia

This is a more fundamental problem than the foregoing and refers to difficulties in learning verbal language itself. In *receptive* dysphasia, the child has difficulty understanding and making sense of the language heard, and by age 5 years may know no words at all. *Expressive* dysphasia – the inability to use language and put words into sentences to express ideas and needs – follows from receptive dysphasia. It may also occur on its own, so that the children can understand what is said but are not able to express their own thoughts. Other intellectual areas of their brains may be functioning perfectly well, and so on the Raven's Matrices visuo-spatial performance problem-solving test (Raven, 1956) they may score above the 95th percentile. If they are very bright in this way, the frustration can be immense. However, their problems are clear to all and it is likely that they will be given specialist tuition at least at school age. The Association for All Speech Impaired Children (AFASIC) publishes advice to parents and teachers which states that from the early pre-school period the children need special tuition and specialized language training.

Developmental dysphasia may also appear on a continuum from mild to severe. Because the facility with language is so fundamental to education, general maintenance in society and social intercourse, even the mildest difficulties, such as word-finding problems and modest difficulties in assembling words and sentences to express ideas, can place children at a severe disadvantage from nursery and reception class onwards. In the course of researches on dyslexia, at least 20 per cent of cases such as this have been identified.

The case studies show both boys and girls who are mildly inarticulate in reception class; some may have had speech therapy, they have dyslexic difficulties, and they have performance quotients on WISC-R often 20–35 points higher than their verbal scores. Their full scores when calculated bring them into the low average range. If we can imagine that in their performance hemisphere a clever intellect is roaring and racketing about, with ideas, explanations and creative solutions to problems, without being able to find an exact means of communicating them, it is little wonder that such children quickly become either aggressive or withdrawn and depressed. They are very much subject to being victims bullied by other children, or bullying others.

As students and adults, they may have mastered their literacy difficulties sufficiently well except when under examination and in unprepared situations. At interviews they also underfunction, whereas in presentations which they can structure and prepare they may shine.

By comparison, academic value is more often associated with the ability to rephrase or rewrite things well than with the ability to initiate and solve problems which other people can convert into policy statements and procedures.

Einstein, unable to use language at 5 and unable to write until he was 10, could well have been one of this group. There are no doubt many highly able individuals in it whose contribution could be converted to positive rather than disruptive ends if we could identify them early on and use appropriate teaching methods to enable them to reveal their true abilities.

Specific learning difficulties in literacy areas

Developmental dyslexia

Pupils with dyslexia have *both* reading *and* spelling problems. It has been rare for their difficulties in spelling to have been as thoroughly investigated as their problems with reading, although the spelling problems are most often much more severe and in need of more attention than the reading difficulties. The incidence of the severest forms of the difficulty is thought to be on average 4 per cent of the British School Population (Rutter *et al.*, 1970). Pupils are reckoned to have 'dyslexia' if their reading (and spelling) is unaccountably low in relation to their intellectual abilities. It is therefore feasible for dyslexia to be found throughout the ability range.

In practice, dyslexia is generally only associated with students of higher academic ability, because researchers set minimum thresholds of 90–100 IQ for their research populations in order to avoid the influence of other secondary variables – in understanding and remembering instructions for example. The IQ threshold of 100 is also often set by remediators for entry of dyslexics into specialist fast-tracking programmes, for obvious reasons.

The Bangor Dyslexia Test by Miles (1991) is useful as a diagnostic tool for use by teachers seeking to identify this group.

Developmental dysorthographia

Pupils with developmental dysorthographia have severe spelling problems but no signs of severely delayed reading. Some such pupils originally had a reading difficulty which has cleared up; others may have learned to read very early and easily but have somehow never mastered spelling and writing to the same standard. Some never really master spelling at all without very specific help.

It is easier for these pupils to bump along in the bottom streams or groups in schools and conceal their difficulties to a large extent, for the same demands are never made upon their spelling as their reading (Peters and Smith, 1986). Spelling is basically a total recall activity and is therefore much more difficult to achieve with accuracy than reading, which is a recognition skill. Hence 'recovered' dyslexics show signs of their problems whenever they are confronted with a new subject or new terminology, as in the early stages of degree programmes. Incidence data is at present difficult to acquire.

The Daniels and Diack or the Schonell Spelling tests are useful diagnostic aids when all the errors made are analysed (Montgomery, in press).

Developmental dysgraphia

Pupils with developmental dysgraphia have a handwriting co-ordination problem, which may be mild or severe. There are a considerable number of pupils, at least 10 per cent of the school population (Gubbay, 1976; Lazslo, 1987), who have difficulties in the fine co-ordination required in handwriting. Their difficulties may bear no relationship to reading and spelling difficulties, but the current methods of primary teaching in Britain, using print script and copy writing, severely disadvantage children with these problems. As they find writing so difficult and time-consuming, it leaves little available cognitive processing time for spelling and writing, and they write very little and usually in a stereotypic form. The lack of practice in spelling and writing to which their difficulty leads can be shown to have a direct impact on spelling development, and so most pupils end up with both handwriting and spelling difficulties. In order to overcome these, it is essential that a cursive handwriting training programme is introduced from the first days in school.

Many highly able students have scribbly handwriting without having a co-ordination problem, because their thoughts run faster than their competence in motor skills can enable them to record. Many teachers expect pupils to produce neat script similar to that printed in early reading books, and downgrade any work which deviates from that model, however good the content may be. Girls in particular are expected to write neatly, whilst more untidy work is tolerated from boys (Good and Brophy, 1982).

Useful for diagnosis is the LDA *Handwriting File* (Alston and Taylor, 1986) and a forthcoming book in the present series, *Spelling*. Montgomery (in press) explores further spelling and handwriting problems and their remediation.

Complex specific learning difficulties

The difficulties already described may be found not only singly but in combination. My researches and those of Peters (1970) show, for example, that at least 30 per cent of all dyslexics have some form of handwriting difficulties. Pupils with reading, spelling *and* handwriting problems are more likely to be referred than those with reading and spelling problems alone who can copy neatly. Some able pupils become adept at subversive copying so that teachers may not be aware that they cannot spell at all. They may read well enough by clever guesswork and use of context clues for their problems to go unobserved until they arrive in secondary schools, where writing skills are heavily used.

Frustration with their learning disabilities leads many to develop emotional and behavioural difficulties which can conceal their underlying problems. Where they become disruptive and 'act out' their frustrations, they obtain faster referral. Once again, a gender factor can operate, for boys are more likely to project their problems outwards and 'blame' their teachers for their lack of success than girls are (Good and Brophy, 1982; Spender, 1981).

'Dyslexic' difficulties and underfunctioning

There are large numbers of children in schools – 25 per cent, according to recent government statistics – who are falling well behind their peers in reading and spelling. Their difficulties in the literacy area are a continuum from mild to severe. Over time, mild difficulties and delays may clear up of their own accord, but there are always a small number whose difficulties are resistant to all but the most specialized tuition. These children, if they are lucky, are referred to a specialist remedial centre which runs a British Dyslexia Association (BDA)-approved programme, or to a private school running a full-time programme. Centres offer tuition in and out of school hours for two or three session per week, whereas the schools offer the fully integrated curriculum essential for those with complex specific learning difficulties. Such provisions are patchy throughout the UK. Other successful programmes are run by the Helen Arkell Centres, some LEAs and Independent dyslexia centres.

Table 7.1 *Discrepancies between IQ, reading and spelling mean scores in 'dyslexics' and matched controls*

Category and numbers	WISC-R VQ	WISC-R PQ	WISC-R Full IQ	Reading Q (D&D)	Spelling Q (D&D)	Chrono-logical age (years)	Male: female ratio
Highly able dyslexic 30	125.3	124.9	126.8	82.8	82.9	10.2	5:1
Dyslexic 288	110.2	108.7	109.6	77.5	73.4	10.1	5:1
Controls 94	N/A (LEA did not permit IQ testing except their schools screen on Young's (1983) Group Test	N/A	108.7 (Young's (1983) Group Tes)	108.3	107.9	8.0	1:1

D&D = Daniels and Diack Reading Test 12 and D and D Spelling Test.
VQ = Verbal Quotient on WISC-R.
PQ = Performance Quotient on WISC-R.
Source: Montgomery, 1994

The 'dyslexic' difficulties are particularly resistant to change, and all of the pupils in the study below are two- or three-time failures already. They have had remedial help within school from class teachers and peripatetic support teachers, and some have had private tutorial help – none of it to any avail. These problems may be present despite very high ability, as can be seen in Table 7.1.

The table shows scores of all pupils referred to a special tuition centre for dyslexia over a three-year period from sixty primary and secondary schools in one local authority. The dyslexic pupils were in mainstream classrooms with the matched controls and had been identified by the schools, tested by the educational psychologists, and referred to the remedial centre for two one-hour tutorials per week. Slower learners were not referred but were given support within their classrooms over a longer period. It was also found that they were less able to profit from the specialist APSL (alphabetic-phonic-syllabic-linguistic) programme (Cowdery, *et al.*, 1983–7).

As can be seen, the majority of dyslexics were in the high average band. As they were likely to have depressed sub-scale scores on information, digit span, coding and arithmetic because of their dyslexic syndrome (Thomson, 1984; Miles, 1993), the WISC-R scores represented an underestimate of their ability. One in ten of these dyslexics were highly able – they were assigned to the highly able group when one of their WISC-R scores was 130 IQ points or over. Their scores were also likely to be an underestimate of their ability, and even so there were amongst them individuals with full-scale scores of 140 plus. The work of one such dyslexic boy is shown in Figure 7.1.

It has been said by Dykstra (1990) that able children are able to compensate for their learning disabilities. The table shows that to some extent this is true, for the highly able as a group are approximately six months ahead of the able dyslexics in reading and almost a year ahead in spelling. But both groups are two or more years behind chronological age peers in reading and spelling, and considerably more than this behind the standard which could be predicted from their mental abilities, even when a regression age is computed. The decrement in performance for the highly able group is more than three years, and up to five years in particular individuals. None of these children could be regarded as functioning anywhere near his or her potential, or as capable of compensating for his or her learning disabilities in any real sense. The Scottish Education Department (SED, 1978) survey by HMI also found a core of 1.5 per cent of pupils with severe problems in basic skills.

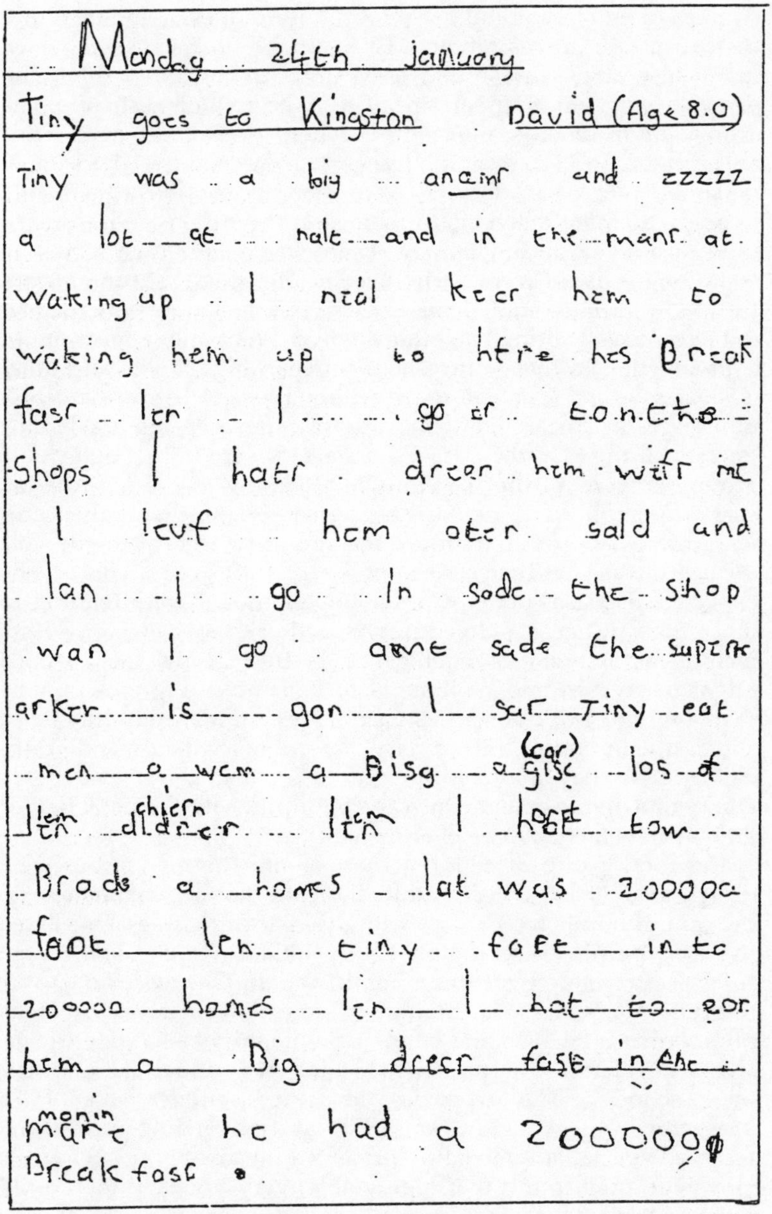

Monday 24th january

Tiny goes to Kingston David (Age 8.0)

Tiny was a big ancimr and zzzzz
a lot at nalt and in the manr at
waking up I nial keer hem to
waking hem up to htre hes Break
fasr len I go or to n the
Shops I hatr dreer hem witr me
I leuf hem oter sald and
lan I go in sode the shop
wan I go aute sade the supem
arker is gon I sar Tiny eat
men a wem a Bisg a gisc (car) los of
lten (lem) didrer (chiern) lten (lem) I hoet tow
Brade a homes lat was 20000a
foot len tiny fa Ft in to
20000a homes len I hat to eor
hem a Big dreer fase in the
mart (monin) he had a 200000
Breakfasr.

Figure 7.1 *The work of an able dyslexic: David, age 8.0 years, IQ 140*

The case histories of the 318 'dyslexic' pupils showed varying degrees of emotional and behavioural difficulties, associated with their response to frustration at being unable to learn skills which many less able peers found easy. Both 'acting out' and 'withdrawal' were common patterns of reaction to their distress. Some school environments and some teachers were more supportive and created less stress in the learners. Some children, because of personality or social factors, were more vulnerable to showing strongly adverse reactions to their learning difficulty, leading to more serious underfunctioning. There was also in each school an even longer list of pupils who needed the specialist tuition from the reading centre staff. Some of these pupils had already made it to the centre's waiting list, others would eventually appear on it.

In addition to these differences between highly able and other dyslexics, there was one more within the age band: there was much greater variability in the ages of referral in the highly able group. All the 6- and 7-year-olds referred were in the highly able group, as were all the 15-year-olds returning to the remediation centre for a top-up of spelling help. When these individuals' scores were removed from the group, the age of referral of highly able dyslexics was later than the rest of the dyslexic group. This is to be expected because, perhaps, their higher scores were tending to mask their difficulties. In education authority areas which do not include assessment of intelligence in the profile, these pupils might be missed and be thought to be functioning more slowly than average, but not seriously so. Highly able pupils may be so successful in coping in ordinary classrooms with dyslexic difficulties that they may be thought to be just about average in ability and achievement. Once again, pupils with the potential for high achievement can be overlooked.

The total group of children from whom these dyslexics were drawn was 20,000. These results indicate that approximately 1.5 per cent of pupils were found with dyslexic difficulties. One in ten dyslexic pupils were in the highly able category. This might suggest that there were more highly able in the 'dyslexic' group, but this was in fact a function of pre-selection processes in which pupils with WISC-R scores below 100 who might also be 'dyslexic' were not referred for specialist teaching; it is undertaken in their own schools. The dyslexics identified entered the TRTS programme (Cowdery, *et al.*, 1983) at the reading centre and received specialist remedial tutorials two or three times per week. However, they found that highly able, very young pupils could quickly learn what they needed from the programme, and so attempts were made to bring them in at 6 years. The earlier they could be identified the more success with the programme was found, for there was so much less for them to unlearn and there were several years of infant education left for them to practise the skills they had learnt. They quickly reached grade level in six months and maintained that progress.

Teacher and school attitudes play a significant role in the eventual careers of 'dyslexic' pupils. Many in this country do not recognize this learning disability at all and regard it as slowness or laziness. They put the 'dyslexics' with the slow learner groups and do not permit them to find areas of achievement for their intellect to manifest itself. Researchers in the area of gifted education often find it difficult to appreciate that a person of 16 or 36 can be highly able and yet are reading and spelling at the level of a 7-year-old. It does in fact defy imagination that an able 6-year-old may not be able to identify and use at least some of the 26 letters of the alphabet to build the simplest of words.

Some of the reasons for the attitudes of professionals about this area of learning disability is that it is not easily amenable to remediation. None of the remedial methods reviewed by Tansley and Pankhurst (1981) actually could be demonstrated as working. As all the dyslexics in my study were two- and three-time failures before referral for APSL tuition, it is not surprising that teachers become disheartened. What became clear in the research was that APSL-based programmes which used multisensory training in the early stages *were effective*. In any summer term, groups of pupils leaving the Centre had improved on average 2.5 years in reading performance and 1.8 years in spelling; prior to this they may have spent one to two years on the waiting list receiving ordinary school-based 'remedial' support and had gained on average four months reading progress and little or no gain in spelling.

If the pupils can be identified in reception class or Year One the remedial programme can be faster and more effective. The pupils do not then have so much to unlearn; there is more work on literacy skills taking place in these early years; and motivation to learn can be maintained as the pupil can experience success, have the difficulties acknowledged, and work with teachers to overcome them. When teachers fail this saps the pupils' conference, and trust and interest in education will be switched to something else in defence.

SENSORY AND PHYSICAL IMPAIRMENT AND UNDERFUNCTONING

The term 'gifted handicapped' first appeared in the 1970s, and the first conference to include the subject was held in the United States in 1976. In 1977, the term was logged in the ERIC (Education Research Index Catalogue) system and was thus officially recognized. However, by the 1980s little further progress was observed, because of the division between funding, administration and educational programmes for the gifted and the handicapped. Those in gifted education found it difficult to cope with 'handicapped' pupils, and the handicapped ethos and stereotypes did not permit of being 'gifted' (Whitmore, 1989). The dual classifications of both highly able and handicapped even now appear to be mutually exclusive except in some areas of good practice.

'Gifted handicapped' includes individuals with visual, hearing, physical and emotional difficulties and learning disabilities. In the UK, there are currently few special programmes and schools for the education of the highly able as understood in the USA, and certainly little government-funded research on the subject. There is variable specialist provision for those with sensory and physical difficulties. Whereas pre-Warnock (1978), this was mainly provided in special schools and units, since this period these pupils have increasingly been integrated into mainstream education, with many units closely associated with the school. The term 'handicapped' is seldom used in educational circles, for it is deemed that the difficulties should not be allowed to handicap the pupil either educationally or socially and all barriers to access should be removed. The integration movement has been proving particularly successful where teachers in the main stream have received the appropriate inservice education from advisory and specialist staff, and where the appropriate learning aids have been purchased. Many pupils with physical impairment have been very pleased with the opportunities offered by integrated education. Pupils with visual and hearing difficulties and those with severe learning disabilities still feel some support from specialists within units or local centres is essential to enable them to profit from their educational experiences. This has proved difficult for providers for those with learning disabilities to accept. Support within mainstream classrooms cannot provide the detailed tutorial knowledge and experience that 'dyslexics' need if they are to develop literacy skills to at least chronological age level within a short period of time.

Despite the accumulated knowledge from research and good

practice, Johnson and Corn in 1989 were still able to conclude from their researches that only a few individuals who were highly able but with sensory, physical or learning disabilities were able to develop their potential giftedness. These individuals were fortunate to have informed and concerned families and/or visionary and innovative educators. The outstanding examples are of course Helen Keller and Christy Nolan.

To be gifted and handicapped means meeting two classificatory identification systems, and needs the resources available from both. Several physically impaired young people said in Learning Difficulties Project Case Studies 'They don't think what our brains can do, only what our legs can't.' This reflects the handicapping stereotyping which they have to suffer sometimes all their lives.

The 'gifted handicapped' individuals who achieve success and acclaim in some sphere of useful human endeavour are characterized by Whitmore and Maker (1985) as:

- having an intense desire to succeed in reaching their goal;
- being capable of devising creative coping strategies for goal attainment.

According to Yewchuk and Bibby (1989), the characteristics of giftedness which teachers perceived in the non-handicapped were found to be similar to those they perceived in severely and profound hearing-impaired pupils. The same can be said to be true of children with physical impairment; their high ability can be identified in the same ways as for pupils without impairment. Where there are barriers to self-expression, however, such as difficulties with motor articulation in speech in cases of cerebral palsy, and with handwriting and co-ordination in a range of motor conditions, there may be delay or even failure in recognizing high ability. In such instances, other modes of assessment will need to be devised.

Where a stereotype is held that the highly able must look 'bright' (Karnes and Johnson, 1991) then those who look different in some way may be considered to be less able than they really are. It is still common for individuals with physical difficulties also to be regarded as mentally retarded. When you push a person in a wheelchair out, it is noticeable that people talk to the pusher and not the wheelchair-bound person: 'How is he feeling today?' or 'Does she take sugar?' In order to avoid overlooking the 'gifted handicapped', Yewchuk and Lupart (1993) drew up the following list of suggestions for guidance in identifying duality and the apparent paradox of giftedness and handicap:

- Be familiar with the characteristics of high ability and talent and how they can be manifested by children with handicaps.
- Use a variety of referral sources and assessment procedures both formal and informal.
- Compare able handicapped with like handicapped peers not with the non-handicapped.
- Create situations where the handicapped can display their abilities.
- Modify assessment procedures to make it possible for the handicapped to reveal their abilities.
- Include examiners in the assessment process who have like handicaps whenever possible.
- If handicaps hinder performance on conventional assessment tasks place greater emphasis on characteristics which circumvent this (e.g. Raven's matrices and WISC-R performance scales where oral/verbal responses are not possible).
- Use a dynamic, interactive assessment procedure to obtain a comprehensive profile of the total functioning.

(p. 715)

We can also add that the teachers and assessors must be trained in identification procedures for identifying both groups – the highly able and the specific area of disability in question.

In Britain, few courses of training have until recently included a consideration of the able and highly able in studies of special educational needs. In the 1981 Education Act, there was certainly no explicit reference to the highly able group. Only those functioning at a level below that of chronological age peers could receive special support. This definition could exclude highly able individuals with learning disabilities and with a range of impairments which could suppress their performance.

At the end of 1993, in a special advisory conference called by the Department for Education, it was finally conceded that the National Curriculum must take account of the needs of the able and highly able under the regulations for equal opportunities. This does not of course entitle the highly able or the schools to any resource provision to cater for their needs, but does make them liable to prosecution if they do not meet them!

What is more important than anything else is that every teacher in school should have a course of inservice training to enable him or her to identify and meet the needs of the able and highly able. All 'theoretical' training such as this has, however, been excised from courses of initial teacher education, and no money has been assigned to inservice training in this area. Training sponsorship for special educational needs has also dried up. Perhaps 2 per cent of teachers have received anything more than awareness training, and that some time ago.

UNDERFUNCTIONING, CULTURAL DIFFERENCE AND DISADVANTAGE

'Culturally different' refers to individuals whose differences are related to their racial/ethnic status, language, religious beliefs, values and/or the way in which they are socialized by the family.

The term 'disadvantage' refers to those brought up in homes and environments where financial resources are limited and educational traditions not strong. Gallagher's (1985) researches showed that both these groups were limited in their representation in gifted programmes in the USA. In 1993, Frasier, in her review of the international perspective, was still able to conclude that there had been little research and evaluation in the area of high ability and cultural difference, and that much of what did exist was focused on the United States. Although several large-scale studies had begun in 1992, they were not due to report until three years later. A significant exception was the work of Feuerstein (1979). As discussed earlier, he devised the learning potential assessment device (LPAD), designed to assess the cognitive potential of individuals. The principle upon which it was based was psychological theory of ability and a test, teach, test process. This enabled the teacher to analyse the child's levels of ability to acquire and demonstrate performance on a variety of psychological components of intelligence/ability tests. In this sense, it can be constructed to be culture free and at least culture fair. His methods, described as instrumental enrichment (Feuerstein, 1980), have enabled many of the students on his programme to achieve very high and quite unexpected levels of cognitive functioning.

What has concerned many working in this area is the major criticism which can be levelled at any instrument and procedure for identification. This is that these tests and procedures reflect and embody the value and critical constructs the dominant culture have for and of high ability. McLeod and Cropley (1989) expressed this problem in the following way:

> Although different subgroups may define exceptional ability according to different criteria, only those of the dominant cultural group may receive recognition; in most countries this means emphasis on language, abstract thinking, listening, sitting quietly and attending, dealing with problems through discussion and respect for authority.
>
> (p. 135)

The intermingling of subcultural values and disadvantages in class and caste systems can prove doubly handicapping, so that high ability easily goes unrecognized. The manifestations of high ability in creative curiosity, intellectually challenging remarks and questions, and a tendency to be physically active and sociable may be generally unacceptable to 'front-line authority' – the teacher. It may be particularly unacceptable and provoking when couched in the language of the subculture in a school and local environment where low expectations of education are held and school work is not valued. In such environs, teachers can become 'blind' to the signs of high ability as their expectations become lowered.

In the Headstart programmes, Karnes and Johnson (1991) concluded that they had improved the chances and services to average children and the 10 per cent in the programmes who were handicapped. The underserved, however, were the 'bright, gifted and talented' 10–20 per cent who were enrolled.

The characteristics of underachievement and cultural factors were summed up by Passow (1982b) in his review as:

- experiential deprivation;
- socioeconomic or racial isolation;
- limited language development.

The school-related factors identified were:

- absence of differentiation;
- labelling and stereotyping;
- low teacher expectation;
- incompatibility between learning experiences and educational needs.

What seems to be required is the retraining and re-education of teachers and those concerned with the administration of the education system, if the potential of a wide range of individuals and groups is to be revealed and in some measure realized. Passow (1981) wrote that what was needed was: 'real commitment on the part of educators and society at large to the concept that talent is not the prerogative of any racial or ethnic group, any social class or any residential area'. (p. 31).

UNDERFUNCTIONING AND GENDER

There is a considerable body of research evidence which shows that girls underfunction and are underrepresented in careers in mathematics, science and engineering, whereas boys tend to underperform in languages and literature studies. When high achievement in a variety of careers is examined, the number of females is small, despite the fact that overt barriers to their progress have been removed. Larger numbers of women than men enter the teaching profession, and yet men far outnumber women as head-teachers, deputies and heads of department. This imbalance becomes more and more noticeable as they progress from primary to secondary to higher and further education. This stratification of an educated profession said to be knowledgeable and concerned about equal opportunities can be regarded as a barometer of the lack of progress which has been made in this area in the fifty years since the 1944 Education Act, which promised education according to individual ability and need.

Women in British society in 1995 were still discriminated against, were not treated as equal citizens, and were consigned to live in poverty in large numbers, according to the Fawcett Society (1995) researches. If most of the overt barriers have been removed, then the implicit values carried by the hidden curriculum and structural inequalities already in society have, it would appear, largely remained. Shakeshaft's (1990) seminal text on *Women in Educational Administration* identifies the same issues and problems in North American society.

Girls, it would appear, learn to underfunction, and all but a few of the able and highly able escape. Spender (1981), in the first of a series of researches and publications, found that the classroom was still 'a man's world', where boys got two-thirds of the teacher's attention even when they were in a minority. They taunted the girls without punishment and received praise for sloppy work that would not be tolerated from girls. Spender found that the boys were accustomed to being 'teachers' pets', and if girls got anything like equal treatment they would protest vehemently and even wreck lessons. Spender argued that discrimination against girls was so deeply embedded in co-educational schools that single sex classes were the only answer.

Her case was based on tape recordings of her own and other teachers' lessons. Many of them, like Spender, had deliberately set out to give girls a fair chance. Spender often felt that she had gone too far and that she had actually spent *more* time with the girls than with the boys. The tapes proved otherwise. In ten taped lessons (in secondary school and college), Spender never gave the girls more than 42 per cent of her attention (the average was 38 per cent) and she never gave the boys less than 58 per cent. There were similar results for other teachers, male and female.

In other words, when teachers gave girls more than a third of their time, the teachers felt that they were cheating the boys of their rightful share. The boys themselves thought the same and insisted that she always asked the girls all the questions. This was in a classroom where 34 per cent of the teachers' time was allocated to the girls. In another class, where boys were receiving 63 per cent of teacher attention, one of them inferred that the boys were not being listened to because the teacher did not like boys. The boys regarded two-thirds of the teachers' time as their fair deal. When they got less, they caused trouble in class and even complained to higher authority. One of the teachers said that he had to give more attention to the boys to stop them playing up.

According to Spender's research, double standards pervaded the classroom. When boys asked question, protested, or challenged the teacher, they were more often treated with respect and encouragement. Girls who engaged in exactly the same behaviour were more often rebuked or even punished. An attention-seeking boy would quickly get a teacher response but girls could hold their hands up for an age and their polite requests for help would go unheeded. The girls often noted the extremes of teacher behaviour in this respect and made wry comments about it. In addition to receiving more teacher attention and support, boys took up more space in the room. Their chairs and desks covered more ground and their bags sprawled across the aisles. They were seen to move about the room more, to cast insulting and abusive remarks at the girls, and were allowed to get away with it.

Boys' written work was also judged by different standards, said Spender. When she asked teachers to mark essays and projects, the *same* work got better marks when teachers were told that it came from boys. Neat and tidy work from girls was treated with some contempt. Teachers would make disparaging remarks about girls' work, suggesting they should spend more time collecting facts than making the work look pretty. But when Spender indicated the work in question came from a boy, the tune changed dramatically.

Spender concluded that in mixed classes, the dice were loaded against the girls. If they were as boisterous and pushy as the boys, they were considered 'unladylike'; if they were docile and quiet they were ignored.

Spender reported that a few schools had introduced single-sex groups for maths and science, and found significant improvement in girls' results. She viewed sexual segregation within schools for certain subjects, rather than a return to single-sex schools, as the most hopeful solution to overcoming underfunctioning by girls.

Spender's results were not unique. There had in fact been a

range of studies which indicated that females learn to underfunc-tion in schools and colleges and that this trend is set from early in the post-natal period. Girl children were found to be handled differently when cross-dressed as boys (Hyman and Mitchell, 1975). Girls were placated, quietened and suppressed when handled, whereas boys were bounced, thrown in the air and encouraged to explore.

Detailed and observational studies in classrooms reported by Good and Brophy (1973, 1977) showed that teachers were more responsive to the questions of boys, gave them more extended information and encouraged them in their work, whereas girls were largely ignored or given monosyllabic controlling and non-informational feedback.

In studies of high ability, girls featured less than boys, although there was no evidence from IQ test data from the Terman studies onwards that there were fewer highly able girls than boys. According to Callahan in 1991 (Cornell *et al.*, 1991), highly able girls still faced inequities, were not achieving at expected levels, and were not choosing options commensurate with their abilities.

In Butler-Por's (1987) study, the top 2 per cent of all the children were invited at Stage One to enrol in the programme. At this stage, boys outnumbered girls by three or four to one in enrolment, although there were equal numbers who were eligible. At Stage Two, when the programme was explained to parents, many failed to enrol their daughters, whereas sons most often were enrolled. At Stage Three, when the pupils transferred from elementary to secondary schools, more girls then dropped out of the programme.

She put these results down to the stereotypic attitudes held towards girls' careers and the stamping in of sex stereotypes, causing the adolescent girls to fear continuing with the programme. She linked this with fear of success in girls, especially the highly able (quoting Horner's, 1968, results), and the motive to avoid success she found in graduate women. In an earlier study, Butler and Nisan (1975) found 68 per cent fear of success in able 17–18 year-old girls, compared with only 10 per cent in boys of the same age. They found that disadvantaged girls developed this fear of success much earlier, at the age of 12–13, which they linked with earlier awareness and acquiescence to the sex-role stereotype.

Interestingly enough, Parson *et al.* (1982) found that parents attributed boys' success to ability whereas girls' success was put down to effort.

Although we may think we have made substantial progress in the area of equal opportunities, this is mostly the outward trap-pings of progress. The glittering prizes are still withheld from all but a token few of half of the human race. In 1996, the Women's Suffrage Movement will be 130 years old, and yet repression and suppression are still widespread in the most cultured of societies. In recent decades, it has been the covert attitudes which have been resistant to change. The language of suppression has been prominent and used to keep women from having aspirations, by questioning their womanliness and self-concept, and by degrading formerly innocent words which may be applied to them and converting them to insults: 'women', 'feminist', 'bra burner' and now 'politically correct'. As Dame Rebecca West said in 1913: 'I myself have never been able to find out precisely what a feminist is. I only know that people call me one whenever I express sentiments that differentiate me from a doormat or a prostitute.'

(Marcus, 1982)

Epilogue: educating the able into the twenty-first century

If we think of giftedness/high ability as innate, then the implication for educative processes are that they shall 'lead out' this quality, in accordance with the literal meaning of the word's root, the Latin *educere*. Educators and researchers would then spend a great deal of time and energy finding tests and inventories to identify highly able individuals, for whom they would provide educational settings which would nurture and enable these talents to develop. This could easily lead us to suggest that special schooling and segregation provision were necessary. Despite what some researchers say about the important contribution of environmental influences to the development and realization of high ability, they can often be observed spending the greater part of their time and energies on testing and identifying strategies. If intelligence is innate, then little can or needs to be done to promote it in the rest of the population.

If we believe that enriching environments and educative experiences contribute in large measure to the expression of high ability in a significant number of those of above average ability, then we might decide to address this in a different way. Our systems and strategies of child rearing and education might be changed or adjusted to enable the individuals to identify themselves through the expression of their capabilities on challenging educative activities. We might rely less on tests and screening devices and focus more upon integrated rather than segregated provision. In a sense, one can feel the strain and conflict between these two approaches in British Education returning.

NURTURE

Whereas the patterns of early socialization and interaction between high ability pre-schoolers and mothers promoted the development of checking, predicting, monitoring and reality testing (Moss, 1990), the interaction patterns of all parents and children are not like this. These scaffolding experiences, Moss argued, facilitated the acquisition of a repertoire of high-level thinking skills as a result of the continuous metacognitive commentary and dialogue. The thinking skills programmes used with disadvantaged groups, and the cognitive process strategies used with a wide variety of pupils in mainstream schools and students in higher education, have shown the ability to enhance cognitive competence in all groups. It is recommended that education for parenthood should be part of the curriculum for all school pupils, and should deal with issues of stereotyping as well as promoting the early development and use of thinking skills.

EDUCATION

> Indeed the urgent need to teach thinking skills at all levels continues, but we should not rely upon special courses and texts to do the job. Instead every teacher should create an atmosphere where students are encouraged to read deeply, to question, to engage in divergent thinking, to look for relationships among ideas and to grapple with real life issues.
>
> (Carr, 1988, p. 73)

In summary, there are six educational developments which I think we need in order to help all children, particularly the able. These are as follows:

- *Mentors*: all children need an adult to identify with who is on their side. In addition, highly able children need to meet and work with experts in fields of common interest and to receive their counsel.
- *CBC*: from an early stage, 'catch children being clever.' Encourage them to feel able and competent, and promote success and the self-concept.
- *CBG*: 'Catch them being good.' Praise and support all positive constructive behaviours rather than focusing on awkward and troublesome behaviours and being negative.
- *Cognitive process strategies*: incorporate these into all teaching across all curriculum areas.
- *Develop a whole-school, college or university policy* towards flexible teaching and learning and the needs of able students.
- *In service and initial teacher education programmes*: the study and use of teaching and learning strategies and cognitive processes should be made an integral part of training programmes for

teachers in schools and for tutors in further and higher education colleges and universities.

The final words are left to Graham Debling, head of Learning Methods Branch at the Employment Department, who had been funding 'Thinking and learning skills' projects at work for a number of years. Their forward thinking needs to be introduced to the Department of Education. This should be facilitated by the merger of the two Departments, now the Department for Education and Employment under the leadership of Gillian Shephard.

Thinking and learning at work
For many years the Employment Department (ED) has sponsored research and development work on learning skills as part of its overall aim to support economic growth by promoting a competitive, efficient and flexible labour market. This means helping to develop potential employees so that they are able to: take on responsibility for managing themselves, show initiative and deal with everyday problems. Employees need to be 'thinkers' at all organisational levels.

Debling, (1994)

References and Further Reading

Adey, P.S. (1991) Pulling yourself up by your own thinking. *European Journal for High Ability* 2, 28–34.

Alston, J. and Taylor, J. (1986) *The Handwriting File*. Wisbech: Learning Development Aids.

Amano, I. (1992) The light and dark sides of Japanese education. *Royal Society of Arts Journal* 145 (5424).

Anderson, H.H. (1960) The nature of creativity. *Studies in Art Education* 1 (2), 10–17.

Anderson, J.R. (1980) *Cognitive Psychology and its Implications*. San Francisco: Freeman.

Annett, M. (1983) 'Lefthandedness'. In M. Jeeves (ed.), *Psychology Survey*. Vol. 3. London: Allen and Unwin.

Arends, R. and Ford, P.M. (1964) *Acceleration and Enrichment in the Junior High School. A Follow Up Study, Research Report 03–05*. Olympia, WA: State Superintendent of Public Instruction.

Aronson, E. (1978) *The Jigsaw Classroom*. London: Sage.

Atkinson, J.W. and Raynor, J. (1974) *Motivation and Achievement*. Washington, DC: Winston and Sons.

Ausubel, D.P. (1961) Learning by discovery: rationale and mystique. *Bulletin of the National Association of Secondary Schools* 45, 18–58.

Bales, R.F. (1950) *Interaction Process Analysis: A Method for the Study of Small Groups*. Cambridge, MA: Addison Wesley.

Bales, R.F. (1961) *Interaction Process Analysis*. Cambridge, MA: Addison-Wesley.

Bannister, J., Sutherland, J. and Brown, J.W. Evaluating college teaching. *Curriculum Reporter Supplement. 1.*

Baumgarten, F. (1930) *Wünderkinder Psychologische untersuchungen*. Leipzig: Johann Ambrosius Barth.

Benn, C. (1982) The myth of giftedness. Part 2. *Forum* 24, 78–84.

Bennett, N. (1986) 'Co-operative learning. Children do it in groups – or do they?' Paper presented to the London Conference of DECP Section of the British Psychological Society.

Bennett, N. and Cass, J. (1986) 'Co-operative learning using computers'. Cited in N. Bennett, op. cit.

Bennett, N. and Jordan, A. (1975) A typology of teaching styles. *British Journal of Educational Psychology* 45 (1), 20–8.

Bereiter, C. and Engelmann, S. (1964) *Teaching the Disadvantaged Child in Preschool*. Englewood Cliffs, NJ: Prentice Hall.

Biermann, K.R. (1985) Indicators of creativity in mathematicians of the 17th to 19th century. *Rostock Mathematics Colloquium* **27**, 5–22.

Biggs, J.B. (1992) *Why and How do Hong Kong Students Learn?* Education Papers 14. Hong Kong: Hong Kong University, Faculty of Education.

Binet, A. (1905) Concerning the assessment of intelligence. *Année Psychologique* **11**, 69–82.

Birenbaum, M. (1994) Towards adaptive assessment – the student's angle. *Studies in Educational Evaluation* **20**, 239–55.

Blackwell, F. (1991) 'A model for curriculum development. A study of a curriculum development in the USA and its subsequent pattern of dissemination and implementation in Britain'. MA Dissertation, University of East London.

Blagg, N. (1987) Instrumental enrichment: an evaluation of a project in three Somerset schools. *Times Educational Supplement*, September, p. 17.

Blagg, N. (1993) *Somerset Thinking Skills Course Handbook. Revised Edition*. Taunton: N. Blagg Associates.

Blakemore, C. (1977) *Mechanisms of the Mind*. Cambridge: Cambridge University Press.

Bloom, B.S. (ed.) (1956) *Taxonomy of Educational Objectives*. Vol. 1 London: Longman.

Bloom, B.S. (1985) *Developing Talent in Young People*. New York: Ballentine.

Bogen, J.E. and Bogen, G.M. (1969) The other side of the brain III. The corpus callosum and creativity. *Bulletin of Los Angeles Neurological Society* **34** (4), 191–220.

Bolanos, P. (1991) Unpublished paper. Cited by H. Gardner (1995c).

Bowers, S. and Wells, L. (1985) *Ways and Means. An Approach to Problem Solving. Handbook of the Kingston Friends Workshop Group*. Kingston: Learning Difficulties Research Project.

Bridges, S.A. (1969) *Gifted Children and the Brentwood Experiment*. London: Pitman.

Bridges, S.A. (1973) *IQ – 150*. London: Priory Press.

Bridges, S.A. (1975) *Gifted Children and the Millfield Experiment*. London: Pitman.

Broadfoot, P. (1986) *Profiles and Records of Achievement*. London: Holt Rinehart and Winston.

Brown, A.L., Bransford, J.D., Ferrara, R.A. and Campione, J.C. (1983) 'Learning, remembering and understanding'. In J. Flavell and E. Markman (eds), *Carmichael's Manual Of Psychology*. Vol. 1. New York: John Wiley.

Bruner, J. (1960) *The Process of Education*. Harvard: Harvard University Press.

Budoff, M. (1967) Learning potential among institutionalized young adult retardates. *American Journal of Mental Deficiency*, 72, 404–11.

Burke, B.S., Jensen, D.W. and Terman, L.M. (1930) *Genetic Studies of Genius. Vol. 3: The Promise of Youth, Follow up Studies of a Thousand Gifted Children*. Stanford, CA: Stanford University Press.

Burkhardt, R.C. (ed.) (1969) *The Assessment Revolution. New Viewpoints for Teacher Evaluation*. Albany, NY: New York State Education Department.

Butler-Por, N. (1987) *Underachievers in School. Issues and Interventions*. London: John Wiley.

Butler, N. and Nisan, M. (1975) Who's afraid of success and why. *Journal of Youth and Adolescence* 4, 259–70.

Buzan, T. (1974a) *Use Your Head*. London: BBC Publications.

Buzan, T. (1974b) *Living Decisions*. London: BBC Publications.

Calder, N. (1970) *The Mind of Man*. London: BBC Publications.

Callahan, C.M. and Hunsaker, S.L. (1991) 'Evaluation of acceleration programmes'. In W.T. Southern and E.D. Jones (eds) *The Academic Acceleration of Gifted Children*. New York: Teacher's College Press.

Callow, R. (1980) 'Recognising the gifted child'. In R. Povey (ed.) *Educating the Gifted Child*. London: Harper Row.

Callow, R. (1981) 'The Southport Inquiry and after'. In D.H.W. Grubb (ed.), *The Gifted Child at School*. Oxford: Society for Applied Studies in Educational Psychology.

Callow, R. (1983) Editorial. *PACE Newsletter*, May, 1.

Carr, K.S. (1988) How can we teach critical thinking? *Childhood Education* 65, 69–73.

Carroll, J.B. (1963) 'Mastery learning principles'. In J.H. Block. (ed.) *Mastery Learning*. New York: Holt Rinehart and Winston.

CATE (1983) *CATENOTE 1*. London: DES.

Cattell, J.M. (1915) Families of American men of science. *Popular Science Monthly* 86, 504–15.

Clarke, B. (1988) *Growing Up Gifted*. Columbus, OH: Merrill.

Congdon, P.J. (1978) *Teaching Able Children. A Handbook of Practical Suggestions*. Solihull: Gifted Children's Information Centre.

Cornell, D.G., Callaghan, C.M. and Lloyd, B.H. (1991) Socio-emotional adjustment of adolescent girls enrolled in a residential acceleration program. *Gifted Child Quarterly* 35 (2), 48–56.

Covington, M.V., Crutchfield, R.S., Olton, R. and Davies, L. (1972) *The Productive Thinking Program*. Columbus, OH: Merrill.

Cowdery, L.L., Montgomery, D., Morse, P. and Prince-Bruce, M. (1983–7) *Teaching Reading Through Spelling*. Vols 1–7. Kingston: Kingston Polytechnic, Learning Difficulties Research Project and now Frondeg Hall Publishers.

Cox, C.M. (1926) *Genetic Studies of Genius. Vol. 2: The Early Mental Traits of 300 Geniuses*. Stanford, CA: Stanford University Press.

Cropley, A.J. (1994) Creative intelligence. A concept of true giftedness. *European Journal of High Ability* 5, 16–23.

Dearing, R. (1994) *National Curriculum Revised*. York: National Curriculum Council.

Debling, G. (1994) Promotional letter about DE funded projects, January. London: Department of Employment.

DES (1968) *Educating the Gifted*. London: HMSO.

DES (1974) *Gifted Children and their Education*. London: HMSO.

DES (1977) *Gifted Children in Middle and Comprehensive Schools*. London: HMSO.

DES (1980) *Statistical Bulletin*. London: HMSO.

DES (1984) *Records of Achievements, A Statement of Policy*. London: HMSO.

de Bono, E. (1970) *Lateral Thinking*. London: Ward Lock Educational.

de Bono, E. (1971) *Lateral Thinking for Management*. Harmondsworth: Penguin.

de Bono, E. (1975) *CoRT (Cognitive Research Trust) Thinking*. Blandford: Forum Direct Educational Services.

de Bono, E. (1976) *Thinking Action*. Blandford: Forum Direct Educational Services.

de Bono, E. (1983) *CoRT Thinking Programme*. Oxford: Pergamon.

De Haan, R.F. and Havighurst, R.J. (1957) *Educating Gifted Children*. Chicago: Chicago University Press.

Denton, C. (1986) 'Identification of able children project results'. DES Oxford Conference Presentation.

Denton, C. and Postlethwaite, K. (1985) *Able Children – Identifying them in the Classroom*. Windsor: NFER-Nelson.

Deutsch, G. and Springer, S. (1986) *Left Brain Right Brain*. 2nd edn. San Francisco: Freeman.

Down, J.L. (1887) *On Some of the Mental Affections of Childhood and Youth*. London: Churchill.

Dransfield, J.E. (1933) Administration of enrichment to superior children in the typical classroom. Contributions to Education **558**. New York: Teacher's College, Columbia University.

Dukes, R.L. and Seidner, C.J. (1978) *Learning with Simulations and Games*. London: Sage.

Dykstra, L. (1990) *Keynote Address on Learning Disabilities*. Washington, DC: Department for Education.

Ediger, M. (1994) Measurement and evaluation. *Studies in Educational Evaluation*, **20** (2), 169–74.

Elliott, C.D. (1983) *British Ability Scales. Handbook and Technical Manual*. Windsor: NFER/Nelson.

Elshout, J. (1990) Expertise and giftedness. *European Journal for High Ability* **1**, 197–203.

Erikson, E.H. (1963) *Childhood and Society*. New York: Norton.

Eriksson, G. (1988) Thinking in visual images in the information age – the changing faces of school. *Gifted Education International* **5**, 97–103.

Fawcett Society (1995) *Equal Citizenship Briefing Pack*. London: Fawcett Society.

Feldhusen, J.F. (1990) 'Conception of creative thinking and creativity training'. Presentation at the 1990 International Creativity and Research Networking Conference, Buffalo, NY.

Feldhusen, J.F. (1992) *Talent Identification and Development in Education*. Sarasota, FL: Center for Creative Learning.

Feldhusen, J.F., Treffinger, D.J. and Balke, K. (1969) *Creative Thinking and Problem Solving in Gifted Education*. Dubuque: Kendall Hunt.

Feldhusen, J.F., Treffinger, D.J. and Balke, K. (1970) Developing creative thinking. The Purdue Creativity Program. *Journal of Creative Behaviour* **4** (2), 85–90.

Feldman, D. (1980) *Beyond Universals in Cognitive Development*. Norwood, NJ: Ablex.

Feldman, D. (1986) *Nature's Gambit. Child Prodigies and the Development of Human Potential*. New York: Basic Books.

Feller, M. (1994) Open book testing and education for the future. *Studies in Educational Evaluation* **20** (2), 235–8.

Feuerstein, R. (1970) 'A dynamic approach to the causation, prevention and alleviation of retarded performance'. In H.C. Haywood (ed.), *Sociocultural Aspects of mental Retardation*. New York: Appleton Century-Crofts.

Feuerstein, R. (1979) 'Learning Potential Assessment Device (LPAD)'. In *The Dynamic Assessment of Retarded Performers*. Baltimore, MD: University Park Press.

Feuerstein, R. (1980) *Instrumental Enrichment*. Baltimore, MD: University Park Press.

Feuerstein, R. (1990) 'Mediated learning keynote presentation'. 2nd International Conference on High Ability, European Council for High Ability, Budapest.

Feuerstein, R. (1993) Mediated learning experience keynote presentation. MLE Conference, February, London.

Feuerstein, R., Klein, P.S. and Tannenbaum, A.J. (1991) *Mediated Learning Experience (MLE): Theoretical, Psychological and Learning Implications*. London: Freund.

Feuerstein, R., Rand, Y., Hoffman, M. and Miller, R. (1980) *Instrumental Enrichment. An Intervention Program for Cognitive Modifiability*. Illinois: Scott Foresman.

Fine, B. (1967) *Underachievers: How Can They Be Helped?* New York: Dalton.

Fisher, R. (1994) *Teaching Children to Think*. Hemel Hempstead: Simon and Schuster.

Flavell, J.H. (1979) Metacognition and cognitive monitoring. *American Psychologist*. 34, 906–11.

Fleming, C.M. (1962) 'Can the pool of talent be increased?' In G.Z. Bereday and J.A. Lauwerys (eds), *The Gifted Child Yearbook on Education*. New York: Harcourt Brace and World.

Flynn, J.R. (1987) Massive IQ gains in 14 nations. What IQ tests really measure. *Psychological Bulletin* **101**, 171–91.

Flynn, J.R. (1988) Japanese intelligence simply fades away. *Psychologist* **1**, 348–50.

Frank, L. (1970) 'The effects of subject controlled learning procedures on performance on Koh's Blocks designs'. Unpublished report cited by H.C. Haywood, J.W. Filler, M.A. Shifman and G. Chatelanet (1975) 'Behavioural assessment in mental retardation'. In P. Reynolds (ed.) *Advances in Psychological Assessment*. Vol. 3. London: Jossey Bass.

Frasier, M.M. (1993) 'Issues, problems and programs in mentoring the disadvantaged and culturally different talented'. In K. Heller, F. Monks and A.H. Passow (eds) *International Handbook of Research and Develop-*

ment of Giftedness and Talent. Oxford: Pergamon.

Freeman, J. (1979) *Gifted Children: Their Identification and Development in a Social Context*. Lancaster: MTP Press, and Baltimore, MD: University Park Press.

Freeman, J. (ed.) (1985) *Psychology of Giftedness*. London: John Wiley.

Freeman, J. (1988) 'The nature of giftedness and high ability'. Presidential Address at the First International Conference of the European Council for High Ability, Zurich.

Freeman, J. (1991) *Gifted Children Growing Up*. London: Cassell.

French, J.L. (1964) *Educating the Gifted*. New York: Henry Holt.

French, S.J. and Cooper, R.M. (1964) *Pilot Project for Improving College Teaching – The Florida Teaching Project*. Tampa, FL: University of South Florida.

Freud, S. (1932) *Leonardo da Vinci: A Psychosexual Study of Infantile Reminiscence*. London: Kegan Paul.

Frostig, M. and Horn, D. (1964) *The Frostig Programme for Development of Visual Perception*. Chicago: Follett.

Fulleylove, E. (1984) *Starting Points for Drama*. Banbury: Kemble Press.

Furneaux, W.D.C. (1962) 'Methods of selection for English universities'. In G.Z. Bereday and J.A. Lauwerys (eds), *The Gifted Child*. New York: Harcourt Brace and World.

Gagné, F. (1985) Giftedness and talent. A re-examination of the definitions. *Gifted Child Quarterly* **29**, 103–12.

Gagné, F. (1994) 'Gifts and talents: the value of peer nominations'. Keynote address, 4th International Conference of the European Council for High Ability (ECHA), October, University of Nijmegen, The Netherlands.

Gagné, R.L. (1973) *The Essentials of Learning*. London: Holt Rinehart and Winston.

Gagné, R.L. (1977) *The Conditions of Learning. 3rd edn*. London: Holt Rinehart and Winston.

Gallagher, J.J. (1969) 'Gifted children'. In R.L. Ebel (ed.) *Encyclopaedia of Educational Research. 4th edn*. New York: Macmillan.

Gallagher, J.J. (1985) *Teaching the Able*. New York: Allen and Boston.

Galton, F. (1869) *Hereditary Genius*. London: Collins.

Galton, M., Simon, R. and Croll, P. (1985) *Inside the Primary Classroom*. London: Routledge and Kegan Paul.

Gardner, H. (1983) *Frames of Mind*. New York: Basic Books.

Gardner, H. (1990) *Frames of Mind. 2nd edn*. New York: Basic Books.

Gardner, H. (1993) *Creative Minds*. London: Basic Books.

Gardner, H. (1994) *The Unschooled Mind*. London: Fontana Press.

Gardner, H. (1995a) Creating creativity. *Times Educational Supplement*, 6 Jan., p. 15.

Gardner, H. (1995b) Machines of the brain. *Times Educational Supplement*, 17 Mar. p. 24.

Gardner, H. (1995c) Creativity – new views from psychology and education. *Royal Society of Arts Journal*, **148** (5459), 33–42.

Gazzaniga, R. (1967) Split brain in man. *Scientific American*, 217, 24–9.

George, R.D. (1992) *The Challenge of the Able Child*. London: David Fulton.

Getzels, J.W. (1970) 'Creative administration and organizational change. An essay in theory'. In L.J. Rubin (ed.) *Frontiers of School Leadership*. Chicago: Rand-McNally, pp. 69–85.

Getzels, J.W. and Jackson, P.W. (1962) *Creativity and Intelligence: Explorations with Gifted Students*. New York: John Wiley.

Gibbs, G. (1980) *Study Methods Group*. Buckingham: Open University.

Gibbs, G. (1981) *Teaching Students to Learn. A Student Centred Approach*. Milton Keynes: Open University Press.

Gibbs, G. (1990) 'Improving the quality of student learning: a summary poster'. Oxford: Oxford Centre for Staff Development.

Gibbs, G. (ed.) (1994) Preface in *Improving Student Learning*. Oxford: Oxford Centre for Staff Development.

Gibbs, G. (ed.) (1995) *2nd International Symposium on Improving Student Learning*, Oxford: Oxford Centre for Staff Development.

Glaser, R. (1985) *Thoughts on Expertise*. (Report No. 8). Pittsburg: University of Pittsburg, Learning Research and Development Center.

Glasser, W. (1965) *Reality Therapy*. New York: Harper and Row.

Glasser, W. (1969) *Schools without a Future*. New York: Harper and Row.

Goldberg, M.L. (1965) *Research on the Talented*. New York: Teachers College, Columbia University.

Good, T.L. and Brophy, J.E. (1973) *Looking in Classrooms*. New York, Harper & Row.

Good, T.L. and Brophy, J.E. (1977) *Educational Psychology: A Realistic Approach*. London: Holt Rinehart and Winston.

Gowen, J.C. and Demos, G.D. (1964) *The Education and Guidance of the Ablest*. Springfield, IL: Charles C. Thomas.

Gubbay, S.S. (1976) *The Clumsy Child*. London: Saunders.

Guilford, J.P. (1950) Creativity. *American Psychologist* **5**, 444–54.

Guilford, J.P. (1959) The three faces of intellect. *American Psychologist* **14**, 469–79.

Guilford, J.P. (1967) Creativity: yesterday, today and tomorrow. *Journal of Creative Behaviour* **1**, 3–14.

Gustad, J.W. (1961) *Policies and Practices in Faculty Evaluation*. Washington, DC: American Council on Education.

Hale, C. (1985) 'Evaluation report on teaching able children'. Kingston: Learning Difficulties Research Project.

Hanf Buckley, M. (1971) Mapping, *Journal of Reading*, January, p. 228.

Hany, E.A. (1993) How teachers identify gifted students: feature processing of concept based classification. *European Journal for High Ability* **4**, 196–211.

Hassenstein, M. (1988) 'Elements of a natural history of intelligence'. Cited in A.J. Cropley (1994) Creative intelligence: a concept of true giftedness. *European Journal for High Ability* **4**, 196–211.

Havighurst, R.J. (1961) *Developmental Tasks and Education. 2nd edn*. New York: Plenum Press.

Haywood, H.C. and Heal, L.W. (1968) Retention of learned visual associations as a function of IQ and learning levels. *American Journal of Mental*

Deficiency, 72, 828–38.

Haywood, H.C. and Heal, L.W. (eds) (1970) *Socio-cultural Aspects of Mental Retardation*. New York: Appleton-Century-Crofts.

Head Start Bureau (1985) *Project Head Start Fact Sheet*. Washington DC: US Administration for Children, Youth and Families.

Hegarty, S., Pocklington, K. with Lucas, D. (1981) *Educating Pupils with Special Needs in Ordinary Schools*. Windsor: NFER-Nelson.

Heim, A. (1970) *Intelligence and Personality. Their Assessment and Relationship*. Baltimore, MD: Penguin.

Heinelt, G. (1974) *Creative Teachers – Creative Students*. Freiberg: Herder.

Heller, K., Mönks, F. and Passow, A.H. (eds) (1993) *International Handbook of Research and Development of Giftedness and Talent*. Oxford: Pergamon.

Herbert, M. (1975) *Problems of Childhood*. London: Pan Books.

Hirst, P. (1966) Language as thought. *Proceedings of the Philosophy and Education Society of Great Britain*, 63–75.

HMI (1979) *Aspects of Secondary Education*. London: HMSO.

HMI (1983) *Science in Primary Schools*. London: HMSO.

HMI (1985) *Education Observed 3: Good Teachers*. London: HMSO.

HMI (1987) *Primary Schools: Some Aspects of Good Practice*. London: HMSO.

HMI (1988) *Ten Good Schools*. London: HMSO.

HMI (1992) *Provision for Highly Able Pupils in Maintained Schools*. London: HMSO.

Hollingworth, L. (1926) *Gifted Children*. New York: World Books.

Hollingworth, L. (1942) *Children Above 180 IQ Stanford-Binet. Origin and Development*. New York: World Books.

Horner, M.S. (1968) 'Sex differences in achievement and performance in competitive and non-competitive situations'. PhD Dissertation, University of Michigan.

Howe, M. (1988) Hothouse children. *Psychologist* 1 (9), 356–9.

Hudson, L. (1966) *Contrary Imaginations*. London: Methuen.

Hurd, S. (1993) 'It'. A conference for the most able youngsters in the Northampton area. *Flying High*, June, 21–2.

Hyman, C.A. and Mitchell, R. (1975) A psychological study of child battering. *Health Visitor* 12 (1), 13–28.

Johnson, D. and Johnson, R. (1975) *Learning Together and Alone*. Englewood Cliffs, NJ: Prentice Hall.

Johnson, H.W. (1964) Another study method: SP3R. *Journal of Developmental Reading* 7, 269–82.

Johnson, S.K. and Corn, A.L. (1989) The past, present and future for gifted children with sensory or physical disabilities. *Roeper Review* 12 (1), 13–28.

Jung, C.G. (1954) 'The gifted child'. In H. Read, M. Fordham and G. Alder (eds), *The Collected Works of C.J. Jung*. Vol. 17. New York: Pantheon Books.

Kanevsky, L.S. (1992) 'The learning game'. In P. Klein and A.J. Tannenbaum (eds), *To Be Young and Gifted*. Norwood, NJ: Ablex.

Kanevsky, L.S. (1994) A comparative study of children's learning in the zone of proximal development. *European Journal for High Ability* 5, 163–75.

Karnes, M.B. and Johnson, L.J. (1991) 'Gifted handicapped'. In N. Colangelo and G.A. Davis (eds), *Handbook of Gifted Education*. Boston: Allyn and Bacon.

Kelly, G.A. (1955) *The Psychology of Personal Constructs*. 2 vols. New York: Norton.

Kellmer Pringle, M. (1970) *Able Misfits*. London: Longman.

Kerry, T. (1981) *Teaching Bright Pupils in Mixed Ability Classes*. London: Macmillan.

Kerry, T. (1983) *Finding and Helping the Able Child*. London: Croom Helm.

Koestler, A. (1966) *The Act of Creation*. Harmondsworth, Middx: Penguin.

Kolb, D.A. (1984) *Experiential Learning: Experience as a Source of Learning and Development*. New York: Prentice Hall.

Koretz, D., Stecher, B. and Deibert, E. (1992) *The Vermont Portfolio Assessment Program. Interim Report on Implementation and Impact 1991–1992 School Year*. Washington, DC: RAND/CRESST.

Kosc, L. (1974) Developmental dyscalculia. *Journal of Learning Disabilities* 7, 46–59.

Kulik, J.A. and Kulik, C.C. (1984) Synthesis of research on effects of accelerated instruction. *Educational Leadership* 42 (2), 84–9.

Larkin, J., McDermott, J., Simon, D.P. and Simon, H.A. (1980) Expert and novice performance in solving physics problems. *Science* 208, 1335–42.

Lawton, D. (1968) *Social Class, Language and Education*. London: Routledge and Kegan Paul.

Lazar, I. and Darlington, D. (1982) Lasting effects of early education: A report from the Consortium for Longitudinal Studies. *Monographs of the Society for Research in Child Development*, 47.

Lazslo, M. (1987) Children with perceptuomotor difficulties in schools. *Times Educational Supplement*, 3 Sept.

Lehman, H.C. (1953) *Age and Achievement*, Princeton, NJ: Princeton University Press.

Lerner, J.W. (1971) *Children with Learning Disabilities*. Boston: Houghton Mifflin.

Linn, R.L., Baker, E. and Dunbar, S. (1991) Complex performance-based assessment. Expectations and validation criteria. *Educational Researcher* 16, 15–21.

Lipman, M. (1991) *Thinking in Education*. Cambridge: Cambridge University Press.

Lombroso, C. (1891) *The Man of Genius*. London: Scott.

Lovell, K. and Shields, J.B. (1967) Some aspects of a study of the gifted child. *British Journal of Educational Psychology*, 137, 201–8.

Mackinnon, D.W. (1965) Personality and the realisation of creative potential. *American Psychologist* 20, 273–81.

MacMillan, E. (1990) 'Teaching able children at the Discovery Centre in Canada'. Paper presented at the London Seminar of Middlesex University and ECHA – European Council for High Ability.

McCarthy, D. (1930) *The Language Development of the Pre-School Child*. Minneapolis: University of Minnesota Press.

McCarthy, D. (1972) *Manual for the McCarthy Scales of Children's Abilities*.

New York: Psychological Corporation.

McClelland, D.C., Atkinson, J.W., Clark, R.A. and Lowell, E.L. (1953) *The Achievement Motive*. New York: Appleton-Century-Crofts.

McClelland, D.C. (1961) *The Achieving Society*. New York: Free Press.

McClelland, D.C., Martin, M. and Richardson, C. (1970) *The Unit Based Curriculum*. Ypsilanti, MI: High Scope Press.

McClelland, D.C., Smith, K. *et al.* (1970) *The DISTAR Model*. Ypsilanti, MI: High Scope Press.

McClelland, D.C., Smith, K. *et al.* (1970b) *The Cognitively Orientated Curriculum*. Ypsilanti, MI: High Scope Press.

McLeod, J. and Cropley, A. (1989) *Fostering Academic Success*. Oxford: Pergamon.

Marjoram, D.T.E. (1985) *Teaching Able Children*. London: Kogan Page.

Marjoram, T. (1986) Better late than never – able youths and adults. *Gifted Education International* 4 (2), 89–96.

Marcus, J. (ed.) (1982) *The Young Rebecca Writings of Rebecca West, 1911–1917*. London: MacMillan.

Maslow, A.H. (1954) The creative attitude. *Structurist* 3, 4–10.

Meek, M. and Thomson, B. (1987) *Study Skills in the secondary School*. London: Routledge.

Miles, T.R. (1983) *Dyslexia, Patterns of Difficulty*. London: Granada.

Miles, T.R. (1991) *Bangor Dyslexia Test*. Wisbech: Learning Development Aids.

Miles, T.R. (1993) *Dyslexia, Patterns of Difficulty*. 2nd edn. London: Whurr.

Miles, T.R. and Miles, E. (1991) *Dyslexia and Mathematics*. London: Methuen.

Miller, G.A. (1960) 'The magical number seven plus or minus two'. In S. Wiseman (ed.), *Intelligence and Ability*. Harmondsworth: Penguin.

Mönks, F.J. (1992) 'Development of gifted children: The issue of identification and programming'. In F.J. Mönks and W. Peters (eds) *Talent for the Future*. Assen/Maastricht: Van Gorcum.

Mönks, F.J. and Mason, E.J. (1993) 'Developmental theories of giftedness'. In K.A. Heller, F.J. Mönks and A.H. Passon *International Handbook of Research and Development of Giftedness and Talent*. Oxford: Pergamon, pp. 89–101.

Mönks, F.J., Boxtel, H.W., Roelofs, J.J.W. and Sanders, M.P.M. (1986) 'The identification of gifted children in secondary education and a description of their situation in Holland'. In K.A. Heller and J.F. Feldhusen (eds), *Identifying and Nurturing the Gifted*. Toronto: Huber.

Montgomery, D. (1957) Unpublished study.

Montgomery, D. (1981) Education comes of age. *School Psychology International* 1, 1–3.

Montgomery, D. (1982) Teaching thinking skills in the school curriculum. *School Psychology International* 3 (4), 105–12.

Montgomery, D. (1983a) *Study Skills and Learning Strategies*. Kingston: Kingston Polytechnic, Learning Difficulties Project.

Montgomery, D. (1983b) Teaching the teachers of the gifted. *Gifted Education International* 2 (1), 32–4.

Montgomery, D. (1984) *Evaluation and Enhancement of Teaching Performance*. Kingston: Kingston Polytechnic, Learning Difficulties Project.

Montgomery, D. (1985) *The Needs of Able Children in Ordinary Classrooms*. Kingston: Kingston Polytechnic, Learning Difficulties Research Project.

Montgomery, D. (1988) Teacher appraisal. *New Era Journal* **68** (3), 85–90.

Montgomery, D. (1989) *Managing Behaviour Problems*. Sevenoaks: Hodder and Stoughton.

Montgomery, D. (1990) *Children with Learning Difficulties*. London: Cassell.

Montgomery, D. (1991) *The Special Needs of Able Pupils in Ordinary Classrooms*. Rev. edn. London: Middlesex University, Learning Difficulties Research Project.

Montgomery, D. (1993) 'Fostering learner-managed learning in teacher education'. In N. Graves (ed.) *Learner Managed Learning*. Leeds: Higher Education for Capability, pp. 59–70.

Montgomery, D. (1994a) 'The promotion of high ability and talent through education and instruction'. In K. Heller and E.A. Hany (eds) *Competence and Responsibility*. *Vol. 2*. Seattle and Gottingen: Hogrese and Huber.

Montgomery, D. (1994b) 'Enhancing student learning in higher education through the development and use of cognitive process strategies'. In G. Gibbs, *Improving Student Learning*. Oxford: Oxford Centre for Staff Development, pp. 227–53.

Montgomery, D. (in press) *Spelling. Remedial Strategies*. London: Cassell.

Montgomery, D. and Hadfield, N. (1989) *Practical Teacher Appraisal*. London: Kogan Page.

Montgomery, D. and Hadfield, N. (1990) *Appraisal in the Primary School*. Leamington Spa: Scholastic.

Morelock, M.J. and Feldman, D.H. (1993) 'Prodigies and savants. What have they to tell us about giftedness and human cognition?' In K. Heller, F. Monks and A.H. Passow (eds) *International Handbook of Research and Development of Giftedness and Talent*. Oxford: Pergamon.

Moss, E. (1990) Social interaction and metacognitive development in gifted preschoolers. *Gifted Child Quarterly* **34**, 16–20.

NACE/DFE (1993–) *Information Leaflet*. Northampton: NACE.

NAGC (1984) *Survey of Able Children's Needs*. London: NAGC (now at Nene College).

NAGC (1989) *Help with Bright Children*. London: NAGC (now at Nene College).

NAGC (1990) *According to their Needs*. London: NAGC (now at Nene College).

Neagley, R.L. and Evans, N.D. (1967) *Handbook for Effective Curriculum Development*. Englewood Cliffs, NJ: Prentice Hall.

Neisser, U. (1967) *Cognitive Psychology*. New York: Appleton-Century-Crofts.

Necka, E. (1986) 'On the nature of creative talent'. In A.J. Cropley, K.K. Urban, H. Wagner and W. Wieczerkowski (eds) *Giftedness: A Continuing World Wide Challenge*. New York: Trillium Press, pp. 131–40.

Nickerson, R.S., Perkins, D.N. and Smith, E.E. (1985) *The Teaching of Thinking*. Hillsdale, NJ: Lawrence Erlbaum.

Nisbet, J.F. (1891) *The Insanity of Genius and the General Inequality of Human Faculty Physiologically Considered*. London: Ward and Downey.

Noller, R.B., Parnes, S.J. and Bondi, A.M. (1976) *Creative Action Book*. New York: Scribner.

O'Connor, N. (1989) The performance of the 'idiot-savant' implicit and explicit. *British Journal of Disorders of Communication*, 24, 1–20.

Ogilvie, E. (1980) *Gifted Children in Primary Schools*. London: Macmillan.

Ornstein, R. (1982) *The Psychology of Consciousness*. 2nd edn. San Francisco: Freeman.

Painter, F. (1982) Gifted secondary pupils in England. *School Psychology International* 3 (4) 237–44.

Palmer, M. (1989) Philosophy at Manchester Grammar School. *Cognito* Spring, 72–5.

Parkyn, G.W. (1948) *Children of High Intelligence*. London: Oxford University Press.

Parson, J. E., Adler, T. F. and MacZala, C. M. (1982) Socialization of achievement attitudes and beliefs: parental influences. *Child Development* 53, 310–32.

Passow, A.H. (1966) *Youth Talent Project: Ventura County Superintendent of Schools Office: Report on 1st Phase Operation*. Ventura County CA.

Passow, A.H. (1981) *Education for Gifted Children and Youth*. Ventura, CA: Ventura County Superintendent of Schools Office.

Passow, A.H. (1982a) *Differentiated Curricula for the Gifted/Talented. Committee Report to National State Leadership Training Institute on Gifted and Talented*. Ventura County CA: Ventura County Superintendent of Schools Office.

Passow, A.H. (1982b) 'Differential curriculum for the gifted/talented. A point of view'. In S.N. Kaplan *et al.* (eds) *Curricula for the Gifted* Ventura County CA: Ventura County Superintendent of Schools Office.

Passow, A.H. (1988) Reflections on three decades of education of the gifted. *Gifted Education International* 1, 1–4.

Passow, A.H. (1990) Needed research and development in educating high ability children. *European Journal of High Ability* 1 (4), 15–24.

Passow, A.H. and Goldberg, M.L. (1951) *The Talented Youth Project: A Progress Report. Horace Mann-Lincoln Institute of School Experimentation*. New York: Teachers' College, Columbia University.

Paul, R. (1990) 'Critical thinking'. In *Critical Thinking Handbook*. Sonoma: Sonoma State University, Centre for Critical Thinking and Moral Critique.

Peters, M. (1970) *Success in Spelling*. Cambridge: Cambridge Institute of Education.

Peters, M. and Smith, B. (1986) 'The productive process: An approach to literacy for children with difficulties'. In B. Root (ed.) *Resources for Reading*. London: UKRA, pp. 161–71.

Piaget, J. (1952) *Origins of Intelligence in Children*. 2nd edn. New York: International Universities Press.

Pickard, P.M. (1976) *If You think Your Child is Gifted*. London: Allen and Unwin.

Plowden Report (1967) *Children and Their Primary Schools*. London: HMSO.

Pole, C.J. (1993) *Assessing and Recording Achievement*. Buckingham: Open University.

Pollard, S. (1989) *A Study of the Use of Cognitive Process Methods in an Ordinary Classroom*. Kingston: Learning Difficulties Research Project.

Poorthuis, E., Kok, L. and Van Dijk, J. (1990) 'A Curriculum assessment tool'. Paper presented at the 2nd Biennial European Conference of the European Council for High Ability (ECHA), Budapest, October.

Pyke, N. (1993) Ablest 'being hindered'. *Times Educational Supplement* 22 Oct., p.7.

Race, P. (1992) 'Developing competence'. In *Professorial Inaugural Lectures*. Glamorgan: University of Glamorgan.

Radford, J. (1990) *Child Prodigies and Exceptionally Early Achievers*. New York: Free Press.

Radford, J. (1993) 'Child prodigies'. Paper presented at British Assocation for Science Conference.

Raph, J.B., Goldberg, M.L. and Passow, A.H. (1966) *Bright Underachievers*. New York: Teachers' College Press.

Raven, J.C. (1956) *The Raven's Progressive Matrices*. London: Lewis.

Rayder, N.F. (1968) College student ratings of instructors. *Journal of Experimental Education* 37 (2), 76–81.

Renzulli, J.S. (1977) *The Enrichment Triad Model. A Guide for Developing Defensible Programs for the Gifted and Talented*. Mansfield Center, CN: Creative Learning Press.

Resnick, L.B. (1989) *Knowing, Learning and Instuction. Essays in Honour of Robert Glaser*. Hillsdale, NJ: Lawrence Erlbaum.

Revesz, G. (ed.) (1925) *The Psychology of a Musical Prodigy*. New York: Basic Books. Reprinted 1970.

Rey, A. (1934) A procedure for evaluating educability. Some applications in psychopathology. *Archives de Psychologie*, 24, 297–337.

Robinson, F.P. (1967) *Effective Reading*. New York: Harper & Row.

Rogers, K.S. and Span, P. (1993) 'Ability grouping with gifted and talented students. Research guidelines'. In K.A. Heller, F. Monks and A.H. Passow (eds) *International Handbook of Research and Development of Giftedness and Talent*. Oxford: Pergamon.

Roth, J.A. and Meyersberg, H.A. (1963) The non-achievement syndrome. *Personnel and Guidance Journal* 41, 500–535.

Royce-Adams, W. (1977) *Developing Reading Versatility*. New York: Rinehart and Winston.

Rutler, M. (1975) *Helping Troubled Children*. Harmondsworth, Middx: Penguin.

Rutler, M., Tizard, J. and Whitmore, K. (eds) (1970) *Education, Health and Behaviour*. London: Longman.

Saunders, L. (1989) *Report on a Study of Conflict Management in Classrooms*. London: ISTD/ Kings College.

Schools Council (1980) *Study Skills in the Secondary School Project Trial Materials*. London: Schools Council.

SED (1978) *The Education of Pupils with Learning Difficulties in Primary and*

Secondary Schools. A Progress Report by HMI. Edinburgh: HMSO.

Selfe, L. (1977) *Nadia, A Case of Extraordinary Drawing Ability in an Autistic Child.* New York: Academic Press.

Selfe, L. (1983) *Normal and Anomalous Drawing Representational Ability in Children.* London: Academic Press.

Shakeshaft, C. (1990) *Women in Educational Administration.* London: Sage.

Shavinina, L.S. (1994) Specific intelligence in intentions and creative giftedness. *European Journal for High Ability* 5, 145–52.

Shayer, M. and Adey, P.S. (1981) *Towards a Science of Teaching.* London: Heinemann.

Shields, J. (1967) *The Gifted Child.* Windsor: NFER.

Shipley, P. and Webster, K. (1988) *CDT Projects for GCSE* London: Heinemann.

Schonberg, H.C. (1970) *The Lives of the Great Composers.* New York: Norton.

Shore, B.M. (1991) How do gifted children think differently? *Journal of the Gifted and Talented Education Council of the Alberta Teacher's Association,* 5(2), 19–23.

Shore, B.M. and Kanevsky, L.S. (1993) 'Thinking processes'. In K.A. Heller, F. Monks and A.H. Passow (eds) *International Handbook of Research and Development of Giftedness and Talent.* Oxford: Pergamon.

Shore, B.M. and Tsiamis, A. (1986) 'Identification by provision'. In K.A. Heller and J.F. Feldhusen (eds) *Identifying and Nurturing the Gifted.* Bern: Huber.

Shore, B.M., Pinker, S. and Bates, M. (1991) Research as a model for university teaching. *Higher Education* 19 (1), 21–35.

Sisk, D. (1991) 'Leadership training for gifted students'. Presentation at the World Council for Gifted Children Conference, The Hague, The Netherlands.

Sisk, D. and Shallcross, D. (1986) *Leadership. Making Things Happen.* New York: Bearly.

Simonton, D.K. (1988) *Scientific Genius. A Psychology of Science.* Cambridge: Cambridge University Press.

Skilbeck, M. (1989) *School Development and New Approaches to Learning: Trends and Issues in Curriculum Reform.* Paris: OECD.

Slavin, R.E. (1977) 'Student team learning techniques: Narrowing the gap between the races'. Report No. 228. Baltimore: John Hopkins Unversity, Center for Social Organization of Schools.

Slavin, R.E. (1987) Ability grouping. A best evidence synthesis. *Review of Educational Research* 60, 471–99.

Slavin, R.E. (1990) *Co-operative Learning. Theory, Research and Practice.* Englewood Cliffs, NJ: Prentice Hall.

Snow, C. P. (1959) *The Two Cultures and the Scientific Revolution.* Cambridge: Cambridge University Press.

Southern, W.T. and Jones, E.D. (1991) 'Academic acceleration. Background issues'. In W.T. Southern and E.D. Jones (eds) *The Academic Acceleration of Gifted Children.* New York: Teachers College Press.

Southern, W.T., Jones, E.D. and Stanley, J.C. (1993) 'Acceleration and enrichment. The context and development of program options'. In K.A.

Heller, F. Monks and A.H. Passow (eds) *International Handbook of Research and Development of Giftedness and Talent*. Oxford: Pergamon.

Spearman, C. (1927) *The Abilities of Man*. New York: Macmillan.

Spender, D. (1981) *Invisible Women: The Schooling Scandal*. London: Writers and Readers.

Springer, S. and Deutsch, G. (1985) *Left Brain, Right Brain*. San Francisco: Freeman.

Stephenson, J. and Weil, S. (1988) 'Higher education for capability'. HEC Launch Presentation. Leeds: Higher Education for Capability Publication.

Sternberg, R.J. (1985) *Beyond IQ. A Triarchic Theory of Human Intelligence*. New York: Cambridge University Press.

Sternberg, R.J. and Davidson, J.C. (1986) *Concepts of Giftedness*. Cambridge: Cambridge University Press.

Sternberg, R.J. and Lubert, T.I. (1991) An investment theory of creativity and its development. *Human Development* **34**, 1–31.

Stonier, T. (1983) *The Wealth of Information*. London: Methuen.

Tannenbaum, A.J. (1983) *Gifted Children*. London: Macmillan.

Tannenbaum, A.J. (1993) 'History of giftedness and gifted education in world perspective'. In K.A. Heller, F. Monks and A.H. Passow (eds) *International Handbook of Research and Development of Giftedness and Talent*. Oxford: Pergamon.

Tansley, P. and Pankhurst, J. (1981) *Children with Specific Learning Disabilities*. Windsor: NFER-Nelson.

Taylor, C.W. (1968) Multiple talent approach: A teaching scheme in which most students can be above average. *Instructor*, 77/8, 142–6.

Taylor, E.A. (1960) *Controlled Reading*. Chicago: Chicago University Press.

Taylor, C.W. (1969) The highest talent potentials of man. *Gifted Child Quarterly* **13** (1), 9–30.

Taylor, K. (ed.) (1991) *Drama Strategies: New Ideas from London Drama*. London: Heinemann.

Teare, J.B. (1988) *A School Policy of Provision for Able Pupils*. Northampton: NACE.

Tempest, N.R. (1974) *Teaching Clever Children 7–11*. London: Routledge and Kegan Paul.

Tennyson, R.D. and Rasch, M. (1988) Linking cognitive learning theory to instrumental prescription. *Industrial Science* **17**, 368–83.

Terman, L.M. (1917) The intelligence quotient of Francis Galton in childhood. *American Journal of Psychology* **28**, 209–15.

Terman, L.M. (1925) *Genetic Studies of Genius. Vol. 1: Mental and Physical Traits of a Thousand Gifted Children*. Stanford, CA: Stanford University Press.

Terman, L.M. and Oden, M.H. (1934) *Genetic Studies of Genius. Vol. 3: Twenty-five Years' Follow-up of a Superior Group*. Stanford, CA: Stanford University Press.

Terman, L.M. and Oden, M.H. (1947) *Genetic Studies of Genius. Vol. 4: The Gifted Child Grows Up*. Stanford, CA: Stanford University Press.

Terman, L.M. (1954) The discovery and encouragement of exceptional talent. *American Psychologist* **9**, 221–30.

Terman, L.M. and Oden, M.H. (1959) *Genetic Studies of Genius. Vol. 5: The Gifted Group at Mid Life: 35 Years' Follow-up.* Stanford, CA: Stanford University Press.

Terrell, I. (1993) 'Student responses to mainstream and distance learning experiences'. Unpublished paper, School of Education, Middlesex University, London.

Thomas, L.F. and Harri-Augstein, E.S. (1971) Project materials used with psychology and teacher education group at Kingston Polytechnic by L.F. Thomas.

Thomas, L.F. and Harri-Augstein, E.S. (1975) *Reading to Learn: Research Project Report.* London Brunel University: Centre for the Studies of Human Learning.

Thomas, L.F. and Harri-Augstein, E.S. (1985) *Self Organised Learning.* London: Routledge and Kegan Paul.

Thomson, M. (1984) *Developmental Dyslexia.* London: Edward Arnold.

Thorndike, E.L. (1913) *The Psychology of Learning, Education and Psychology.* Vol. 2. New York: Teacher's College Press.

Thurstone, L.L. (1938) 'Primary mental abilities'. Psychometric Monograph No. 1. Chicago IL: University of Chicago Press.

Tilsley, P.J. (1981) 'Attitudes and opinions on gifted children and their education'. In A.H. Kramer (ed.) *Gifted Children Challenging their Potential.* New York: Trillium Press.

Torrance, E.P. (1962) *Guiding Creative Talent.* New York: Prentice Hall.

Torrance, E.P. (1963) *Education and the Creative Potential.* Minneapolis: University of Minnesota.

Torrence, E.P. (1965) *Gifted Children in the Classroom.* New York: Collier Macmillan.

Torrance, E.P. (1966) *Torrance Tests of Creative Thinking.* 1st edn. Princeton, NJ: Personnel Press.

Torrance, E.P. (1971) 'Long range predictive studies of creative thinking and their international extensions'. Paper presented at the 17th International Congress of Psychology, Belgium.

Torrance, E.P. (1975) Sociodrama as a creative problem solving approach to studying the future. *Journal of Creative Behaviour* 9 (3), 182–5.

Torrance, E.P. and Hall, I.K. (1980) Assessing the further reaches of creative potential. *Journal of Creative Behaviour* 14, 1–19.

Treffert, D.A. (1989) *Extraordinary People. Understanding Idiot-savants.* New York: Harper and Row.

Trent, J.W. and Cohen, A.M. (1973) 'Research on teaching in higher education'. In R.M.W. Travis (ed.) *Second Handbook of Research on Teaching.* Chicago: Rand-McNally, pp. 997–1071.

Urban, K.K. (1990) Recent trends in creativity research and theory in Western Europe. *European Journal of High Ability* 1, 99–113.

Urban, K.K. and Jellen, H.G. (1986) 'Assessing creative potential via drawing production. The test for creative thinking and drawing productivity'. In A.J. Cropley, K.K. Urban, H. Wagner and W.H. Wiecz-erkowski (eds) *Giftedness. A Continuing World Wide Challenge.* New York: Trillium Press.

Usborn, A.F. (1953) *Applied Imagination, Principles and Procedures of Creative Thinking*. New York: Scribner.

Van Tassel-Baska, J. (1985) 'Acceleration'. In J. Maker (ed.) *Critical Issues in Gifted Education*. Rockville, MD: Aspen Publications.

Van Tassel-Baska, J. (1993) 'Theory and research on curricular development for the gifted'. In K.A. Heller, F.J. Mönks and A.H. Passon, *International Handbook of Research and Development of Giftedness and Talent*. Oxford: Pergamon.

Vellutino, F.R. (1979) *Dyslexia Theory and Research*. New York: MIT Press.

Vernon, P.E. (ed.) (1970) *Creativity: Selected Readings*. Harmondsworth. Penguin.

Vygotsky, L.S. (1962) *Thought and Language*. Trans. E. Haufmann and G. Vakar. Boston: MIT Press.

Vygotsky, L.S. (1978) *Mind in Society*. Cambridge, MA: Harvard University Press.

Walberg, H.J. (1995) 'Nurturing children for adult success'. In M.W. Katzco and F.J. Monks (eds), *Nurturing Talent: Individual Needs and Social Abilities*. Assen: Van Gorcum.

Wallace, A. (1986) *The Prodigy: A Biography of William James Sidis, the World's Greatest Child Prodigy*. London: Macmillan.

Wallace, B. (1983) *Teaching the Very Able Child*. London: Ward Lock.

Wallach, M.A. and Kogan, N. (1965) *Modes of Thinking in Young Children*. New York: Holt, Rhinehart & Winston.

Wallach, M.A. and Kogan, N. (1968) *Modes of Thinking in Young Children*. New York: Holt Rinehart and Winston.

Wallas, G. (1926) *The Art of Thought*. New York: Harcourt Brace.

Walmsley, J. and A. Margolis, (1987) *Hothouse People: Can We Create Super Human Beings?* London: Pan.

Wang, M.C. and Lindvall, O.M. (1984) 'Individual differences and school learning environments'. In E.W. Gordon (ed.) *Review of Research Education*. Vol. 2. Washington, DC: American Educational Research Association.

Warnock, M. (1978) *The Report of the Special Committee on Children with Special Educational Needs*. (Warnock Report.) London: HMSO.

Wechsler, D. (1945) *The Bellevue Intelligence Tests*. New York: Psychological Corporation.

Wechsler, D. (1974) *Manual for the Wechsler Intelligence Scale for Children – Revised (WISC-R)*. New York: Psychological Corporation.

Weikart, D., Deloria, D., Lawser, S. and Weigerink, R. (1970) 'Longitudinal results of the Perry Pre-School Project'. Monograph No. 1. Ypsilanti, MI: High Scope Press.

Weikart, D., Rogers, L., Adcock, C. and McClelland, D. (1971) *The Cognitively Orientated Curriculum. A Framework for Preschool Teachers*. Urbana, IL: National Association for the Education of Young Children.

Weisberg, R.W. (1988) *Problem Solving and Creativity. The Nature of Creativity*. Cambridge: Cambridge University Press.

Westinghouse Learning Corporation (1969) *The Impact of Head Start – An Evaluation of the Effects of the Head Start Experience on Children's Cognitive and Affective Development*. Springfield, VA: Department of Commerce Clearing House. PB 184 328.

Wheldall, K., Morris, M. and Vaughan, D. (1981) Rows versus tables: an example of the use of behavioural psychology in two classes of eleven year old children. *Educational Psychology* 1, 171–84.

Whitmore, J.R. (1980) *Giftedness, Conflict and Underachievement*. Boston: Allen and Bacon.

Whitmore, J.R. (1981) Gifted children with handicapping conditions: a new frontier. *Exceptional Children* 48, 106–14.

Whitmore, J.R. (1989) Four leading advocates for gifted students with disabilities. *Roeper Review* 12 (1), 5–13.

Whitmore, J.R. and Maker, C.J. (1985) *Intellectual Giftedness in Disabled Persons*. Rockville, MD: Aspen.

Wilgosh, L. (1991) Underachievement in culturally different children. *European Journal for High Ability* 2, 166–73.

Witty, P.A. (1958) 'Who are the gifted?' In N.B. Henry (ed.) *Education of the Gifted*. 57th Yearbook of the National Society for the Study of Education. Chicago, University of Chicago Press, pt 2, pp. 41–63.

Xenos-Whiston, M. (1989) 'The distinguishing characteristics of demonstration teachers of the gifted'. Unpublished PhD thesis, University of Montreal. Cited in B.M. Shore and S.L. Kanevsky (1993) 'Thinking processes'. In K.A. Heller, F. Monks and A.H. Passow (eds), *International Handbook of Research and Development of Giftedness and Talent*. Oxford: Pergamon.

Yamomoto, K. and Dizney, H.F. (1966) Eight professors. A study on college student's preferences among their teachers. *Journal of Educational Psychology* 57, 146–50.

Yashin-Shaw, I. (1994) Cognitive structure of creativity. Implications for instructional designs. *European Journal of High Ability* 5, 24–38.

Yewchuk, C. and Lupart, J. (1993) 'Gifted handicapped: a desultory duality'. In K.A. Heller, F. Monks and A.H. Passow (eds) *International Handbook of Research and Development of Giftedness and Talent*. Oxford: Pergamon.

Yewchuk, C.R. and Bibby, M.A. (1989) The handicapped gifted child: problems of identification and programming. *Canadian Journal of Education* 14 (1), 102–8.

Young, D. (1983) *Young's Group Tests of Intelligence*. Sevenoaks: Hodder and Stoughton.

Young, P. and Tyre, E. (1991) *Gifted or Able? Realizing Children's Potential*. Buckingham: Open University Press.

Ziehl, D.C. (1962) *An Evaluation of an Elementary School Enriched Instructional program*. Ann Arbour, MI: University of Michigan. Microfilms N 62–4644.

Name index

Subject index